VIRGINIA WOOLF AND THE DISCOURSE OF SCIENCE

The Aesthetics of Astronomy

Holly Henry investigates how advances in astronomy in the early twentieth century had a shaping effect on Virginia Woolf's literature and aesthetics as well as on the work of modernist British writers including Vita Sackville-West, H.G. Wells, Olaf Stapledon, Bertrand Russell, and T.S. Eliot. The 1920s and 1930s witnessed a pervasive public fascination with astronomy that extended from the US, where Edwin Hubble in 1923 definitively determined that entire galaxies existed beyond the Milky Way, to England, where London's intellectuals discussed Sir James Jeans's popular astronomy books and the newly explored expanses of space. In re-evaluating the cultural context out of which modernism emerged, Henry contends that Woolf, through her own fascination with astronomy, formulated a global aesthetics that helped shape her fiction and her pacifist politics. Henry's study includes examinations of unpublished scientific and literary archival material and sheds new light on Woolf's texts and on recent re-evaluations of Modernism.

HOLLY HENRY is Assistant Professor of English at the California State University, San Bernardino. Her research has appeared in publications in both the humanities and the sciences including contributions to *Virginia Woolf in the Age of Mechanical Reproduction* (2000) edited by Pamela L. Caughie and *Astronomy & Geophysics: The Journal of the Royal Astronomical Society*.

VIRGINIA WOOLF AND THE DISCOURSE OF SCIENCE

The Aesthetics of Astronomy

HOLLY HENRY

CAMBRIDGE
UNIVERSITY PRESS

PUBLISHED BY THE PRESS SYNDICATE OF THE UNIVERSITY OF CAMBRIDGE
The Pitt Building, Trumpington Street, Cambridge CB2 1RP, United Kingdom

CAMBRIDGE UNIVERSITY PRESS
The Edinburgh Building, Cambridge, CB2 2RU, UK
40 West 20th Street, New York, NY 10011-4211, USA
477 Williamstown Road, Port Melbourne, VIC 3207, Australia
Ruiz de Alarcón 13, 28014 Madrid, Spain
Dock House, The Waterfront, Cape Town 8001, South Africa

http://www.cambridge.org

First published 2003

Printed in the United Kingdom at the University Press, Cambridge

Typeface Adobe Garamond 11/12.5 pt   *System* LATEX 2$_\varepsilon$ [TB]

A catalogue record for this book is available from the British Library

ISBN 0 521 81297 6 hardback

Dedicated to
Christine, Wilbur, Chip, Cherie and John

Contents

Illustrations

Preface

Astronomy has been a personal passion from childhood. It was my dad who fastened a telescope with radiator hose clamps to a homemade tripod so that we could observe a lunar eclipse, or who would pause on a summer's night to point out a passing satellite. Somehow I don't remember what I saw through that army issue telescope our grandfather gave us, only it always being cold and that as children we were breaking the rules by staying up late. It was not exactly what I saw, but what I was inspired to dream – of other worlds whirling through space – that launched me on a career path that has culminated in the writing of this book. It is with great delight that I recognize some of the people and institutions that have made this research project possible. I wish to thank Christopher Vincent Jeans of 10 Adams Road, Cambridge, who so generously invited me to sift through his father's very carefully kept notebooks and papers. Christopher hosted me at his home on two separate occasions, and I am greatly touched by his kind and gentle spirit. In coming to know Christopher, I feel I have glimpsed, if only in part, something of the character of his father Sir James and mother Susi.

This book resulted from my graduate research directed by Susan Squier at the Pennsylvania State University. Susan invigorated the graduate program with her fascination with the interconnections of literature and science, and showed me the possibility of pursuing this interdisciplinary research. I am deeply grateful to Susan for her encouragement and inspiration, and for tirelessly reading and responding to multiple drafts of the manuscript in various stages. Lee Smolin, Robert Lougy, and Rich Doyle graciously served on my dissertation committee. Rich invited me to audit his seminars through which I came to read Haraway, Latour, Deleuze, and Guattari, and to dream about cryogenics and technologies of the future.

I wish to thank The Royal Society, the Royal Astronomical Society, the BBC Written Archives Centre, the British Museum, the British Library, the British Library Newspaper Library at Colindale, King's College,

Cambridge, the Huntington Library, the Beckman Institute at the California Institute of Technology, the Observatories of the Carnegie Institution of Washington, and the Mount Wilson Observatory for granting me access to papers and archives related to this project.

I am grateful to the California State University, San Bernardino, for granting me in 2001 a course release so that I could complete final research on the manuscript, also to the Department of English at Cal State for supporting my travel to England to research materials at the British Library at Colindale, King's College, Cambridge, and James Jeans's private papers at the home of Christopher Jeans. I also wish to express my gratitude to the Penn State Research and Graduate Studies Office, and to the Penn State Department of English, for making possible a trip to research the James Jeans archives at The Royal Society in London, the Royal Astronomical Society in London, the BBC Written Archives Centre, and the British Library. In addition, I am deeply grateful to William L. and Josephine Berry Weiss, and the Weiss Graduate Fellowship Program at Penn State University. As a Weiss Fellow, I was granted a teaching release and given opportunity to research and write most of the chapters. Through funding by the Penn State Office of International Programs and the Penn State Department of English, I presented selections of my research at the Inspiration of Astronomical Phenomena Conference (INSAP) in Malta in January 1999, and at several International Virginia Woolf conferences.

Many colleagues, friends, and family members supported my research. Regarding content on astronomy and cosmology, I consulted several astronomers, cosmologists, and historians of astronomy, many of whom became personal friends. Lee Smolin graciously explained difficult concepts related to cosmology. Ray White was partly responsible for my being able to present a portion of my research at the INSAP Conferences in Malta and in Palermo, both of which were remarkable experiences. Chris Impey, Leo Connolly, and Larry Webster offered genuine conversation explaining astronomical phenomena, and patiently listened to me talk about this project. I wish to thank Don Nicholson, historian of the Mount Wilson Observatory, for spending two afternoons giving me a guided tour of the Observatory and talking with me about Edwin Hubble and the history of the observatory. Peter Hingley, historian of the Royal Astronomical Society in London, deserves a special note of appreciation for important insights with regard to the historical and scientific material.

Many Woolf scholars answered queries related to my research. These include Stuart Clarke, Ann Banfield, Maggie Humm, Susan Squier, Mark Hussey, Jane Marcus, Pamela Caughie, Judith Killen, and so many others.

Thanks also to my colleagues Lisa Roney, Harvey Quamen, Christina Jarvis, Julie Vedder, Fiona Paton, Pat Malay, and Carl "Pete" Ricker who read and responded to drafts of the chapters and offered provocative suggestions throughout. Robert Whitehead assisted in reproducing the illustrations. Harold and Lynne Schweizer, and Michael Payne, gave advice and encouragement. Rob Dunham and Phil Page made me believe this book would actually materialize. Lance Bush inspired me with remarkable stories of his own experiences with the NASA program, and reasons for dreaming of our human future in space. I am deeply grateful to Lance for encouraging me to attend the Space Generation Forum (SGF) in Vienna, Austria in 1999. As a result of SGF, I have had the privilege to work with a team of space professionals at the United Nations Offices in Vienna and elsewhere on issues related to the peaceful uses of outer space. I also wish to thank Richard Devon for inviting me to teach the Space Colonization course in the Science, Technology and Society Program at Penn State University.

This project would not have been possible without my mother, Christine, and her endless hours of consultation and piquant suggestions for revisions. It is she who taught me to never fear failure. Wilbur, my brother, scanned science articles and quoted alternatively Shakespeare or Twain, depending on the present need. My sister, Cherie, never minded when I phoned out of sheer frustration, and patiently recalled her own delight in the wonders of literature and reading. My father, Wilbur, reminded me that writing is not so very different from more technical pursuits – it all comes down to a little detective work and some trouble-shooting.

I am very grateful to Cambridge University Press, Jane Goldman, readers of the manuscript, and copy editor Sara Barnes, all of whom offered valuable suggestions. It is a delight that this book appear by the same Press that published the work of James Jeans. And most especially, I wish to thank Ray Ryan for helping me in realizing this project and for his tremendous patience in the final preparation of the manuscript.

Acknowledgements

Excerpts from letters and papers of the James Jeans Papers archived at The Royal Society and at the home of Christopher Jeans reprinted by permission of Christopher Jeans of Cambridge. Excerpts of Jeans's letters archived at the BBC Written Archives Centre reprinted by permission of Christopher Jeans and the BBC Written Archives Centre. Studio photograph of Virginia Woolf (c. 1927) reprinted by permission of the Mortimer Rare Book Room, Smith College. Images from James Jeans's *The Universe Around Us* reproduced by permission of the Observatories of the Carnegie Institution of Washington. An excerpt from a letter by E.M. Forster to Virginia Woolf reprinted by permission of the Society of Authors as agent for the Provost and Scholars of King's College Cambridge. An excerpt from the letters of George Ellery Hale reprinted by permission of the Institute Archives of the California Institute of Technology. Excerpts from the correspondence and memoirs of Edwin and Grace Hubble from the Edwin Hubble Papers reprinted by permission of the Huntington Library, San Marino, CA. An excerpt from Clive Bell's letter to Saxon Sydney-Turner held in the Leonard Woolf Papers reprinted by permission the Huntington Library, San Marino, CA. *Punch* cartoons reproduced by permission of *Punch* Cartoon Library & Archive. An excerpt from Jill Graham's e-mail to the VWoolf listserv is reprinted by permission of Jill Graham. Illustration by Mervyn Peake reproduced by permission of David Higham Associates. Graphic accompanying article titled "The Star Stuff that is Man" reproduced by permission of the Photo Sales Department of the *New York Times* Agency. Illustration titled "Measuring the Stars" reproduced by permission of the *Illustrated London News* Picture Library. Excerpts of correspondence between Marie Stopes and James Jeans reprinted by permission of the British Library. Excerpts of correspondence between Charles A. Siepmann and James Jeans reprinted by permission of the BBC Written Archives Centre and Christopher Jeans.

Abbreviations

AROO	*A Room of One's Own*
BTA	*Between the Acts*
CE	*Collected Essays* by Virginia Woolf
D	*The Diary of Virginia Woolf*
DM	*The Death of the Moth and Other Essays*
E	*The Essays of Virginia Woolf*
GR	*Granite and Rainbow*
HH	*A Haunted House and Other Short Stories*
JR	*Jacob's Room*
L	*The Letters of Virginia Woolf*
MD	*Mrs. Dalloway*
ND	*Night and Day*
PA	*A Passionate Apprentice*
TG	*Three Guineas*
TTL	*To the Lighthouse*
TW	*The Waves*
TY	*The Years*

Introduction: Formulating a global aesthetic

At the age of 26, while on summer holiday in Sussex, Virginia Woolf could most likely be found on a clear evening peering through a telescope at the moon and stars. "Tonight we speculated upon the stars;" wrote Woolf, "fancied ourselves moored, one of an innumerable fleet; & saw the earth shrink to the size of a button, its rim just over there where the lighthouse marks the sea. This shrinkage was the result of seeing the moon close at the end of a telescope, like a globe of frosted silver..." (*A Passionate Apprentice* 368). This single diary entry, written on an August evening in 1907, swells with themes that would become major preoccupations throughout her life's work. As she looked out into the night sky, Woolf became keenly aware of the earth as a tiny inhabited speck in the vast reaches of the intergalactic depths. Often she imagined the earth as a ship, tumbling and adrift in an incredible expanse – the abyss of space. Such an image magnified that drastic "shrinkage" of earth she sensed when peering at "the moon close at the end of a telescope."

The apparatus of the telescope had a powerful shaping effect on Woolf's aesthetic imagination. Through it she glimpsed tiny images of other worlds. The dusty craters of the moon reminded her of water drops in plaster of Paris, and in her diary she recorded observing the "cardboard collar" rings of Saturn. More importantly, those other worlds came to life for her at the end of her telescope. On that summer evening in 1907 the globe of the moon reminded her that somewhere, on the other side of the earth's globe, communities thrived under the warmth of an afternoon sun. The moon, she wrote,

was, for the first time, a visible token, shining in dead of night, that the sun was still blazing somewhere, in an August sky. You could fancy hard blue & white, on the other side of the world; all the palms flashing, & the drone of heat; people sleeping under umbrellas; great melons, & donkeys with water skins, men lounging within the limits of hard black shadows - while here we walked in the vast darkness, & the

I

tobacco plants gleamed pale & their fine perfume powdered the air with sweetness. But through the telescope it is no longer moonlight; but the hot sun. . . . (*PA* 368)

Glimpsing the moon and stars against the hard black of the night sky indelibly impressed upon Woolf a vision that would help shape what I call her global aesthetic, as well as her pacifist politics. By that, I mean that those other worlds suggested to her something of what earth must look like from space, and, too, that the earth was indeed a planet moving through interstellar wastes. She realized that earth's inhabitants must rely on this small, fragile globe for their future survival.

This study offers an investigation of the interconnections between modernist British fiction and a pervasive popular interest in astronomy in the 1920s and 1930s in Britain and in the US. In the pages ahead, the cultural elements that gave rise to that interest are investigated. Grounded in the cultural studies of science, this study explores how modernist writers, and particularly Virginia Woolf, engaged and disrupted discourses of science within popular culture.

The networks that link Woolf's literary texts to the sciences have been of interest as early as May 1938 when Elizabeth Nielsen, an American literature student, visited with the Woolfs to discuss, Virginia noted, "Einstein, & his extra mundane influence upon fiction" (*D*5: 146). Woolf described Nielsen as "entirely distracted by Einstein" (*D*5: 146). At the time she first contacted Woolf, Nielsen was studying at Oxford. Woolf exchanged a few letters with her in October 1938 to say she had "not read Einstein; I should not understand it."[1] Since then Woolf scholars have investigated her interest in physics, Darwinian evolution, psychoanalysis, and the philosophy of science.[2] This study, alternatively, theorizes how Woolf's aesthetic perspectives, as well as her pacifist politics, were shaped by advances in astronomy and by emerging visualization technologies, ranging from large astronomical telescopes to the inexpensive hand-held camera. I have chosen Woolf's work as the particular site for my research as her texts represent a significant interface between literature, popular culture, and the sciences; however, the study additionally offers close readings of fiction, poetry, and non-fiction prose by an array of modernist British authors and science writers in the context of these converging phenomena.

Woolf's global aesthetic vision was inspired in part by her father, Leslie Stephen, who read widely in the natural sciences and was particularly interested in astronomy. A serious mountain climber in his younger years, Stephen claimed that the view of earth's surface from the top of Mont Blanc gave one a sense of the scale of things, of the "littleness" and "ephemeral existence" of humankind (*The Playground of Europe* 262). Stephen's contemplation of humans in relation to the scale of things became an important theme for Woolf's writing. Then too, she was thinking about humanity's minute existence in relation "to the immensity of the sky" (*PA* 387) when, while traveling in Italy in 1908, she read Thomas Hardy's *Two on a Tower* (1882). Woolf described the novel as setting in "contrast the stars with minute human loves" (*PA* 386). In the novel, the astronomer Swithin St. Cleeve describes for Lady Constantine the "[t]wenty millions" of stars visible with a powerful telescope, as well as the great "voids and waste spaces of the sky" (*Two on a Tower* 31, 33). He explains that the stars "burn out like candles" to become "invisible cinders" (*Two on a Tower* 34, 35). Swithin, who studies variable stars which by the early 1920s would become the means of measuring the great distances of intergalactic space, tells Lady Constantine, "Of all the sciences, [astronomy] alone deserves the character of the terrible" (*Two on a Tower* 34, 35). The very terminology Hardy used to depict the vastness of space and the life cycle of stars would be echoed in James Jeans's popular science books of the 1920s and 1930s. A British mathematician and cosmologist, Jeans described the stars as the "unwanted ends of lighted candles burning themselves out," and characterized the universe as "terrifying because of its vast meaningless distances."[3] Woolf's sense of the insignificance and the ephemerality of humans on the cosmological scale may also have been inspired by the French astronomer and popular science writer N. Camille Flammarion, who wrote of the possibility of human extinction in some future eon when the sun's energy had dissipated. An illustration from his *Astronomie Populaire* (1881) depicts the last human family to expire as earth freezes over in the dim light of our dying sun (Figure 0.1).

As a new generation of astronomical telescopes in the early decades of the twentieth century opened up new vistas of space, popular audiences were awed by the immensity and seeming lifelessness of the universe. Earth, by comparison, was depicted by Jeans to be no more than a granule of sand, whirling blindly through the vast and uninhabitable vacuum of space. Popular science writers such as Jeans, Cambridge astrophysicist Arthur Eddington, mathematician Bertrand Russell, and physiologist J.B.S. Haldane explored the implications of the advances in astronomy that had effected what I call a modernist human decentering and re-scaling. Fascinated with the new vistas of space, Woolf read the work of these scientists and began developing literary strategies that responded to this re-scaling, and that offered possibilities for a radical rethinking of the social and political structures of her day.

Figure 0.1 **The Last Human Family.** This illustration published in Camille Flammarion's *Astronomie Populaire* (1881) was captioned: Surprised by the cold, the last human family has been touched by the finger of death, and soon their bones will be buried underneath the shroud of the eternal ice fields (translated by author).

Of the scientists she read, James Jeans particularly captivated Woolf's imagination. By the late 1920s, Jeans garnered international attention with the publication of his non-technical astronomy texts, which topped the best-seller booklists in Britain and in the US. With the release in 1929 of *The Universe around Us*, Jeans was catapulted into the public eye. By January 1931, the famous cartoonist Will Dyson had parodied the swiftness with which Jeans gained widespread attention. In one Dyson cartoon that ran in papers in Britain and the US, two Londoners gaze skyward. One exclaims, "How mysterious is the Universe!" in reference to Jeans's recently published volume *The Mysterious Universe* (1930), while his colleague replies, "Ah, indeed – almost as mysterious as Jeans's book!"[4] In England, Jeans became a national celebrity through his non-technical texts, as well as his public lectures and BBC broadcasts on developments in astronomy and the new physics. A serious mathematician highly respected by colleagues in mathematics, cosmology and observational astronomy, and in physics, Jeans in all probability was the most widely read of Britain's popularizers of astronomy and physics. His non-technical science books, illustrated with numerous photographs of far-flung galaxies, sparked a public fascination with stars and nebulae, as well as a concern regarding humans' decentered and ephemeral existence in a universe far older than even most scientists imagined. Woolf's fiction and essays demonstrate her own response to Jeans's work, and the images of intergalactic space she glimpsed in the pages of his non-technical publications.

In fact, Jeans's books, lectures, and BBC broadcasts are crucial in re-imagining the popular milieu against which I read Woolf and other modernist writers. This study explores the breadth of his public appeal as well as the ways his non-technical texts shaped popular, literary, and artistic responses to the new vistas of space. The musical compositions of the prolific British composer Gustav Holst, for instance, were partly inspired by Jeans.[5] Holst read both *The Mysterious Universe* and Jeans's *Through Space and Time*, an expansion of public lectures given in 1933 (*Gustav Holst* 164). Interested not only in astrology but also in the science of astronomy, Holst had gained international visibility with a well-received sequence titled *The Planets* (1914–17), the music of which evoked the immensity and mysteriousness of the huge gaseous planets of our solar system.[6] He had also written a collection of songs based on poems by Humbert Wolfe, including one titled "Betelgeuse" after the red supergiant star in the Orion constellation.[7] It was largely due to Jeans, Holst's daughter Imogen has noted, that "Betelgeuse" became one of her father's favorite poems. "Betelgeuse, he knew, was the brightest star in Orion. And he knew that Sir James Jeans had said: 'If Betelgeuse were to replace our sun we should find ourselves inside it, its radius being greater than that of the earth's orbit'" (*Gustav Holst* 139). Holst set these lines from Wolfe's poem to music in 1929:

> On Betelgeuse
> the gold leaves hang in golden aisles
> for twice a hundred million miles,
> and twice a hundred million years
> they golden hang, and nothing stirs,
> on Betelgeuse.
> (quoted in *Gustav Holst* 139)

The phrases regarding "twice a hundred million miles" refer to the colossal size of red giant stars, and red supergiants such as Betelgeuse, the diameter of which had been calculated in 1920 to equal 240 million miles. Virginia Woolf most likely knew of Holst either through BBC broadcasts of his compositions or his appointment as music director at Morley College in 1907 where she, for two previous years, had been teaching composition and literature courses (*L6*: 419, n. 3). Like Holst's, Woolf's own work reflects the inspiration she drew from Jeans.

However, evidence that would place Virginia Woolf in a room sipping tea and discussing the stars with James Jeans has not yet been found. Nigel Nicolson recalled that his mother Vita Sackville-West, Woolf's dear friend and one-time lover, "was also caught up with the fascinated love of astronomy, and [that] she did meet Jeans."[8] Jeans, in fact, once gave Nicolson one of his popular astronomy books. "I forget where it was," wrote Nigel, "but he gave me a copy of *The Universe around Us* in 1930, when I was 13, and I have it still."[9] Although Jeans clearly knew some of Virginia's friends and associates, he remained at the fringe of Bloomsbury. While at Cambridge, Jeans became friends with mathematician Godfrey Harold Hardy, who was in turn a colleague of Leonard Woolf and Saxon Sydney-Turner.[10] Having entered Trinity College in 1896, G.H. Hardy was elected to the Apostles two years later, "The Society" of which Leonard Woolf, Sydney-Turner, Roger Fry, Bertrand Russell, and many of Virginia's closest associates were members.[11]

An additional connection between Jeans and Leonard Woolf was Russell Kerr Gaye (1877–1909). Hardy and Gaye were Cambridge colleagues and both were members of a group called the Sunday Essay Society who met to discuss theological issues.[12] In February of 1903, R.K. Gaye wrote to his colleague Jeans, who had been recuperating from an illness: "The Sunday Essay is maintaining its character as a battleground between the rival factions of its scholars."[13] One of those factions was "the mystico-nebular school consisting of [Saxon] Sydney-Turner, [Leonard] Woolf, and [Lytton] Strachey...."[14] Yet, despite his oblique connections to what became Bloomsbury, Jeans and his popular science writing, as this investigation will show, was to play a considerable role in Woolf's formulation of a global aesthetics.

THEORETICAL FRAMING

Virginia Woolf and the Discourse of Science investigates how advances in astronomy, made possible by a new generation of telescopes in the early decades of the twentieth century, had a shaping effect on work by Woolf and other British writers who were her contemporaries, including Olaf Stapledon, Vita Sackville-West, Roger Fry, Bertrand Russell, H.G. Wells, T.S. Eliot and others. What follows is a study in Woolf's narrative experiments, her passion for science, especially astronomy, as well as those moments where her writing traversed advances in visualization technologies, astronomy and cosmology, and the technologies of global war. The study explores how large astronomical telescopes like the 100-inch at Mount Wilson Observatory, with which American Astronomer Edwin Hubble worked, brought into the purview of popular audiences spectacular vistas of spiral nebulae whirling millions of light-years from earth. Interdisciplinary in approach, this investigation ranges across a broad spectrum of cultural moments and literary works. Its scope extends from phenomena such as Halley's comet and Hubble's extra-galactic nebulae to a variety of modernist literary works and popular science texts.

Deleuze and Guattari proposed that a literary text might be considered a "little machine" that "must be plugged [in] in order to work" (*A Thousand Plateaus* 4). I have attempted to plug Woolf's texts into the literary, cultural, scientific, and technological networks associated with advances in astronomy in the early decades of the twentieth century. In so doing, it seems evident that Woolf's fiction and essays contributed to, and at times resisted, the popular response to discourses related to technology and the sciences. The methodology of my investigation is based on the work of Joseph Rouse, Donna Haraway, Bruno Latour, and others working in the cultural studies of science.[15] Using Latour's model of tracing "science in the making," this investigation concerns itself less with science as theory (i.e., astrophysics, evolution, relativity), than with science as an activity, and the facts and artifacts discourses of astronomy produced (*Science in Action* 15). Like Latour who attempts to articulate the "imbroglios" or networks of interconnection between scientific practices and public and political discourse, I have set out to imagine the imbrication of advances in astronomy, emerging visualization technologies, and popular science writing, with discourses among modernist artists that produced in part Woolf's experiments in fiction (*We Have Never Been Modern* 3). Woolf's texts demonstrate how the new vistas of space emerged at the same time that modernist writers were forging new literary forms that might account for a modernist human decentering and re-scaling.

The research presented here situates itself within the current re-assessment of modernism, and of Bloomsbury as effete and disconnected from the concerns of public audiences. Literary study of the interconnection between modernist texts and the sciences has focused on psychology, eugenics, physics, film technologies, and more recently the philosophy of science, but not as thoroughly on the import of advances in astronomy and cosmology. This study provides evidence of how significant these sciences were to the formulation of British modernism, and specifically links Woolf's work to the pervasive popular interest in cosmology. Letters exchanged between Virginia and Vita Sackville-West indicate their shared fascination with astronomy. Vita, for instance, while traveling through Persia in January 1926, wrote to Woolf that the landscape surrounding the tomb of Tutankhamen, in Luxor, Egypt, reminded her of "[d]esolation like the mountains of the moon."[16] A year later, while again in Persia, Vita mused in a letter to Virginia: "[T]here is one little asteroid, called Ceres I think, only four miles across, the same size as the principality of Monaco, on which I have often thought I should like to live, revolving in lonely state round the sun. It would be even better than my island in the South Seas. Did you know I had got an island in the South Seas? It has a banana tree on it."[17] A month later Vita reported: "There was a new moon over the poplars in the Isfahan garden...curtseying away from a star like the one we saw when we went for walk at Long Barn...but in a very different sky."[18] From Smoke Tree Ranch near Palm Springs, California, Vita wrote of her delight in seeing "[m]agnificent stars overhead, and mountains all around"; she commented that nature's fury had been following her with "hurricanes in the Atlantic, blizzards in Chicago, earthquakes in California...and a meteor which lit up five states for half an hour and came to rest in Arizona."[19] Recent scholarship on Woolf and technology has demonstrated the extent to which Woolf, Eliot, and other modernist writers were captivated by new technologies related to photography, cinema, radio, the gramophone, and motoring. Vita, in fact, reported to Virginia on the motor speed records set at Daytona by Sir Henry Seagrave.[20] While Woolf has traditionally been considered detached from, even disdainful of, elements of popular culture, her fascination with the new vistas of space reflect that she too was immersed in this popular milieu. She was nevertheless critical at times of the deployment of some advances in technology and the sciences. Chapter Six examines her critique of specific instances of aggression in scientific practice, and explores her proposal in *Three Guineas* of feminist strategies for a scientific praxis that adopts a more global perspective.

Michael Whitworth points out that what is called popular science "can refer to 'best-sellers' with a genuinely popular sale, and to non-technical books of science which were never intended to have, or which never reached, a large audience."[21] While the term "popular" has multiple applications, in this study the term denotes public interests prevalent within a cultural milieu. In the study that follows, the term "popular" refers to expositions on the sciences that proliferated in a variety of media, some of which targeted a broad spectrum of readers. While readers of literary journals like the *London Mercury* or the *Athenaeum* may not have represented the same audiences who learned of advances in astronomy through daily newspapers, the variety of venues in which popular science expositions appeared illustrates the diversity of audiences fascinated with the new vistas of space. This fascination with astronomy, as this study will show, appeared to be irrespective of class and educational differences.

There were, of course, radically different formations of modernism and of popular culture in the US and in Britain. However, in Chapter One, I suggest that a transnational response to the work of Hubble, Jeans, and Eddington emerged as a result of the enhanced vistas of space made possible by a new generation of telescopes. That shared public experience might be identified as a participation in what Rita Felski calls the "popular sublime." She invokes the term to "highlight the significance of the aspiration to the transcendent, exalted, and ineffable as a central impetus of modern mass culture" (*The Gender of Modernity* 119).[22] Felski contends that the critical bracketing of the sublime as a "a high culture tradition stretching from Romantic poetry to the twentieth-century avant-garde has served to obscure the centrality of sublime imagery and vocabulary in many of the texts of modern mass culture" (*The Gender of Modernity* 120). She asserts that "literary representations of the aspiration to infinitude, transcendence, and boundlessness assume a much wider variety of forms than has usually been acknowledged in the critical literature" (*The Gender of Modernity* 120). Felski co-opts the sublime, associated with that which simultaneously inspires awe and terror, to identify in modern mass culture a desire for a "loss of self that ha[s] historically been gendered feminine rather than masculine" (*The Gender of Modernity* 120). As an example of this, Felski cites a novel by Marie Corelli, *A Romance of Two Worlds* (1887), in which the female protagonist escapes her body to glimpse alien worlds in outer space: "I gazed upon countless solar systems. . . . I saw planets whirl around and around with breathless swiftness. . . . I could scarcely perceive the Earth from whence I had come – so tiny a speck was it – nothing but a mere pin's point in the burning whirl of immensities" (quoted in Felski 135). The romantic aspiration for the sublime that Felski locates in Corelli's novels, she claims, "emerges as a key element of the modern" (*The Gender of Modernity* 120, 121).

Felski's notion of a popular sublime perhaps best articulates the varied aesthetic, journalistic, and parodied responses to the great expanses of outer space that unfolded before an eager public in the pages of James Jeans's texts and to some extent in the daily press. Vita Sackville-West commented, in a review of Jeans's *The Mysterious Universe*, that the stars had an appeal that characters in a novel did not: "[I]n everyday life we are concerned with what affects our fellow-beings, and not with what goes on in outermost space. . . . Nevertheless, there is some grandiose suggestion about the path of a star which is lacking in the career of Mrs. Smith."[23]

The new vistas of space evoked something of the sense of the sublime that drew so many British climbers to mountaineering in Switzerland in the 1860s and 1870s, and to Nepal in the 1920s. Several English climbers, inspired in some cases by the sublime poetry of the British Romantics, were among the first to reach the peaks of the Swiss, Italian and French Alps, many of which topped 10,000 feet. As Chapter Three will show, Leslie Stephen ranked among the best of Britain's climbers. Jeans and Hubble would both travel to the Alps, but never climbed with the rigor of Stephen, or of the celebrated George Mallory, friend to John Maynard Keynes and Duncan Grant, and whose death on Mount Everest in 1924 made sensational news in the British press. Jeans, in fact, met his second wife Susi Hock in 1935 while climbing in the Alps; Susi had completed a climb to about 10,000 feet (*Sir James Jeans* xiv). And his first wife, Charly, published a poem about Kanchenjunga (28,146 ft.), the third highest mountain in the world, located in the East Himalayas.[24] The poem associated the mountain's imperviousness to human life with the cold light of the stars, and concluded with an image of the mountain's "white peaks cleav[ing] the deep skies" with its "company of stars" which "gleam down, enormous, liquid, bright,/Out of the black profundity of night" (*"Driftweed" and Later Poems* 94). A similar fascination with the sublime evoked by the unexplored regions of space filtered into popular culture in England and the US, as a result of powerful telescopes brought on line in the early decades of the twentieth century. I want to suggest that Jeans's popular astronomy books represent a genre that has not been fully acknowledged as having a shaping effect on modernist literary works, and yet provoked the kind of sublime imagery and language that Felski identifies as central to modernism.

Besides its contributions to modernist literary studies, the significance of this investigation resides in a certain iteration at the turn of the twenty-first century of events of more than seventy years before. Each new generation of telescopes opens up an age of discovery and helps to shape popular perceptions of the human relation to cosmological phenomena. In the 1920s, Hubble's findings radically altered accepted theories on the structure, size and age of the universe and, perhaps more importantly, the human place within it. Today with the Hubble Space Telescope, the Chandra X-Ray telescope, establishment of an array of other orbiting telescopes, as well as the Keck Observatories in Hawaii, and the Hobby–Eberly Telescope at the McDonald Observatory, astronomers and cosmologists verge on a similar informational threshold regarding the earliest formation of the universe. Images from the Hubble Space Telescope have produced an increase in recent articles in national newspapers and popular journals that raise questions regarding the probability of life existing on extra-solar planets, and in other galaxies. Astronomers hope to discover clues that might explain the effects of dark matter in the universe, as well as reveal a more comprehensive view of how galaxies initially formed or how entire solar systems are born and die out. And the answers to their questions will inevitably filter into the literature and popular culture of our own lifetimes.

Stars and nebulae in popular culture

Splashed across the front page of the *New York Times*, a resplendent, multi-colored photograph reveals two galaxies colliding in the depths of space, 63 million light-years from earth. The spectacular image of the explosive collision between the Antennae galaxies was captured by the Hubble Space Telescope, and appeared in multiple newspapers and on magazine covers. The cover of *Newsweek*, for instance, sported a dramatic image of the cosmic crack-up. Headlined "Galaxies: How the Universe Began – How it might End," the magazine featured a report on galaxies as colossal whirls of stars and solar systems racing through space at tremendous speeds.[1] Hubble's lens has glimpsed not only how stars are born, but also how worlds die out, and the massive collision between the Antennae galaxies suggests what the future ultimately holds for human existence. Astronomers now say the Milky Way is likely to find its demise in a similar galactic conflagration. According to the *New York Times*, "The Milky Way and Andromeda are approaching each other with a speed of 300,000 miles an hour."[2] But given the vast distances between the galaxies no such collision, the news report assures, will occur for another five billion years, and by then earth will have been consumed in an enormous expansion of our dying sun. As the Hubble Space Telescope continues to relay never before seen cosmic events into the popular purview, the images beamed back from space have captivated public attention.

Similarly, nearly a century ago, as a new generation of telescopes began producing stunning photographs of extra-galactic phenomena, a popular fascination with astronomy emerged in the US and in Britain. On an October night in 1923, Edwin Hubble, working with the new 100-inch reflecting telescope at Mount Wilson Observatory, photographed the spiral nebula Andromeda. One particular photograph taken that evening would lead to a monumental discovery. By calculating the distance to a variable star identified on the photographic plate, Hubble determined that the Andromeda nebula appeared to be located nearly a million light-years beyond our galaxy.[3] Prior to this, astronomers rigorously debated whether the Milky Way marked the extent of the entire universe.

The suggestion that the universe extended beyond our galaxy had been put forward as early as 1785, when British astronomer William Herschel contended that nebulous astronomical objects were "distant stellar systems."[4] Later in the 1840s William Parsons, known as Lord Rosse, working with a 72-inch reflecting telescope, found that what were known as nebulae often had a spiral structure (Ronald Brashear and Daniel Lewis, *Star Struck* 159). Lord Rosse was able "to distinguish individual stars in some of the larger ones [which] helped strengthen the belief that spirals were galaxies (sometimes called 'island universes') like our own Milky Way" (*Star Struck* 159). However, when in 1918, Harlow Shapley measured the Milky Way at three-hundred thousand light-years across, he consequently "doubted that the spiral nebulae were distant galaxies as they could hardly be so far away as to be outside [our own] galaxy" (*Star Struck* 161).

The debate was settled in January 1925 with an official announcement of Hubble's findings at a joint meeting of the American Astronomical Society and the American Association for the Advancement of Science held in Washington, DC.[5] Two months earlier, in November 1924, the *New York Times* ran a short article headlined: "Finds Spiral Nebulae Are Stellar Systems. Doctor Hubbell [sic] confirms view that they are 'Island Universes' similar to our own."[6] Hubble's confirmation of the existence of extragalactic nebula or galaxies external to the Milky Way, was said to have "expanded one hundred fold the known volume of the material universe."[7] Before the end of the decade, Hubble and his assistant Milton Humason would announce yet another earth-shaking find. The universe, they reported, was expanding at an incredible rate. Light emitting from the faintest galaxies indicated they were receding from the Milky Way at speeds upwards of 12,000 miles per second (Edwin Hubble, *The Realm of the Nebulae* 119).[8] Galaxies located further away, Hubble's velocity/distance relation indicated, were receding at even greater speeds.

Disclosure of Hubble's findings sparked widespread popular interest in emerging telescopic technologies and cosmology in both the US and in Britain. Public fascination with the new discoveries in astronomy changed Mount Wilson Observatory, where Hubble conducted his research, "from a quiet enclave of astronomers into a bustling tourist attraction" (Gale Christianson, *Edwin Hubble* 212). By the early 1930s, the observatory opened for public viewing of stars and nebulae, and became a mecca for celebrities and public audiences alike drawing by the mid-thirties as many as 4,000 visitors on a holiday weekend (Christianson 213). Offering accommodations in cabin-like bungalows for $1.50 per night, the observatory provided opportunities for gazing at the stars through the 60-inch telescope and occasionally the large 100-inch Hooker telescope (Christianson 212). Tours of a small museum hung with photographs of stars and nebulae whirling millions of light-years from earth, as well as lectures on astronomy, were also available while the observatory's recently installed swimming pool provided an added attraction (Christianson 212).

Launched by his discoveries into the Hollywood set, Hubble was sought out by renowned scientists, actors, and literati alike. Hollywood celebrity Anita Loos, author of the novel that became the Broadway smash *Gentlemen Prefer Blondes*, screen and stage star Helen Hayes, British novelist Aldous Huxley, British actor George Arliss, as well as Albert Einstein himself ranked among Mount Wilson's more visible guests (Christianson 212). Each made the journey seeking the chance to peer through the observatory's powerful telescopes. "We were intrigued," Hayes later noted, "by the fact that a tiny bit of glass, which could fit into the socket of one man's eye, could swell out to embrace the whole universe. It seemed to put us in hailing distance of all eternity" (quoted in Christianson 259).

VIRGINIA WOOLF AND THE NEW VISTAS OF SPACE

What has not been recognized is the powerful shaping effect advances in astronomy in the early decades of the twentieth century had on Britain's literary artists and intellectuals. Nor has the scientific and personal collaboration between scientists in the US and in Britain been explored explicitly in relation to the British fascination with astronomy in the 1920s and 1930s. Virginia Woolf, in particular, was deeply curious about the sciences, especially astronomy. Her fiction and essays reveal that she read best-selling, non-technical science texts covering cosmology, relativity, and the new physics. Developments in astronomy and cosmology were reported in daily newspapers, as well as the eclectic weekly literary reviews in which Woolf published her short fiction and essays. As Gillian Beer notes, "Virginia Woolf, like most educated people of the 1920s, was well aware of Einstein as an intellectual presence."[9] Not only would she have read about galaxies whirling in the abysses of space, the nearly unimaginable size of the star Betelgeuse, and Clyde Tombaugh's discovery of a new planet, Pluto,[10] but she also knew, and in some cases socialized with, some of Britain's most prominent mathematicians and science writers.

Through her association with Ottoline Morrell at both Garsington Manor and in London, Woolf became part of a network of intellectuals many of whom published multiple non-technical science books on advances in mathematics, the new physics and in cosmology.[11] There she had opportunity to discuss science and mathematics with Cambridge mathematicians Bertrand Russell and Alfred North Whitehead. Leonard Woolf's description of the Garsington gatherings suggests that astronomy and cosmology may have been typical topics of discussion:

The zenith of the Garsington week-end in late spring and early summer was Sunday afternoon.... [T]here was always a galaxy of male stars, from ancient red giants like [W.B.] Yeats to new white dwarfs from Balliol and New College.... The Oxford generations of the nineteen tens and nineteen twenties produced a remarkable constellation of stars of the first magnitude and I much enjoyed seeing them twinkle in the Garsington garden. (*Beginning Again* 202–3)

Two scientists who played a significant role in heightening Britain's popular interest in astronomy and cosmology were British mathematician and cosmologist James Jeans and Cambridge astrophysicist Arthur Eddington. Woolf clearly had read their popular science books and, as Gillian Beer suggests, may have known their work through their BBC wireless broadcasts.[12] Thus, Woolf's literary and polemical writing represents a significant site for discovering the interconnections between British literary artists and the scientists who were their colleagues and associates.

While Woolf's personal and intense fascination with cosmology will unfold in the chapters that follow, this chapter explores the pervasive public preoccupation with astronomy that Britain experienced in the 1920s and 1930s, as well as how this interest was generated. Chapter One examines the cultural impact of Hubble and Einstein's reconfiguration of modern cosmological models of the universe, and reconstructs in part the popular milieu within which Woolf was formulating her global aesthetics. The chapter in addition explores the social and literary networks through which Woolf found opportunity for exchange with renowned scientists and popular science writers of her day.

THE ATHENAEUM: WOOLF'S LITERARY CONNECTION TO THE SCIENCES

Popular audiences in Britain were amazed at the new vistas of intergalactic space captured by improved telescopic technologies. Photographs of spiral nebulae and distant stars, published largely in non-technical astronomy texts, and to a limited extent in the daily press, brought into the public purview spectacular images of intergalactic space. Topics related to cosmology and the physical sciences became inextricably interwoven into public discourse. Daily newspapers such as *The Times* [London] and the *London Illustrated News*, as well as review journals including the *English Review, London Mercury*, and the *Review of Reviews*,[13] eagerly engaged the public with articles on cosmology, relativity, and the new physics. Such literary journals enjoyed a wide circulation in the early decades of our century largely, as Adrian Smith has noted, because "[t]he cinema was in its infancy and the wireless still a decade away. Television was the stuff of science fiction... Thus the only competition was the daily press" (*The New Statesman* 49–50). Readers found in these publications essays on physics, cosmology, and the atom as readily as articles on homemaking. A January 1929 issue of the *Hibbert Journal*, for instance, featured essays on "The Human Value of the New Astronomy" and "Relativity in Prayer" alongside an essay titled "Homemaking as a Key Industry."

One journal in particular dedicated to bringing both the arts and the sciences to its readers was the eclectic British weekly the *Athenaeum*. From its earliest inception in 1828, the *Athenaeum* had been devoted to providing a forum for intellectual interchange between artists, scientists, economists, and politicians. In its second issue, the journal announced its subjects: "literature, art, and science."[14] By the 1910s, the *Athenaeum* ran regular sections on book reviews, entertainment reviews, music and drama, poetry, and recently released gramophone recordings. While the science content had been somewhat reduced, the journal continued to publish articles and essays on advances in technology and the sciences. In 1923 the *Athenaeum* was subsumed into the *Nation & Athenaeum*, under John Maynard Keynes, and maintained a reputation throughout the decade as "one of the foremost weeklies in the country."[15]

Some of Virginia Woolf's best and earliest short fiction, essays, and literary reviews received top billing in the *Athenaeum*, and its later configuration the *Nation & Athenaeum*. "Solid Objects" and "Kew Gardens" were first published in the *Athenaeum*, while her treatise on a modern prose poetics, "Mr. Bennett and Mrs. Brown," appeared in the *Nation & Athenaeum*.[16] In fact, prior to 1925, Woolf published largely in these journals or anonymously in the *Times Literary Supplement* (Hermione Lee, *Virginia Woolf* 559). Her husband, Leonard, also made significant editorial contributions to the *Nation & Athenaeum* while serving as literary editor from 1923 through 1931.

The *Athenaeum* quickly developed as a vital part of the intellectual life of Virginia and Leonard Woolf and their colleagues. As Michael Whitworth points out, "Intersecting with the Garsington circle was one which formed around the literary weekly the *Athenaeum* under the editorship of John Middleton Murry between 1919 and 1921."[17] Indeed, Woolf wrote in March 1919 to her sister Vanessa Bell: "Our amusement now is Murry and the Athenaeum.... It is rather fun about the Athenaeum, as every one is to write what they like..." (*L2*: 341). Many within the Woolfs' circle published book reviews, original literary work, and essays in the publication. These included Woolf's brother-in-law Clive Bell, art critic and friend Roger Fry, T.S. Eliot, Aldous Huxley, E.M. Forster, Bertrand Russell, Lytton and James Strachey, and Katherine Mansfield. The later *Nation & Athenaeum* became so central to the Woolfs' social circle that Vanessa complained to Roger Fry in December 1923: "Talked a great deal about the Nation. It seems to me like a drug. Everyone reads it and discusses it in and out and theres always a lot of gossip about each article or review – one is quite out of it if one hasnt seen it for some weeks as I generally havent" (quoted in Lee, *Virginia Woolf* 447). Woolf biographer Hermione Lee has also noted the importance of the journal to the Woolfs: "With Leonard at the *Nation* and Virginia as his frequent contributor, and with the [Hogarth] Press expanding at the same time, the Woolfs settled, as a couple, into the centre of the London literary network. Virginia's relationships were greatly entangled in this..." (*Virginia Woolf* 447).

Both the *Athenaeum*, and the *Nation & Athenaeum*, developed as crucial sites for Virginia Woolf's access to science writers, and for her reading of popular science. "Literary journals and publishing houses," Whitworth comments, "create imaginary communities, geographically disparate, but possessing some degree of cultural or ideological agreement."[18] The *Athenaeum* brought Virginia and Leonard, if only by virtue of their association with the publication, into conversation with several prominent popular science writers. In fact, "a number of the most respected scientists of the times were contributors during the later years of the magazine."[19] In addition, Leonard Woolf, as literary editor of the *Nation & Athenaeum*, reviewed popular science texts by scientists and science writers including Bertrand Russell, J.B.S. Haldane, Gerald Heard, and James Jeans.[20]

Often the Woolfs' articles and essays and those of their colleagues, published in the *Athenaeum*, appeared on pages adjacent to non-technical essays on advances in the sciences. This stark juxtaposition of scientific exposition and the literary essay was standard fare. For instance, an essay titled "Matisse and Picasso" by Clive Bell was published back-to-back with a review of books on Einstein's theory of gravitation.[21] One of Roger Fry's essays, "Art and Science," appeared next to an article on Einsteinian relativity titled "The Equivalence Principle."[22] Notice of Ernest Rutherford's lecture on "Atomic Projectiles and their Collisions with Light Atoms" appeared in a June 1919 issue, while an announcement for T.S. Eliot's talk on "Poetry" for the Arts League appeared in an October issue that same year. Although Jeans and Eddington, two of the nation's most celebrated popularizers of astronomy, did not publish in the journal, their books and public lectures were regularly reviewed by *Athenaeum* writers. For instance, their public debate on the viability of Einsteinian relativity held at the Royal Society in 1920 was recreated for public audiences through *Athenaeum* coverage.

Particularly from 1919 through the early 1920s, astronomy and the new physics were featured topics in the *Athenaeum*. At that time, John William Navin Sullivan, a mathematician, science writer, and assistant editor for the journal, published numerous essays on astronomical experiments, Einstein's general relativity theory, and on cosmology. In 1919 alone, J.W.N. Sullivan featured articles on the importance of the British Eclipse Expeditions of that year, the magnitude and apparent brightness of stars, the relation of the sciences to art and literature, as well as on the "island-universe" debate regarding the question of whether the Milky Way was only one of innumerable galaxies. In an essay titled "Stellar Universes," Sullivan concluded, "It is difficult to avoid the hypothesis that the spiral nebulae are separate universes, 'island universes[,]' ... existing at distances unimaginably greater than the dimensions of our own lens-shaped system and Milky Way."[23] This he wrote six years prior to the announcement of Hubble's discovery that the Andromeda nebula was indeed an entire galaxy located outside the Milky Way.

In a recent reassessment of Sullivan's work, Michael Whitworth credits Sullivan with having "pioneered the craft of scientific journalism."[24] Sullivan became acquainted with Ottoline Morrell's circle, including Aldous Huxley, in the summer of 1918 when he moved next door to Garsington Manor to work as a conscientious objector.[25] Convinced of the importance of astronomical discoveries for literature, Sullivan criticized modernist fiction writers for their inability to adopt a "cosmic" perspective and to address the issues of an age in which humans were grappling with their position "amid the great spaces of astronomy."[26] Popular science books would become "serious rivals of modern novels and poetry," argued Sullivan, because "[t]hey are more dramatic, they open up larger vistas, they are as well written, and they are cheaper."[27] Sullivan's assessment, as this study will show, was not that far from the truth.

STANDING ON THAT "GLOBE OF GLASS":
RELATIVITY AND ECLIPSE MANIA[28]

In June of 1927, when a total solar eclipse was to be visible in England, the event was so widely celebrated by the British public that special overnight train and bus services from London to Yorkshire, Lancashire and other locations within the belt of totality were provided (Lee 508; *L3*: 377). It was the first, and probably only, time that most living in England would have the opportunity to witness a total eclipse of the sun. Virginia Woolf and Vita Sackville-West were among those fascinated millions armed with smoked glass who flocked to the path of totality in hopes of glimpsing the event.[29]

In the weeks leading up to the eclipse, as science writer Sylva Norman noted, "the word 'eclipse' was the Hail and Farewell of every conversation."[30] Days just prior to the eclipse, *The Times* [London] ran multiple articles on predicted weather conditions, designated scientific observing posts, special train schedules, tips for safe observation, as well as detailed maps of motor routes to areas of totality. Celebrations on the eve of the eclipse were widespread. At Richmond, located very near the central line of totality, a week-long list of entertainment was planned to include "a lecture; a dance in the castle grounds...competitions; whist drives... [and] a cricket match."[31] In London, "there was the Crystal Palace, with room on its terraces for thousands of people."[32] For those traveling to England's western coast, *The Times* reported: "Southport will carry out its elaborate arrangements for entertaining the visitors during the small hours. Cinemas, cafes, and dancing places will be open besides the sands."[33] From Blackpool, the Bickerstaffe steamer was "to leave the pier for a cruise into the centre of the belt of totality."[34] One Yorkshire community held an "Eclipse Dance" scheduled to conclude with the eclipse itself.

Advertisements and editorial cartoons that appeared in daily newspapers and weekly publications demonstrate the extent to which this particular eclipse was celebrated. Distributors of Barclay's Lager, for instance, cashed in on the intense popular interest with a full-page advertisement which read: "Light or Dark? For those who dwell outside the area of teetotality there is no drink to eclipse Barclay's Lager" (Figure 1.1). The Barclay's advertisement appeared in a June 1927 issue of *Punch*, which published several editorial cartoons that month parodying the public fascination with the eclipse.[35] One cartoon, lampooning the public appetite for details related to the eclipse, depicted a gentleman dropping in on an "eminent official" at the Royal Astronomical Society to say, "Excuse me, Sir, but I thought

Figure 1.1 **Barclay's lager capitalizes on eclipse.** Barclay's lager cashed in on the widespread public interest in the June 1927 eclipse. This full-page advertisement appeared in the 29 June issue of *Punch*.

Caller (to eminent official of Astronomical Society). "EXCUSE ME,
SIR, BUT I THOUGHT IT MIGHT BE OF INTEREST TO YOU TO KNOW THAT THERE WILL
PROBABLY BE AN ECLIPSE OF THE SUN ON THE TWENTY-NINTH OF THIS MONTH."

Figure 1.2 ***Punch* cartoon on the 1927 solar eclipse.** A *Punch* editorial cartoon (15 June)
parodies the widespread public interest in, and knowledge about, the total solar eclipse to
be visible in England. Courtesy of *Punch* Cartoon Library and Archive.

it might be of interest to you to know that there will probably be an eclipse
of the sun on the twenty-ninth of this month" (Figure 1.2). In another,
titled "The Eclipse," a woman, who stands looking skyward through her
piece of smoked glass, reprimands her unruly son, "If you don't behave
yourself, Osbert, I shan't bring you next time" (Figure 1.3). The cartoon's
humor lies in the fact that it was widely known this was the first total solar
eclipse to be visible in England for more than 200 years. As Woolf herself
had noted, another would not be seen in Britain's skies until 1999 (*D*3: 144;
also 142, n. 16).[36]

THE ECLIPSE.

"IF YOU DON'T BEHAVE YOURSELF, OSBERT, I SHAN'T BRING
YOU NEXT TIME."

Figure 1.3 **"The Eclipse."** This *Punch* cartoon (29 June issue) suggests the degree of
public fascination with events related to astronomy. A mother, who observes the total solar
eclipse through smoked glass warns her unruly son, "If you don't behave yourself, Osbert,
I shan't bring you next time." The humor of the cartoon's caption inheres in the fact that
there would not be another total solar eclipse visible in England until 1999. Obviously
many in Britain were aware of the scientific details regarding the eclipse. Courtesy of
Punch Cartoon Library and Archive.

In those early morning hours of 27 June, under the eerie and haunting sky of the eclipse, Woolf witnessed a dramatic 24 seconds when darkness swept over Bardon Fell and the Yorkshire Dales. The skies, Woolf noted, "became darker and darker as at the beginning of a violent storm; the light sank & sank...when suddenly the light went out. We had fallen. It [the earth] was extinct. There was no colour. The earth was dead" (*D3*: 143). Deeply moved by the experience despite the cloud cover that prohibited her seeing a fully blackened sun, Woolf recorded details of the event in her diary (*D3*: 142–4), and later reworked that account for her essay "The Sun and the Fish," and her novel *The Waves* (237).

From her vantage point, the cloud cover that morning was considerable. "We began to get anxious," wrote Woolf; "We saw rays coming through the bottom of the clouds. Then, for a moment we saw the sun, sweeping – it seemed to be sailing at a great pace & clear in a gap; we had out our smoked glasses; we saw it crescent, burning red; next moment it had sailed fast into the cloud again; only the red streamers came from it; then only a golden haze..." (*D3*: 143). Woolf clearly knew the science of the event she was observing. She noted the crescent sun partly obscured by the moon. Those "red streamers" she glimpsed were most likely coronal streamers or solar prominences. One of the poignant aspects of this particular eclipse was the sheer element of chance, due to the unsettled weather, in seeing the eclipsed sum during the 23 or 24 seconds of totality. "The moments were passing," wrote Woolf, "We thought we were cheated...Nothing could be seen through the cloud. The 24 seconds were passing" (*D3*: 143). Nor was she alone in reporting the strange light produced by both the eclipse and cloud cover. Special correspondents for *The Times* at Giggleswick, Southport, West Hartlepool, and Swanage, and on board an Imperial Airways plane chartered by the news firm, also offered detailed reports on the strangeness of the pale eclipsed light. *The Times* correspondent at West Hartlepool, where totality was obscured by clouds, commented on the silence of the crowds as they stood in the moon's shadow: "As there was no spectacle to watch in the sky, the darkness was all the more impressive. There was a strange eerie stillness in nature and in the vast gathering of men. No sound was heard but the breaking of the small waves on the sands."[37]

Standing in the pale light, Woolf mused how the world seemed on the verge of extinction. She understood the very real possibility that life on our planet might easily be extinguished. The "darkness" was like "a sudden plunge, when one did not expect it" and had evoked for her a sense of humans "at the mercy of the sky" in an ancient struggle for survival (*D3*: 144). In "The Sun and the Fish," Woolf reflected on her sense, as the light turned achromatic, of earth's fragility. She envisioned the earth as a dessicated "frail shell" or as a "globe of glass":

The shadow growing darker and darker over the moor was like the heeling over of a boat, which, instead of righting itself at the critical moment, turns a little further and then a little further on its side; and suddenly capsizes.... It [the earth] hung beneath us, like a cage, like a hoop, like a globe of glass. It might be blown out; it might be stove in. (*CE*4: 181)

Upon the sun's reappearance, she recalled in her diary, it was "with a great sense of relief. It was like recovery. We had been much worse than we had expected. We had seen the world dead" (*D*3: 144).

Interestingly, Woolf's diary entry on the eclipse, dated 30 June, is remarkably similar to Sylva Norman's published account that appeared in the 9 July issue of the *Nation & Athenaeum*. Both women noted similar motifs and images, namely, the sense of the earth withering under the strange silver light of an eclipsed sun, and a feeling of connection with humanity's primitive past. Norman compared the "credulous savage [who] beats drums to scare off the devourer of the sun" to the revelers at a local "Eclipse Dance" who "use[d] drums and saxophones to herald [the eclipse's] approach and celebrate its swallowing."[38] Woolf too had noted, "I thought how we were like very old people, in the birth of the world – druids on Stonehenge" (*D*3: 143). Likewise in "The Sun and the Fish" Woolf observed: "We were very, very old; we were men and women of the primeval world come to salute the dawn" (*CE* 4: 180). Jane Goldman, in *The Feminist Aesthetics of Virginia Woolf*, comments that it is the "sense of shared experience which comes across most powerfully in Woolf's description" of the eclipse (29).[39] Indeed, Woolf noted, "Never was there a stranger purpose than that which brought [so many millions] together that June night..." (*CE* 4: 179). The solar eclipse catalyzed for Woolf a vision of earth as a fragile oasis of life for all humankind.

At least four widely-publicized events related to astronomy and cosmology, in the early decades of the twentieth century, had a significant impact on popular culture in Britain and the US. Besides Hubble's determination that entire galaxies existed beyond the Milky Way and that the universe is expanding, two other events related to astronomy attracted public attention: the return of Halley's comet in 1910, and the British Eclipse Expeditions of 1919 which demonstrated the viability of significant tenets of Einstein's General Theory of Relativity.

In the summer of 1910, Halley's comet once again approached the sun in its roughly 75-year cycle, and this time the earth was to pass through the comet's tail.[40] "Two years earlier, astronomers had detected cyanogen gas, a known poison, in the tail of comet Morehouse"; consequently, public concern mounted regarding the possibility of world-wide poisoning as earth traversed Halley's tail (Christianson 61). "Comet pills," intended to counter the effects of the comet's potentially poisonous gases, found a viable market.[41] In the US, claims of the possibility of a collision with the comet fueled apprehension regarding Halley. One American science writer warned of the effects of such a cataclysmic event:

[T]he year 1910, with its return of Halley's comet, is by some looked upon with fear and dread.... What will happen if the astronomers have made a slight mistake in their calculations and the comet should come into collision with the earth? With the earth traveling in space at the great speed of 18 1/2 miles per second, and the comet in the opposite direction with a velocity even greater, such a head-on collision would be appalling; the earth might possibly be blown to pieces![42]

It was speculated further that Halley might "strike Earth somewhere between Boston and Boise, knocking the planet into the depths of outer darkness and dooming every creature on its surface" (Christianson 61). In addition to concerns regarding a planetary collision, there were warnings that hydrogen in the comet tail could ignite the earth's atmosphere: "Some sealed their windows against the predicted fallout while others," suggestive of the tragic events surrounding the cult deaths associated with the March 1997 passing of Comet Hale-Bopp, "saved the comet the trouble by committing suicide" (Christianson 61).[43]

England, too, experienced a pervasive public anxiety over Halley's return. One British postcard depicted a fireball streaking across the sky. A face painted on the fireball included fangs and claws, which grasped human victims as it swooped over a crowd.[44] Actually, the possibility of a comet colliding with earth, and the terrifying consequences of such an event, had been looming in the British imagination as early as 1897 with the publication of H.G. Wells's short story "The Star." In Wells's tale, an asteroid slams into Neptune and accumulates into a flaming mass that hurtles toward earth. Like Halley's comet, the asteroid garners international attention and is featured in newspaper headlines in London and other capital cities. "[N]ewspaper readers of two hemispheres were made aware for the first time of the real importance of this unusual apparition in the heavens. 'A Planetary Collision,' one London paper headed the news..." (H.G. Wells, "The Star" 681).[45] With uncanny accuracy, Wells's story not only anticipated a decade earlier the kind of comet panic experienced over Halley in Europe and the US, but also speculated on the widespread natural disasters that would result from the impact or even near-miss of a passing asteroid. In "The Star," a "master mathematician," a kind of Einstein-like figure at whom many initially scoff, predicts global warming (caused by an increase in earth's temperature as the "blazing mass" neared earth) as well as "[e]arthquakes, volcanic outbreaks, cyclones, sea waves, [and] floods" ("The Star" 686).[46] However, just as "the star" approaches, the moon passes between the asteroid and earth, forcing the asteroid to veer into the sun.

The plot of "The Star" was later reworked by Wells for his novel *In the Days of the Comet* (1906). In the novel version, the earth's passage through a comet's gaseous green tail has a mesmerizing effect and causes humans to desist from aggression and war. Wells's story and his subsequent novel share extremely similar details with an earlier novel by the French astronomer and popularizer of astronomy N. Camille Flammarion. In the English translation titled *Omega: The Last days of the World* (1894), Flammarion envisioned a comet of greenish hue striking the Earth centuries in the future. Public panic ensues when it is learned that the comet is comprised of carbonic-oxide gas, and concerns are raised regarding "whether the mixture of this noxious gas with the atmosphere would poison the entire population of the globe" (*Omega* 22–3). In Flammarion's version an "illustrious astronomer," like the unnamed "master mathematician" of Wells's short story, describes how the moment of impact will produce simultaneously "an earthquake… a volcanic eruption, [and] a cyclone" (*Omega* 49, 48–9). However, in Flammarion's tale there is no rescue for humanity. While the comet, on impact with earth, causes limited devastation, humanity eventually faces extinction millions of years later. Yet the closing lines of the novel reassured readers that in the vast expanse of the universe, life abounded on distant planets circling far-flung stars: "infinite space remained, peopled with worlds, and stars, and souls, and suns; and time went on forever" (*Omega* 287).

If Halley's comet raised public awareness regarding earth's vulnerability in the depths of space, Einstein's "general theory of relativity demolished the conventional sense of stability of the entire material universe."[47] Einsteinian relativity had largely reconfigured nineteenth-century conceptions of space and time. The theory's dynamical model for space and time provided the basis for entirely new models of the universe, both then and now. Whereas Newtonian physics defined gravitation as an actual force of attraction, Einstein contended that astronomical objects instead moved in relation to the contours of space itself. According to his then highly controversial and contested theory, planets orbited the sun because the fabric of space surrounding the sun was warped or curved by the sun's mass, and that even star light, as a result of the sun's mass, would be deflected by such curvature.

While completing his general theory of relativity, Einstein had hoped to find means of testing the theory, which predicted that light would be deflected by the gravitational field of astronomical objects. "Einstein wrote to George Ellery Hale, the leading American solar astronomer, in 1913 asking him whether, in his experience, someone could detect the offset location of a star that happened to be just to the side of the Sun during normal daylight hours. Hale responded that this could not be done with instruments available at the time and that one would have to wait for a solar eclipse to view a star next to the Sun" (*Star Struck* 52).

Six years later, Arthur Eddington, and Charles Rundle Davidson of the Royal Observatory at Greenwich, led the British Eclipse Expeditions to determine the viability of Einstein's claims of the curvature of space, and whether star light passing near the sun would be deflected to the degree Einstein had calculated. In preparation for the total solar eclipse in May of 1919, Eddington and Davidson traveled to Africa and Brazil, respectively, to telescopically photograph the Hyades stellar group in order to confirm Einstein's calculations for the deflection of light by the sun's gravitational field. These stars, whose light normally is occluded by the sun's brilliance, would be visible during the eclipse and their apparent distance from the sun's limb could be calculated. Despite unfavorable weather conditions, at least for Eddington, both British astronomers nevertheless obtained photographic evidence that confirmed displacement of the Hyades stellar group to the degree Einstein had predicted.[48]

Their findings, announced in November 1919 at a joint meeting of the Royal Astronomical Society and the Royal Society in London, made headlines across Europe and the US. Light appeared to have mass; space could bend. Observational confirmation of these tenets of relativity suggested that Einstein's general relativity provided a more viable and accurate model for understanding the dynamics of space. Eddington's apt analogy of the physicist's predicament prior to Einstein's theories points up the significance of the expeditions:

In default of a better framework, [a Newtonian model of the universe] was still used, but definitions were strained to purposes for which they were never intended. We were in the position of a librarian whose books were still being arranged according to a subject scheme drawn up a hundred years ago, trying to find the right place for books on Hollywood, the Air Force, and detective novels.[49]

Thus Einstein was launched into the public limelight. "The speed with which his fame spread across the world, down through the intellectual layers to the man in the street," according to Ronald Clark, "created a startling phenomenon..." (*Einstein: The Life and Times* 246). Prior to the

Eclipse Expeditions, Einstein had not been taken entirely seriously, even by many physicists. But once the results of the Eclipse Expeditions reached the pages of *The Times* [London] and the *New York Times*, he had attained celebrity status. Following the Expedition reports in *The Times*, "the paper carried something concerning Einstein and his celebrated theory... more or less daily for the rest of the year."[50] The media attention was so intense that Einstein "complained to Max Born that he felt like a man plagued by the Midas touch – only, instead of turning into gold, everything he touched turned into newsprint!" (David Cassidy, *Einstein and Our World* 64). In London, relativity limericks and cartoons appeared in local papers, and one apparently could purchase relativity pottery.[51] One British cartoon featured a detective nabbing a bank robber with "a flashlight whose light rays turned corners"; the cartoon was captioned, "Elementary, my dear Einstein" (Clark 248). Even London's Palladium music hall attempted to book Einstein for a "three-week 'performance'" (Clark 248).[52]

By 1929, Einstein's work had been so widely absorbed into popular culture in Britain and in the US that upon publishing a short paper in a German publication, Einstein received an odd letter from Eddington, stating: "You may be amused to hear that one of our great department stores in London (Selfridges) has posted on its window your paper (the six pages pasted up side by side) so that passers-by can read it all through. Large crowds gather around to read it!"[53] The following year, in an incident at Manhattan's Museum of Natural History, guards had to dispel a "near riot" when more than 4,000 people rushed to see a film that explained relativity (Denis Brian, *Einstein: A Life* 191).

Part of Einstein's popularity was born of sheer confusion. Attempting to cater to the pervasive demand for articles on relativity, newspapers were willing to pay high fees for concise, non-technical expositions (Clark 238). However, not all explications were equally rigorous or elucidating. For instance, Alexander Moszkowski, a writer in Berlin who published in 1921 his interviews with Einstein, recalled that European news coverage of the Eclipse Expeditions included "full-page beautifully coloured pictures intended to give the reader an idea of the paths pursued by the rays for the stars during the total eclipse of the sun" (*Einstein, the Searcher* 14–15).[54] Despite the newspapers' "large illustrations," which Moszkowski noted, "must certainly have cost the authors and publishers much effort and money," the illustrations were often inaccurate (*Einstein, the Searcher* 14). "These afforded Einstein much amusement, namely, *e contrario*, for from the physical point of view these pages contained utter nonsense. They showed the exact opposite of the actual course of the rays..." (*Einstein, the Searcher* 15).

Likewise, in 1920, *The Times* [London] offered in an issue of its educational supplement a three-page spread on relativity, one article of which was written by Dr. Herbert Wildon Carr. Carr had that year published a nontechnical, book-length exposition on Einstein titled *The General Principle of Relativity*, which apparently revealed less about Einstein's theory than Carr's own limited understanding of the topic. J.W.N. Sullivan, a strong proponent of Einstein's controversial theories, wrote a rather scathing review of Carr's book:

> We admit that the theory of Relativity is a mysterious subject; Professor Carr, to us, makes it more mysterious than ever. For instance, he introduces two trains, one travelling at sixty miles an hour and the other at thirty miles an hour. We knew that something complicated was coming, because we are always meeting these trains in expositions of Relativity. But never before have we encountered Professor Carr's remark about them: "According to the principle of Relativity, the velocity of each is identical, because in each train the observer is at rest."[55]

Noting Carr's absurd inference that "every velocity is equal to every other," Sullivan sympathized with more conservative British physicists who remained skeptical of relativity: "We can understand that Sir Oliver Lodge dislikes the theory."[56]

Whether as fallout from public confusion or the increase in popular expositions on astronomy and relativity, terms like "gravitational fields," "space-time," and "light-years" fell into common parlance. "Women lost sight of domestic worries and discussed co-ordinate systems, the principle of simultaneity, and negatively charged electrons," wrote Moszkowski regarding the public response to Einstein (*Einstein, the Searcher* 14). By popular estimation the universe was reeling. Virginia Woolf had commented that the year 1910 marked an irreversible change in the way humans negotiated their world. In the essay "Character in Fiction" she noted the profound inability of conventional literary forms to articulate the world revealed presumably by the new physics and the new astronomical vistas of space. "Thus it is that we hear all round us, in poems and novels and biographies, even in newspapers articles and essays, the sound of breaking and falling, crashing and destruction. It is the prevailing sound of the Georgian age..." (*E*3: 433–4).[57] Mark Hussey notes that while Woolf intended to comment on "shifts in European aesthetic practices," the early decades of the twentieth century witnessed "profound changes in scientific conceptions of the universe."[58] Yet it seems likely that Woolf also meant to suggest the ways in which the new vistas of space were shaping modernist literature. Leonard Woolf observed of the same time period those advances in science and technology that had reconfigured the popular perception of the human place in the universe: "[I]t was exciting to be alive in London in 1911 and... there was reason for exhilaration. The revolution of the motor car and the aeroplane had begun; Freud and Rutherford and Einstein were at work beginning to revolutionize our knowledge of our own minds and of the universe" (*Beginning Again* 37).

CAMBRIDGE PUBLISHES SCIENCE FOR GENERAL AUDIENCES

Rapid developments in cosmology and astronomy in turn sparked a tremendous market for popular expositions on relativity, the new physics, and astronomy. Science writer F.S. Marvin observed, "Recent speculations on the nature of the stars have aroused so much interest that books on the subject have been selling like novels, and people have been arguing more about fundamental questions than they have ever done since Darwin."[59] By the mid-1920s, Cambridge University Press realized the potential market for affordable non-technical expositions on astronomy and cosmology. S.C. Roberts, secretary of the Press, recalled the point at which he stumbled upon the idea "that cosmogony might contain the potentialities of best-selling beyond the dreams of academic avarice" ("A Memoir," *Sir James Jeans*, ix). Roberts had been reading the conclusion to *Astronomy and Cosmogony* (1928), a highly respected technical text by James Jeans. The final chapter described the saga of humanity's nascent position in an ancient and vast universe, and read as dramatically as any novel or play: "Man may have appeared on the scene rather late in the history of the universe," warned Jeans; "possibly the main drama of the universe is over, and our lot is merely to watch the unwanted ends of lighted candles [the stars] burning themselves out on an empty stage" (*Astronomy and Cosmogony* 421).[60]

Jeans's writing appealed to a wide range of audiences in that the kinds of inquiry even his textbooks pursued had been formerly left largely to poets and philosophers. At the close of *Astronomy and Cosmogony*, Jeans had queried:

What is the relation of life to that universe, of which, if we are right, it can occupy only so small a corner? What, if any, is our relation to the remote nebulae, for surely there must be some more direct contact than that light can travel between them and us in a hundred million years? Do their colossal uncomprehending masses come nearer to representing the main ultimate reality of the universe, or do we?... Or is our importance measured solely by the fraction of space and time we occupy – space infinitely less than a speck of dust in a vast city, and time less than one tick of a clock which has endured for ages and will tick on for ages yet to come?(422)

Jeans emphasized the fact that humans have existed for only a fraction of the time the universe has endured. Jeans's popular books on astronomy, in particular, invited the reading public to likewise contemplate the new vistas of space and their meaning for humankind.

Anticipating the exploding market for popular accounts of advances in astronomy, Roberts proposed that Jeans, who initially had published largely technical texts, write a popular exposition on astronomy. Jeans replied that although Cambridge had a reputation as "the finest mathematical printers in the world," he was convinced the Press "couldn't sell a popular book" ("A Memoir," *Sir James Jeans* x). He couldn't have been more wrong. In September of 1929, Jeans published through Cambridge *The Universe Around Us* and consequently was catapulted into the public eye. "The first edition...was sold out during October. By the end of 1929, 11,300 copies had been sold" ("A Memoir," *Sir James Jeans* x). A year later, the *Evening Standard* [London] reported that the book had sold more than 40,000 copies in English, and that the publication was to be translated into seven additional languages.[61] Traditionally devoted to publishing only scholarly texts, Cambridge University Press saw the opportunity for cashing in on popular science, and emerged as the "Press that made science a best seller."[62]

By the time Jeans had prepared a sequel, *The Mysterious Universe* (1930), *The Times* was asking to publish advance copy of the final chapter.[63] To say the book sold well would be an understatement. According to Roberts, "For the next few weeks our chief concern was to keep *The Mysterious Universe* in stock" ("A Memoir," *Sir James Jeans* xi). Selling 1,000 copies a day in the first month, *The Mysterious Universe* was also later translated into at least thirteen languages including Czech, Bengali, and Burmese (E.A. Milne, *Sir James Jeans* 77). In his history of the Cambridge University Press, Roberts recalled, "Undoubtedly the largest measure of purely popular fame came to the Press as a result of its publication of the reflections of mathematicians and philosophers on the ultimate problems of the universe."[64] The Press had published popular science books prior to this. Alfred North Whitehead's *The Concept of Nature* (1920) as well as his *Science and the Modern World* (1926) had been successful expositions on investigations into the nature of material phenomena and on the new physics, and Arthur Eddington's *The Nature of the Physical World* (1928), according to Michael Whitworth, "lifted popular-science publishing to new heights."[65] Yet none of these texts reached the initial sales volume of Jeans's non-technical publications. Jeans made a significant contribution to the popularization of, in particular, astronomy. Even the daily newspapers repeatedly commented on his rapid rise to fame. Headlines in the *Sunday Express* [London] in March 1931 read:

"SCIENCE AND SENTIMENT ARE BEST SELLERS!" The accompanying news article led off with a discussion of Jeans's recently published volume *The Stars in Their Courses*: "One of the most significant events in recent publishing history is the overwhelming success of the popular scientific books of Sir James Jeans..."[66]

Jeans kept meticulous notebooks of clippings of news articles, book reviews, and announcements of his publications, as well as news coverage of his public lectures and BBC broadcasts. The notebooks, totaling fifteen in all, demonstrate his national and international acclaim, as attested by the press coverage his publications and presentations earned in the US, Britain, and around the world. For instance, Jeans preserved a total of 206 reviews and announcements, filling two ledger notebooks, on just the first edition of *The Universe Around Us*. That figure includes only those reviews that appeared in domestic British newspapers, and not the additional 188 clippings of reviews and book announcements published in newspapers in the US, India, Australia, New Zealand, and South Africa, or even those that Jeans simply did not collect. As an indication of his international renown, book reviews and notices for *The Universe Around Us* appeared in the *Times of India*, the *Malay Mail*, the *Delhi Daily Chronicle*, the *Hindu*, the *Bombay Chronicle*, and the *Johannesburg Star*.

News clippings on the release of *The Mysterious Universe* fill four more notebooks that include 334 reviews and announcements published just in domestic British papers; one notebook is dedicated to US reviews while another was needed for news clippings from other countries. Whitworth reports that Jeans's *The Mysterious Universe* sold 148,000 copies between 1930 and 1937, and he attributes the high sales partially to the popular science market established by Eddington and J.W.N. Sullivan.[67] However, it is also the case that the subject of Jeans's texts and the numerous photographs he used to illustrate his books attracted a wide audience. The topic of astronomy and its visual appeal, as this chapter will show, were factors that also contributed to the high sales of Jeans's texts.

Prior to the turn of the twentieth century, many serious scientists would not have considered publishing popularizations. As a result, women scientists and science writers largely dominated the market in non-technical science publication. Women popularized science for adult and children readers in areas such as botany, chemistry, and natural history, and published many of the best popular astronomy texts of the nineteenth century.[68] Women's interest in astronomy and other sciences and their acumen for science writing resulted in part from the science curricula instituted in women's schools in Britain. By the mid-nineteenth century, one well-respected women's institution, the North London Collegiate School, offered students courses in "the property of matter, the laws of motion, mechanical powers, simple chemistry, electricity, geology, botany, natural history and astronomy" (Patricia Phillips, *The Scientific Lady* 248). Agnes Clerke's *A Popular History of Astronomy during the Nineteenth Century* (1885) ran to 500 pages and was so well researched and documented it was read by lay readers as well as by working astronomers. "Clerke was not merely a mediator between the scientific experts and an uninformed public," as Bernard Lightman comments, she "also stood as an interpreter of the larger meaning of recent astronomical discoveries to the professional astronomers themselves."[69] Her books were admired by George Ellery Hale, founder and director of Mount Wilson Observatory. Clerke, an astronomer and historian of astronomy, corresponded with Hale over technical concerns related to astronomy, and in 1903 submitted to him at least one article for review and possible publication in the prestigious *Astrophysical Journal* published by the American Astronomical Society. Hale in turn asked for her recommendations regarding research at Mount Wilson, then one of the world's leading astronomical observatories, granted her permission to use Mount Wilson photographs in her publications, and made sure that her books held a prominent place in the observatory library.[70]

Several women scientists, however, conducted serious scientific work in astronomy and astrophysics in the early decades of the twentieth century. One example is Henrietta Leavitt, who was the first to determine the relation between the period of variable stars and their luminosity. Given that variable stars pulsate or increase in brightness and size at regular intervals, Leavitt, working at the Harvard Observatory, was able to determine by 1912 that stars with the longest period between such increases in brightness also had the greatest luminosity. Though Leavitt was prevented from fully exploring the period-luminosity relation she had discovered, it was soon realized that in knowing a variable star's period, and its absolute luminosity, the distance to the star could be calculated with accuracy.[71] It was Leavitt's findings, as Hubble himself acknowledged, which afforded him the means for determining a distance to the Andromeda nebula (*The Realm of the Nebulae* 14–15).

More closely associated with Virginia Woolf was Elizabeth Williamson, her friend Ethel Smyth's great niece. While Williamson apparently was not an observational astronomer on par with Leavitt, she worked as an assistant in astronomy at University College London. On at least one occasion in 1938 Woolf visited the observatory where Williamson worked, and later wrote in her diary: "[W]ent to see the moon at Elizabeth Williamson's observatory,

& did not see it" (*D5*: 190)."[72] Although University College London built a substantial observatory at Mill Hill in 1929, it is most likely that Woolf visited one of the three small rooftop observatories or domes then operational at the university's Gower Street site.[73] Woolf considered Williamson remarkable, and praised her "terse and muscular mind" to which Woolf thought hers no match (*L4*: 179, 181; *L6*: 109). Woolf admitted to Smyth regarding Williamson reading her novels, "I do like Eth [Elizabeth] to like them" (*L5*: 384). Yet, despite women's important scientific work in astronomy and in science popularization in the nineteenth century, by the early twentieth century popular publishing in astronomy became the purview of recognized scientists and researchers like Eddington and Jeans.[74]

A TRANSNATIONAL FASCINATION WITH ASTRONOMY

While clearly there was not an undifferentiated public response in Britain and the US to the new vistas of space, media attention in both nations given to advances in astronomy suggests that a popular fascination with astronomical discoveries developed as a transcontinental preoccupation. Frequent and consistent collaboration between British and American astronomers, in the early part of the twentieth century especially, allowed for the sharing of data. Mount Wilson Observatory hosted scientists from around the world, and provided opportunity for a cadre of British and American astronomers and cosmologists to fraternize and work together. Hubble, Jeans, and Eddington corresponded, visited, and hosted each other. George Ellery Hale, of Mount Wilson Observatory, corresponded with British astronomers Robert Ball, Agnes Clerke, George Darwin, Astronomer Royal Frank Dyson, physicist J.J. Thomson, Jeans, and many others. One reason for the frequent professional exchange between British and American astronomers was the fact that, at the time, several of the most powerful telescopes in the world were located in the US. The 60-inch and 100-inch telescopes at Mount Wilson became operable in 1908 and 1917 respectively.[75] The 100-inch Hooker telescope was the largest reflecting telescope in the world and remained so for roughly 30 years. The degree of collaboration between British and American astronomers is evidenced in part by a letter Hale sent Jeans reporting that Jeans's text *Problems of Cosmogony and Stellar Dynamics* (1919) would be used to determine the research program for the newly operational 100-inch telescope: "We are now at work on the definitive observing programme of the 100-inch telescope, and it is hardly necessary to say that your book, which I admire so much, is our chief guide in preparing the attack on the spiral nebulae and on many other questions.

I hope you will send me suggestions from time to time as our programme will be elastic enough to permit us to follow them. Give my kindest regards to Mrs. Jeans..."[76]

Hubble and Jeans were among those astronomers instrumental in shaping a transnational response to the human decentering evoked by the new vistas of space. It was partly through Jeans that Hubble's important discoveries were popularized in Britain. Hubble and Jeans shared a close and long-standing professional and personal friendship. Grace Hubble, Edwin's wife, was an eloquent writer and keen observer of conversation. Noting in her diaries cherished memories of Jeans, Grace tells a story of Jeans, on one occasion while visiting the US, having received a phone call at his hotel room:

> 'Yes,' said Jeans peremptorily, 'send the reporter along and when you send him, send along tea, – bread and butter, cake, all that sort of thing, you know.'
>
> 'Why,' he exclaimed presently, 'doesn't that reporter come up, and where is the tea?' and he rang the desk. You were speaking, said the desk, with the Editor of the Los Angeles Times, the reporter is on his way from Los Angeles.
>
> 'Heavens!' said Jeans to us, as he hung up. 'I have told the editor of the newspaper to send along our tea. It won't be in the paper, do you think?' Yes it will, I said. And it was.[77]

Both Jeans and Hubble had developed a classification system for the formation of galaxies.[78] And from 1923 on, Jeans served as a research associate at Mount Wilson Observatory, where, in 1919, Hubble began investigating extra-galactic nebulae. Jeans carried out research at the observatory on several occasions, and Hubble in turn made extended trips to England in 1934 and 1936 to present his own findings. During such visits, the astronomers at times provided accommodations for each other. Jeans often cited Hubble's research in his publications and frequently requested photos from Mount Wilson to illustrate his books as revealed by a letter to Hubble dated February 1938: "As usual with my writings I shall have to quote you and your work rather largely, and I hope you will not mind my doing this. I may also in due course write and ask you if you can spare me copies of certain photographs which I may be wanting."[79]

Having achieved celebrity status on both sides of the Atlantic, Jeans was so widely known in the US his name readily appeared in newspaper headlines and his books were reviewed in the daily newspapers. In December 1929, for instance, his volume *The Universe Around Us* topped the best-seller lists.[80] In fact, in April 1930 *The Universe Around Us* was presented to the President of the United States along with several other books to be placed in his White House study: "A delegation of American booksellers and a select committee of judges today presented to President [Herbert] Hoover the first twelve of 500 books, which are to be the nucleus of a White House library."[81] *The Universe Around Us* ranked among the list of twelve.

By the early 1930s, Hubble too was a recognized public figure in both countries. In 1934 at the close of a trip to England, Grace commented in her diary on Hubble's fame: "At 7:30 the porter got our trunk to the roof of the taxi & we drove past James's Palace into the Mall murmuring, Farewell, a long farewell to our greatness. Edwin said, It won't seem bad to be incog for awhile."[82] Two years later Hubble was again in England to give the Rhodes Lectures at Oxford. Grace recorded their jaunt to a bookshop to find "pictures of old astronomers": she noted that upon the employees' query regarding Hubble's name, "they said, Oh, a household word, sir! & became ever so interested."[83] During that same trip, Sir Carleton Allen had written Edwin regarding the success of Hubble's lectures: "You certainly seem to have a wide appeal; it is a bit of a record to have established yourself in a *Times* sub-leader, *Punch, The Children's Newspaper* and *The Evening News!*"[84]

The Hubbles established several important and longstanding British ties, some of which were peripheral to, but connected nonetheless to Virginia Woolf's circle of colleagues. Hugh Walpole became a close and dear friend to Grace, and corresponded with the Hubbles from the time they met in 1934, when Hugh visited Hubble at Mount Wilson Observatory. Afterwards Hugh scribbled a thank you note to Edwin on Metro-Goldwyn-Mayer Studio letterhead: "It was one of the great nights of my life and this is... no exaggeration – I shall never forget Saturn so long as I live... Please let me come and see the moon!"[85] Grace recorded how one particular visit by Hugh to the observatory evolved into a scene in Walpole's novel *Roman Fountain* (1940):

In "Roman Fountains" [sic] Hugh wrote of a night on Mt. Wilson. That night, when we left the 100-inch, he and Harold [Cheevers] and I walked to Dan Tracy's cabin.... He played the records Hugh asked for, the Brandenberg Concertos, Brahm's first and fourth symphonies.... The Milky Way streamed across the star-filled sky, the nightwind stirred the trees, a deer's tread rustled near us. Are there any animals up here? Asked Hugh. Yes, I said, bob-cats, mountain lions. Are the mountain lions little animals? He asked. I took them to their door...[86]

Walpole actually gave a signed copy of *Roman Fountain* to Virginia Woolf.[87]

Aldous and Maria Huxley were by far the Hubbles' closest British colleagues. In August 1937, Edwin and Grace met the Huxleys when they, along with British science writer Gerald Heard, moved to California, as Aldous had planned to do scripts for MGM Studios (Christianson, *Edwin Hubble* 261).[88] The Huxleys met the Hubbles at a party hosted by Anita Loos and in very short order developed a close relationship (Christianson 260). Grace recorded in her diary several accounts of the Huxley's visits to the observatory as well. An avid amateur astronomer herself, Grace noted on one such occasion:

After dinner we walked to the 100-inch – The moon and a globular cluster. Then we came out into enchanting moonlight, a glow in the west, a haze of moonbeams and shadow, all the domes and towers [of the telescope observatories] washed with shining silver. Went to the 60-inch & E[dwin] trained it on the ring nebula and other far-off things.... Matthew [Huxley's son] said, what do you expect to find with the 200-inch [telescope], sir? and E[dwin] – We hope to find something we didn't expect. And Aldous chuckled. Outside the 60-inch Aldous said, "Look at the pilasters and the fluting. It is Roman, it is like the tomb of a great queen." And it was, under the magic of the moon.[89]

Grace apparently edited at least one of Aldous's novels as evidenced by letters to her from Maria Huxley: "The novel is coming on slowlier and slowlier as it grows which is usually the case. – Why should we not let you have the proofs in Aberdeen? You are [supposed to be] so good at it and it does wear Aldous to do it and nobody even thinks I could be good."[90] Again in January 1944, Maria wrote to Grace reporting that Aldous "is within the last twenty pages of finishing the novel. Then it will be typed and then your work will start."[91] Thus, Grace's diary entries and correspondence offer valuable insight into the friendships the Hubbles maintained with their British associates and colleagues.

A MODERNIST HUMAN DECENTERING AND RE-SCALING

We peer out into the universe, observed Jeans, to discover that the "inconceivably long vistas of [cosmological] time...dwarf human history to the twinkling of an eye" (*The Mysterious Universe* 3–4). The new astronomical vistas provoked a very different sense of spatial relationships, and pointed up humans' relative insignificance in the larger universe. The increase in popular science publishing noted by S.C. Roberts further contributed to this public sense of a modernist human decentering. What made Jeans so tremendously popular was not only his literary eloquence in making

Figure 1.4 **Spectacular image of a galaxy from *The Universe Around Us.*** This photograph of the Nebula N.G.C. 891 in Andromeda was taken at Mount Wilson Observatory. Jeans often wrote to Edwin Hubble or George Ellery Hale to obtain remarkable images for his popular and technical publications. Courtesy of The Observatories of the Carnegie Institution of Washington.

difficult astronomical and physical concepts accessible for readers, but also his penchant for illustrating his books and public lectures with numerous photographs of distant stars and swirling galaxies. Notes from Jeans's public presentations reveal that he used as many as thirty-five to forty-five slides to illustrate a single lecture.[92] He incorporated into his books multiple photographs of stars and galaxies, many of which were supplied by Mount Wilson Observatory, despite the fact that including the photographs was labor intensive and presumably costly (Figure 1.4). S.C. Roberts reported that especially for Jeans's non-technical books Cambridge University Press "took a good deal of trouble over the illustrations" (*Sir James Jeans* x). By comparison, Jeans's immediate competitor in popular publishing at the Press, Eddington, had used very few images of stellar and galactic phenomena. From 1927 through 1935, Eddington published at least five non-technical science texts. Combined, these five books contained a total of nine photographs, perhaps in part because of their subject matter. The texts were *Stars and Atoms* (1927), *The Nature of the Physical World* (1928), *Science and the Unseen World* (1929), *The Expanding Universe* (1933), and *New Pathways in Science* (1935).

However, with the publication of Jeans's popular astronomy books, large numbers of people had access to breath-taking images of comets, globular clusters, and spiral galaxies whirling through space millions of light-years from earth. Although British astronomer Isaac Roberts's photographs of the Andromeda spiral displayed in 1888 at a meeting of the Royal Astronomical Society in London "created a sensation," this was for a limited audience largely within the scientific community.[93] Jeans, on the other hand, provided a wide readership access to the new vistas of space (Figure 1.5). *The Universe Around Us* (1929) included thirty-two images, many of which were photographed with the 100-inch telescope at Mount Wilson Observatory. *The Stars in Their Courses* (1931), an expansion of Jeans's BBC broadcasts on astronomy and cosmogony, offered seventy-two spectacular photographs of stars and nebulae, meteors, and planets. At the back of the text were maps of the constellations appearing in Britain's northern and southern skies. Another publication *Through Space and Time* (1934) was based on a series of public lectures Jeans had given at the Royal Institution and incorporated 106 photographs and figures including images of solar eclipses, as well as artistic renditions of the lunar landscape. Even the photograph used as the frontispiece to *The Mysterious Universe*, which covered both astronomy and the new physics, showed a cluster of nebulae not unlike the Hubble Deep Field images of galaxy clusters. It was not that nineteenth-century astronomy texts hadn't included photographs or that the British public had never

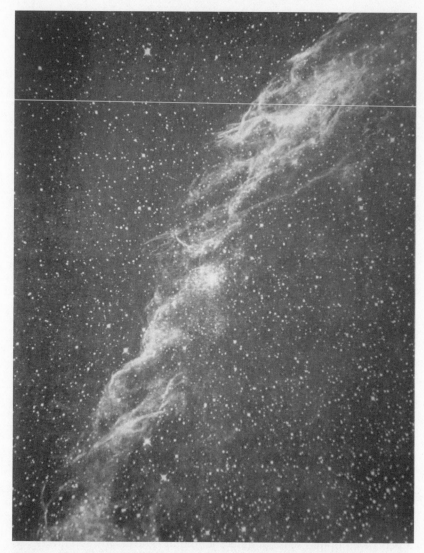

Figure 1.5 **Nebula in Cygnus from** *The Universe Around Us.* Images like this one, taken at Mount Wilson Observatory, illustrated Jeans's books and provided the public with remarkable views of astronomical phenomena, as well as a sense of the innumerable stars scattered across the wastes of space. Courtesy of The Observatories of the Carnegie Institution of Washington.

seen images of spiral nebulae. Agnes Clerke's *Problems in Astrophysics* (1903) touted eighty-one illustrations and photographs of stars and nebulae. But photographic technology had advanced so greatly by the early 1920s that the later images were stunning by comparison, and consequently fostered public interest in astronomy in much the same way as the Hubble Space Telescope's full-color exposures of colliding galaxies, stellar explosions, and six-trillion-mile-high clouds of dust have garnered front-page coverage in national newspapers and magazines.

As photographic images of remote galaxies whirling through space proliferated in non-technical science books, and in a few newspapers like the *Illustrated London News*, cosmic phenomena began to take on a reality for popular audiences. However, in surveying those photographs, it becomes clear that a certain tension resides at the heart of the science popularization project. On the one hand, the photographs were included in order to make accessible the far reaches of the universe; yet, what resulted from the photographs was an increasing realization of a human decentering within the vastness of the universe. Attempting to place into perspective earth's relation to the unbelievable distances then only recently calculated to exist between nebulae, Jeans wrote in *The Mysterious Universe*, "Indeed our earth is so infinitesimal in comparison with the whole universe, we, the only thinking beings, so far as we know, in the whole of space, are to all appearances so accidental, so far removed from the main scheme of the universe that it is *a priori* all too probable that any meaning that the universe as a whole may have, would entirely transcend our terrestrial experience, and so be totally unintelligible" (152). Within such a scenario, earth had been relegated to what Jeans described as "an exceedingly small corner of the universe" (*Eos* 85).

The new generation of large astronomical telescopes, like the 100-inch at Mount Wilson, had effected a modernist decentering and re-scaling of humans. Questions of astronomy became implicitly linked with a public concern regarding the future of human existence. By far, the most persistent question raised by the print media in Britain and in the US had to do with a pervasive popular sense of a decentering of humans in the universe. In covering the Rede Lecture Jeans gave at Cambridge in November 1930, the *Evening Standard* [London] ran the headline "Do We Matter?" The accompanying article reported:

The ancient view that the earth was not only the center of the universe, but also the largest part of it, has disappeared.... More recently it was supposed, on good astronomical grounds, that we were, in fact, as nearly as possible at the centre of the observed system of stars. That, too, has gone. It now seems, according to the latest advices, that we lie a little to the right of the centre of one gigantic system of stars among many.[94]

The *Daily Herald* [London], also covering the Rede lecture, ran the following headline on its front page: "MANKIND JUST AN ACCIDENT: Ice Age of Universal Death Must End the World." Describing Jeans as the "most eminent of British physicists," the news article cited verbatim passages from Jeans's lecture "concerning man and his place in the universe."[95]

Similar headlines, just the previous year, regarding humanity's place in the universe had been sweeping newspapers in the US. "The old speculation and inquiry as to man's place in the universe – and with that *his position in the scale of living creatures* – have again arisen," reported the *New York Times* in 1929, the year Hubble announced the expansion of the universe.[96] Science writer H. Gordon Garbedian wrote:

Our forefathers thought we were the centre of the universe. Now we know that we are but a small part of one universe among a million universes. It is the newly discovered universes – the outer galaxies, or spiral nebulae – that have forced upon us the new estimate of the size of the cosmos....[97]

The print media as well as the reading public turned their attention to the human position within the incredible expanses of the universe.

Jeans, and his popular publications, further contributed to the public sense in both the US and in Britain of this modernist human decentering. In his texts, as well as in public lectures and BBC broadcasts in London, Jeans spoke of the new vistas of space as "terrifying." He was convinced of the accidental nature of human existence, and of the rarity of life in the universe:

Standing on our microscopic fragment of a grain of sand, we attempt to discover the nature and purpose of the universe which surrounds our home in space and time. Our first impression is something akin to terror. We find the universe terrifying because of its vast meaningless distances, terrifying because of its inconceivably long vistas of time which dwarf human history to the twinkling of an eye, terrifying because of our extreme loneliness.... Into such a universe we have stumbled, if not exactly by mistake, at least as the result of what may properly be described as an accident. (*The Mysterious Universe 3–4*)

Jeans depicted the universe as disinterested in, even inimical, to life: "Perhaps indeed we ought to say [the universe] appears to be actively hostile to life like our own. For the most part, empty space is so cold that all life in it would be frozen..." (*The Mysterious Universe* 4). Given such a picture of the cosmos, Jeans claimed life in the universe assuredly was rare. "Millions of millions of stars exist which support no life," wrote Jeans, "which have never done so and never will do so" (*The Universe Around Us* 323). Jeans had theorized that our solar system was formed by a tidal disruption of material whipped from the sun by the gravitational pull of a random passing star. In what he called the Tidal Theory, Jeans posited that the solar system was formed by the close approach of a star near our sun, setting in motion "exaggerated forms of high mountains of matter moving over the surface of the star" (*The Universe Around Us* 224). These mountains supposedly ejected from the sun into long arms or filaments that eventually condensed into planets. Given the vast distances in outer space, Jeans contended, such an event would be statistically highly improbable. Thus, he theorized, life in the universe emerged on planets formed by sheer accident and must therefore be extremely rare.[98]

Then too, Harlow Shapley claimed that humans were nothing more than molecular waste cast off from the stars. In January 1925, the Harvard Observatory, headed by Shapley, coordinated a series of twenty-two radio talks on the latest developments in astronomy. Such a claim only heightened the public concern over a modernist human decentering produced by the new astronomical findings. "[W]e are made out of the same materials that constitute the stars," Shapley declared.[99] In a *New York Times* article headlined, "The Star Stuff that is Man," Shapley similarly reported, "We are made of the same stuff as the stars, so when we study astronomy we are in a way only investigating our remote ancestry and our place in the universe of star stuff. Our very bodies consist of the same chemical elements found in the most distant nebulae...."[100] Shapley's assertion, later formalized as the theory of nucleosynthesis, classified humans as mere by-products of stellar fission, haphazard accidents of natural processes.[101]

Several news stories, headlined in the *New York Times* in 1928 and 1929, further demonstrated the public angst in the US regarding a perceived decentering and re-scaling of humans within the universe. In November 1928, front page headlines declared: "Center of the Universe Located by Shapley." It was reported that Shapley had located the center of the *universe* in the constellation Sagittarius and at "about 47,000 light years away from the sun."[102] What the article intended readers to understand was Shapley's calculation for the distance to the center of the Milky Way, not the universe. The abstruseness of terms was indicative of the historical moment. That is, until 1925, our galaxy was believed to comprise the entire universe, and it was not until several years later that the universe was *popularly* understood to extend beyond the Milky Way. Even *The Times* [London], in a January 1925 news article on Jeans, described the Milky Way as the "universe": "Our universe, so far as observation goes, is limited to about 1,500,000,000 stars, thinning out definitely with their distance from the sun, which is approximately in the centre."[103]

Again, in February 1929, the *New York Times* featured another lengthy report on Shapley's calculation. "Our Universe Bares its Heart," the headline read, "Dr. Harlow Shapley, Who Plumbed Space to Find the Cosmic Centre, Explains the Significance Of This Discovery...."[104] The headline alone, with its promise of exposing the "cosmic centre" of the universe, suggested a certain anxiety about where humans find themselves in the vast abyss of space. That anxiety is further evidenced in Shapley's description of our solar system as ephemeral and minute. "Instead of being the centre of this universe," Shapley claimed, "our sun is but an insignificant speck around which flits a shadow called the earth...."[105] The center of the galaxy, Shapley reported, was at least some 50,000 light-years away. Thus, he noted, "[T]he light which we see coming from it now left the centre of the universe a long, long time before man began to live on this planet in his present form."[106]

Illustrations for the story were equally telling. The lead graphic for the article sported a full-page illustration of an astronomer peering through a huge telescope at a band of stars representing our galaxy. Below this illustration, which is located center-page, the caption reads, "Looking at the Centre of the Universe (Marked with a Dot in Circle) in the Milky Way." And there, midway across the top portion of the illustration, is a circled white dot indicating the center of the galaxy. That illustration, with its white dot, not only marks an anxiety about the modernist human decentering this chapter has been elaborating, but also demonstrates the media's response to the public anxiety regarding the new understanding of humanity's place in the universe. If humans must accept their decentered position within the abyss of intergalactic space, at least they could identify the "centre" of their own galaxy. A similar apprehension inheres in the illustration for a previously cited *New York Times* article titled "The Star Stuff that is Man." Central to the artist's sketch accompanying the report is a male figure, standing on a barren earth, silhouetted against a background of whirling galaxies, racing comets, and revolving planets (Figure 1.6). The image of the human silhouette appears as large as a single galaxy in the illustration, yet the text accompanying the image reads: "In so vastly enhanced a picture a human being becomes smaller – almost infinitesimally – physically, though

SUNDAY, AUGUST 11, 1929. TWENTY-FOUR PAGES

THE STAR STUFF THAT IS MAN

Out of the Surveys of the Far-flung Universe, Science Presents a New Vision of the Cosmos in Which We Are Pictured as Part of a Magnificent Creation, Startling in Its Gigantic Expanses

Figure 1.6 **"The Star Stuff that is Man."** The human figure in this *New York Times* illustration stands on the barren rock of earth in purposeful contrast to the whirling galaxies and streaking comets of intergalactic space. Centered in the illustration, the figure is depicted as large as a galaxy. This unusual use of scale points up the pervasive public anxiety about a modernist human decentering and re-scaling that this chapter elaborates. Courtesy of the Photo Sales Department of the *New York Times*.

intellectually man may be said to have increased in stature, for in a sense he increases in size mentally as his conception of the cosmos approaches to the truth."[107] The writer's angst about a human re-scaling and decentering becomes evident in the assertion of the increased intellectual stature of the infinitesimally small human.

Newspapers in Britain seemed to rely less on visuals or graphics and more on multi-tiered bold headlines to convey the implications of the human decentering suggested by Jeans. The *Illustrated London News* was one of the few newspapers in Britain committed to publishing photographs and paintings of the new vistas of space.[108] To illustrate a review of Jeans's *The Mysterious Universe*, the newspaper published a two-page spread of spectacular color paintings, by French astronomer Lucien Rudaux, of Jupiter as seen from one of its moons.[109]

ASTRONOMY'S MESSAGE OF POSSIBILITY

While Jeans indeed wrote of the terrifying vastness of space, he ultimately emphasized the long eons ahead in which humans might make tremendous advances. To illustrate this point, Jeans included in *The Universe Around Us* a table as seen below which compared the age of the earth to the age of telescopic astronomy:

Age of earth . . . . about	2,000,000,000 years	
Age of life on earth . . . . "	300,000,000	"
Age of man on earth . . . . "	300,000	"
Age of astronomical science . . . . . . "	3,000	"
Age of telescopic astronomy . . . . . . "	300	" (13)

"And perhaps a final item," reported *The Times* in a review of the book, "might have assigned something like 30 years to astronomical photography."[110] *The Times* article, as if to emphasize humanity's littleness, noted that this "short table concerning our little earth itself shows in almost diagrammatic form how recently we have begun to acquire knowledge...."[111] While Jeans intended to point up the long future in which humanity might make even greater astronomical discoveries, the media's interpretation of his work often only further heightened the public sense of the minuteness of human existence.

Jeans explained what he saw as the implications of the new astronomical vistas: "As the earth has already existed for 2000 million years, it is *a priori* reasonable to suppose that it will exist for at least something of the order of 2000 million years yet to come, and humanity and astronomy with it" (*The Universe Around Us* 14). He embraced a hopeful vision for the future of humankind. "Looked at in terms of space, the message of astronomy is at best one of melancholy grandeur and oppressive vastness. Looked at in terms of time, it becomes one of almost endless possibility and hope.... We have come into being in the fresh glory of the dawn, and a day of almost unthinkable length stretches before us with unimaginable opportunities for accomplishment" (*The Universe Around Us* 331).

Despite Jeans's vision of the possibilities for humanity, news headlines in Britain frequently reflected what many interpreted as Jeans's dismal view of human ephemerality. On publication of *The Universe Around Us*, one London paper ran a story headlined: "INTERESTING THEORIES OF A FAMOUS ASTRONOMER. Universe Which is Melting Away. Sun Slimming at Rate of 360,000 Million Tons a Day."[112] The media's emphasis on the ephemerality of humans in comparison to the cosmological eons tended to obscure Jeans's positive vision for the future of humankind.

WOOLF'S "LIBERATING & FRESHENING" VISTAS OF THE STARS

Such was the cultural milieu in which Woolf developed her own responses to the new vistas of intergalactic space. The new cosmology, unfolded in the pages of eclectic literary journals, the daily newspapers, and in popular science expositions captivated, inspired and terrified popular and literary audiences, and helped shape Woolf's own experiments in developing new prose forms. As science writer F.S. Marvin observed in 1929, the public passion for astronomy was heightened to such a level that people had "been stampeded ... by the appearance of a planet."[113] Even J.W.N. Sullivan found cause to lament the science he so aggressively popularized: "To the general mind the result [of advances in astronomy] has been to make the universe bigger and man smaller, and this is, perhaps, no unfair summary. It is probably difficult, after hearing a duet sung by an astronomer and a psycho-analyst, not to feel depressed."[114] By the late 1920s, Hubble and Jeans might be added, along with Freud, to the list of scientists including Copernicus, Galileo, and Darwin, whose work produced earlier moments of human decenterings.

Leonard Woolf, too, had commented on the bleak future for humanity that the new cosmology suggested. In a review of Jeans's *Universe Around Us* (1929), Leonard quailed before the broad vistas of intergalactic space that the world's great telescopes revealed:

The glimpse which one gets of these universes of myriads of stars flaming through space is, if regarded from the point of view of man's aspirations, depressing and humiliating. One may gape at the stupendous figures of space and time and speed, one may win little cold comfort from wondering at man's surprising ingenuity in robbing the universe of some of its fantastic secrets, but the spectacle, from every human point of view, is horrible and terrible in its meaninglessness.[115]

Virginia, on the other hand, found Jeans's descriptions of the seemingly infinite reaches of intergalactic space productive in formulating her global aesthetics and her anti-war politics.

While the print media persistently drew attention to what Jeans described as the "melancholy grandeur and oppressive vastness" of space, Woolf seems to have gravitated toward Jeans's claims of the possibility for a hopeful human future in the long eons to come (*The Universe Around*

Us 331). She knew well Jeans's analogy regarding the positive possibilities for humankind, having noted in her diary, "You know what Jeans says? Civilisation is the thickness of a postage stamp on the top of Cleopatra's needle; & time to come is the thickness of postage stamps as high as Mont Blanc" (*D4*: 65).[116] Woolf was citing the conclusion to *The Universe Around Us*, in which Jeans attempted to demonstrate "the length of the future which, so far as astronomy can see, probably stretches before civilised humanity" (330). Jeans suggested that if past geological ages of the earth might be represented by the height of Cleopatra's Needle, and the span of human existence were indicated by the thickness of a penny, then a postage stamp stuck to the penny might represent the period of established human civilizations. An entire stack of postage stamps equaling the height of Mont Blanc, Jeans argued, would be necessary to depict the long ages ahead in which humankind might excel. "[T]he first postage-stamp represents what man has already achieved; the pile which outtops Mont Blanc represents what he may achieve, if his future achievement is proportional to his time on earth" (*The Universe Around Us* 330–1).

Rather than inspiring a sense of isolation or depression, those photographs of intergalactic space printed in Jeans's popular science texts afforded Woolf fresh perspectives that informed her experiments in narrative form, as well as her radical pacifist stance on human aggression. "What shall I think of that[s] liberating & freshening?" she wrote in March of 1940, even as war planes flew over her home, Monk's House. "I'm in the mood when I open my window at night & look at the stars. Unfortunately its 12.15 on a grey dull day, the aeroplanes are active..." (*D5*: 276). Far from being unnerved by advances in astronomy, she was inspired by the stars. The new vistas of intergalactic space suggested to her a hopeful future for humankind. Somehow, in what Jeans had characterized as a nearly lifeless universe, humans had evolved and had achieved some civility. And somehow, Woolf seemed to believe, deep within humans stirred a tenacious capacity for survival.

In the interwar years, the talk among British intellectuals had focused on the seemingly imminent demise of human civilization. In February 1940 as World War II raged, Woolf recorded a dinner party conversation in which T.S. Eliot, Saxon Sydney-Turner, and Clive Bell discussed their concerns about the decimation of civilization. She, however, had rejected the general consensus:

But our talk? – it was about Civilization. All the gents. against me. Said very likely, more likely than not, this war means that the barbarian will gradually freeze out culture. Nor have we improved. Tom & Saxon said the Greeks were more thoroughly civilised. The slave was not so much a slave as ours are. Clive also pessimised – saw the light going out gradually. So I flung some rather crazy theories into the air. (*D5*: 268)

Her resistance to Eliot and Bell's pessimism marked in part her own conflicted relationship to the high culture of Oxbridge they espoused. Regardless of Woolf's exact point of opposition to the conversation that evening, it is clear that she consistently resisted assertions of the necessary demise of human civilization, either as a result of evolution, human aggression, or the "heat-death" of the universe as suggested by Clive's comment on the "light going out gradually."[117] In a letter written in 1908 to Saxon Sydney-Turner, Bell once commented: "What does a star or two, a world or two . . . signify. What do all the stars & systems signify. All that is not permanent is futile, and nothing is permanent, save perhaps time & space. If so, time & space alone are significant."[118]

Despite her awareness of earth's fragility and its minuscule size in a universe Jeans had described as inimical to life, Woolf recalled in "The Sun and the Fish" the lizards she had observed at the London Zoological Gardens, and how their silent resilience denoted the possibility for life in ages far hence:

After destruction calm; after ruin steadfastness. . . . One lizard is mounted immobile on the back of another, with only the twinkle of a gold eye-lid or the suction of a green flank to show that they are living flesh, and not made of bronze. All human passion seems furtive and feverish beside this still rapture. Time seems to have stopped and we are in the presence of immortality. (*CE4*: 182)

If humans could avoid destroying each other through global conflict, Woolf apparently believed, they too might persist throughout the universe's long ages with the same resilience as those ancient and long surviving reptiles.

Nevertheless, like many of the science writers who were her associates, Woolf understood the very real possibility of human extinction. And certainly, like her husband Leonard, her fascination with technology and the sciences was at times conflicted. But in opposition to modernist doomsday plots and headlines that lamented the inevitable demise of humanity, Woolf instead explored in her fiction and essays alternatives for human survival into the far future. In *Jacob's Room* (1922), as old Mr. Clutterbuck invites the guests at Mrs. Durrant's party to gaze through his telescope, Miss Eliot, turns to him and asks, "Doesn't it make you melancholy – looking at the stars?" (50). But Clutterbuck resists the perspective articulated by Leonard Woolf and in news headlines regarding the terrifying meaninglessness of the universe. Mr. Clutterbuck replies, "Why should it make me melancholy? Not for a moment – dear me no" (*JR* 50). Chapter Two examines how Woolf's fascination with telescopic technologies inspired her experiments with narrative and her pacifist politics. What becomes clear in the pages that follow is that Woolf maintained a hopeful vision for the future of humanity, based in part on the "liberating & freshening" vistas of the stars, both as she saw them in James Jeans's popular astronomy books, and through the lens of her own telescope.

2

From Hubble's telescope to "The Searchlight"

In 1929, the same year Edwin Hubble and Milton Humason reported that the universe was expanding as galaxies raced away from each other at phenomenal speeds, Virginia Woolf began drafting a short story about stars, telescopes, and war. The story, later titled "The Searchlight," suggests not only that Woolf was aware of Hubble's radical reconfiguration of the universe, but that the new astronomical vistas had a powerful shaping effect on her aesthetic practices and pacifist politics. Reconstructing in part the interconnections between Woolf's writing and Britain's public interest in astronomy, this chapter charts Woolf's exploration of alternative aesthetic and political perspectives suggested to her through emerging telescopic technologies. Her fiction and essays materialized out of a complex network of events extending from new developments in cosmology to the eruption of the World War II. Woolf drew upon the popular interest in cosmology and telescopic technologies as a means of experimenting with narrative. The chapter theorizes how Woolf's own fascination with cosmology and with telescopes helped shape what I define as her narrative scoping strategies. She deployed these scoping strategies in her fiction, particularly in her story "The Searchlight," both at the level of sentence structure, and, more generally, by staging her plots and characters against the backdrop of the broad vistas of intergalactic space. The apparatus of the telescope, given the reversibility of its visual fields, reveals where she learned these scoping strategies and how she used them to support her pacifist politics.

WOOLF'S REFRAMING OF EDWIN HUBBLE'S ANDROMEDA RESULTS

J.W. Graham, who has done extensive research on the multiple typescript drafts of "The Searchlight," has identified the source for Woolf's story as an autobiographical account by Sir Henry Taylor, a friend and photographic subject of Woolf's great-aunt, Julia Margaret Cameron. Taylor had recorded how in the summer of 1822 while visiting his father's estate, he would journey "in the middle of the summer's nights" to a nearby "uninhabited castle, partly ancient, partly modern" (*Autobiography of Sir Henry Taylor* 45). There he would spend his days in the castle tower with a telescope watching ongoing events at an adjacent farm. The crucial scene of Taylor's account, at least for Woolf, is the moment in which he recalled spying two young people embrace. "Through this telescope," wrote Taylor, "I saw once a young daughter of the farmer rush into the arms of her brother, on his arrival after an absence, radiant with joy" (*Autobiography* 45). The telescope, through which Taylor recalled witnessing the embrace, sparked Woolf's imagination as is evidenced by early titles for her story, which included "Seen through," "What the telescope discovered," and "The Telescope."[1] Even years after she initially drafted the story, Woolf referred to her piece as the "old Henry Taylor telescope story" (*D5*: 204). Woolf, however, extensively reworked Taylor's account in multiple drafts she sketched over the course of twelve years.[2] What has not been explored is how those revisions suggest Woolf's increased interest in centering her story on the apparatus of the telescope. Not only does the telescope figure prominently in the story's later versions, it becomes the device that best exemplifies Woolf's narrative scoping strategies.

Under Woolf's pen, the siblings' embrace of Taylor's story is transformed into a passionate kiss between a young woman and a mysterious man. In the first typescript draft, an omniscient narrator simply recounts a scene in which a young man, from the tower of a ruined castle, spies through a telescope a servant girl and boy kissing "violently, brutally, passionately" (quoted in J.W. Graham 383). In later versions, the teller of the telescope story has been transmuted into the character of Mrs. Ivimey, who relates the kiss as glimpsed by her great-grandfather as a youth. The setting of Taylor's story also gets reworked to a summer's night during which Mrs. Ivimey and her husband along with other guests attend a dinner at a private British club. While the guests are having coffee on the balcony of the club's revamped eighteenth-century mansion, the beam of a nearby air force searchlight sweeps across the balcony. Upon seeing a "bright disc" of light reflected presumably by "a mirror in a ladies' hand bag," Mrs. Ivimey declares, "You'll never guess what *that* made me see!" ("The Searchlight," *HH* 120). Thus begins Mrs. Ivimey's tale and Woolf's reconfiguration of Taylor's account into her narrative of telescopes, searchlights, and war.

Perhaps the most significant revision to the final drafts of "The Searchlight" was Woolf's adoption of a dramatic narrative style. Mrs. Ivimey relates the story of her great-grandfather as a youth, sitting at the window of an abandoned castle tower and "looking though [a] telescope at the stars," as she too gazes into the night sky (*HH* 122). "Jupiter, Aldebaran, Cassiopeia," she recalls, as she pauses to look out over the mansion balcony "as if she were up in the tower looking from the window that swung open" (*HH* 122). Gesturing toward the evening sky, she exclaims, "There they were... the stars" (*HH* 122). The immediate effect of this dramatic enactment of the story, her pointing to the stars as if she were in the castle tower of her great-grandfather's youth, is that the dinner guests inevitably become part of the performance: "They all looked at the stars that were coming out in the darkness over the trees. The stars seemed very permanent, very unchanging [...] A hundred years seemed nothing [...] They seemed to be with [the boy], in the tower, looking out over the moors at the stars" (*HH* 122–3).[3] The guests are further drawn into the drama largely through Mrs. Ivimey's peculiar collapsing of narrative time in which the past becomes conflated with the present. As she peers at the stars, Mrs. Ivimey suddenly "seemed puzzled, because she could not find the telescope" (*HH* 122), even as she had not been able to find her great-grandfather's telescope during a visit to the castle ten years earlier. Her supposed confusion regarding the whereabouts of her great-grandfather's telescope conflates her telling of the story with two distinct, but past events: her previous visit to the castle tower, and the event of her great-grandfather's own peering through the telescope at some point in the 1820s.

The audience participation inherent in Mrs. Ivimey's dramatic narration, however, extends beyond the guests on the balcony to actual readers of the story. Mrs. Ivimey's narration positions the reader on the mansion balcony, and simultaneously behind the lens of Mrs. Ivimey's imaginary telescope. This can be demonstrated by examining the moment in which Mrs. Ivimey has pivoted the lens of her make-believe telescope from the stars to the earth: "Then she made a movement, as if she swung something into position. 'But what did the earth look like through the telescope?' she asked" (*HH* 123). Miming the act of focusing a hand-held telescope, Mrs. Ivimey made "another quick little movement with her fingers as if she were twirling something" (*HH* 123), and began to describe what the boy of her story presumably glimpsed through his scope: "He focussed it upon the earth [...] He focussed it so that he could see... each tree... each tree separate... and the birds... rising and falling... and a stem of smoke... there... in the midst of the trees.... And then... lower... lower... (she lowered her eyes)... there was a house..." (*HH* 123–4). The very structure of the sentences evokes the view made possible by a telescope. The ellipses, repetitions, and lacunae require that the reader encounter the text in a sense similar to the experience of looking through the restrictive lens of a scoping device. The elliptical interruptions, for instance, limit the reader's view to only one tree at a time, then the birds, then the farmhouse. Albeit only momentarily, the reader nevertheless must physically pause as the sentence is focused through the mechanisms of the ellipses and repetition of the words "focussed," "each," and "lower." Thus reading "The Searchlight" becomes a participatory, embodied, and dramatic experience for Woolf's readers by means of the narrative structure.

Woolf's scoping strategies, however, operate at a level beyond sentence structure. Stephen Spender's literature students once complained that Woolf's characters seem to view the world "from a very great distance, [and] as though through the wrong end of a telescope."[4] Despite the intended derogatory tone of their critique, Spender's students were in part correct. What is significant about telescopes, at least for hand-held models, is the reversibility of their visual fields.[5] That is, when one looks through the opposite end of a telescope, objects observed, instead of being magnified, look very small and very far away. Woolf effects a similar reversal of the telescopic visual field in "The Searchlight," especially in the moment that the reader glimpses the kiss between the young woman and the mysterious man who appears "from around the corner" of the farmhouse (*HH* 125). Despite the fact that "every brick" of the house is telescopically visible, the kiss is seen not in close-up, but as if through the opposite end of the telescope. Mrs. Ivimey declares, "It was the first time [her great-grandfather] had seen a man kiss a woman – in his telescope – miles and miles away across the moors!" (*HH* 124). Not only do Woolf's characters seem to view the world through the wrong end of a telescope, but her characters themselves are often depicted as if *observed* through a telescope's opposite end. This visually obverse narrative strategy may have suggested itself to Woolf in May 1932, during an excursion to Greece with art critic Roger Fry and his sister Margery. Woolf noted that one evening, while on a hill above Delphi, Margery had invited a "goat girl" to "look through her [field]glasses, first the right way, then the wrong" (*D4*: 95).

This penchant for scaling between close-up and distant views of her characters suggests Woolf's awareness of, and response to, a public concern regarding a modern human re-scaling due in part to a new generation of large astronomical telescopes that had demonstrated the vast distances of intergalactic space. Woolf saw, too, that the telescope is a time machine of sorts, in that looking out into space always marks a looking back in cosmological time. Thus, Mrs. Ivimey, who narrates her tale while miming the act of peering through an imaginary telescope, looks back in time to glimpse a crucial moment which marks the beginnings of her life: "And then a girl came out of the house . . . wearing something blue upon her head . . . and stood there [. . .] And then . . . look . . . A man . . . A man! He came round the corner. He seized her in his arms! They kissed . . . they kissed" (*HH* 124). In glimpsing the kiss, Mrs. Ivimey witnesses to some extent her own genesis, in that her great-grandfather ends up marrying the "girl" spied through his scope. Attributing her very existence to the apparatus of the telescope, she explains, "Because if there hadn't been a telescope, I shouldn't be sitting here now" (*HH* 122). Woolf's appreciation of large astronomical telescopes as devices for looking back in time is evidenced by other early titles for the story which included "Scenes from the Past," "A Scene from the Past," and "Incongruous Memories," later revised to "Inaccurate Memories."[6] Woolf's dear friend E.M. Forster also associated the telescope with looking back in time, and with memory. He wrote to Virginia regarding her novel *The Waves*: "Although I knew your way of remembering the past was very different from my own, I'd never realised it consciously till I came on your handling of Percival. I didn't think it inadequate or 'wrong' – only felt with a good deal of emotion that we don't use the same telescopes."[7]

Woolf understood the telescope as a device that allows for a simultaneous co-existence of the past and present, and experimented in "The Searchlight" with contemporary cosmological theories on light as it traverses the universe. There is, for instance, that curious moment when Mrs. Ivimey claims that the young woman glimpsed through the telescope " 'was my –' . . . as if she were about to say 'myself' " (125). And like the young woman, Mrs. Ivimey too wears "something blue on her head" (125) so that it is as if Mrs. Ivimey sees herself, and not her great-grandmother as she looks through her imaginary scope. The possibility of the simultaneity of past and present was posited in part as a result of Einstein's model of the universe. Einstein had posited a finite, but unbounded model of the universe, which might be conceived of as the surface of a ball or planet. Light traveling along the surface of space, so to speak, must return to its starting point, and thus astronomical events of the past might be observed in the present. Jeans explained, "As a consequence of space bending back on itself, a projectile of a ray of light . . . cannot go on for ever without repeating its own tracks" (*The Universe Around Us* 69). It was argued that because of the curvature of space, light would eventually travel around the entire universe and as a result astronomers should be able to see the beginnings of the universe.[8]

Jeans's popular astronomy texts and BBC lectures had sensitized Woolf to humans' ephemeral and non-privileged position within the frame of cosmological space and time. Indeed, Hubble demonstrated that the universe was far older and more vast than even cosmologists had previously imagined. Woolf understood the larger implications of Hubble's reconfiguration of the universe, and the implicit decentering of humans that the 100-inch Mount Wilson telescope helped produce. Those images of spiral galaxies whirling millions of light-years from earth and published largely in popular astronomy books like those by Jeans only further diminished "that confidence in human centrality which was already being abraded in her father's generation by evolutionary theory."[9] Woolf's own experimentation with a re-scaling of humans in the universe is denoted by Mrs. Ivimey's great-grandfather's boyhood attempts to understand himself in relation to vastly remote cosmic phenomena: " 'There they were,' [Mrs. Ivimey] went on, 'the stars.' And he asked himself, my great-grandfather – that boy. 'What are they? Why are they? And who am I?' as one does...looking at the stars" (*HH* 122). Jeans similarly had questioned at the close of *Astronomy and Cosmogony*: "What, if any, is our relation to the remote nebulae, for surely there must be some more direct contact than that light can travel between them and us in a hundred million years?" (422).

Woolf's telescopic depiction of the kiss invited her readers to focus on the ephemerality of humans in relation to the long ages of the cosmological past while at the same time pointing up the inanity of global conflict. Indeed, in an early draft of the story, titled "Incongruous Memories," the boy ventures off to the castle tower to read about "wars in Hungary & all the ancient lore of the ancient world–about chemistry & astrology & [then] about battles, policies & dead men's doings–until he thought himself the only survivor in the world of the dead."[10] It is specifically his father's books on war that leads the boy to turn his telescope to the stars. "Now every night he swept the skies...& imagined the abysses through which he in his tower, & the sleeping house, were sweeping so incessantly."[11] Ultimately, what Woolf's readers see through Mrs. Ivimey's imaginary telescope is a moment marking the beginnings of a human life, namely Mrs. Ivimey's, silhouetted against the backdrop of the abysses of space. It is life, as the narrator of "Incongruous Memories" specifically noted, which is glimpsed through the telescope: "There was life, there was love, there was passion!"[12] But it is the beginnings of a life seen against the backdrop of imminent war, which, in the story's final version, has invaded the dinner party by means of the searchlight that catches Mrs. Ivimey in its beam. In order to appreciate Woolf's response to the popular concern regarding a human decentering and re-scaling discussed in Chapter One, her own engagement with emerging telescopic technologies and advances in cosmology must first be explored.

WOOLF AND THE TELESCOPE

Evidence of her fascination with telescopes and with astronomy surfaces throughout Woolf's diaries and letters. In April 1929, for instance, Woolf wrote of having viewed the "craters of the moon" through a telescope owned by Vita Sackville-West: "These I saw silver white & like the spots that are made by water dropping into plaster of paris through Vita's telescope the other day" (*D3*: 222). So great was Woolf's interest in astronomy that Vita investigated the possibility of installing a planetarium at her home, Long Barn – until Vita learned it would cost roughly £20,000. While touring Berlin, Vita wrote to Woolf in February 1929: "I'll tell you about the Planetarium. I wanted to have one at Long Barn, but on enquiry I discovered that they cost £20,000. I am therefore going to devote all my energies to getting one put up in London. It is another aspect of Virginia's World. I shall try to write an article about it, but it is a subject for you, not for me."[13] Two years earlier, the women traveled by train from London to Yorkshire to view the total solar eclipse of 1927. Later, in 1938, Woolf was invited by her friend Elizabeth Williamson, an assistant in astronomy at University College London, to one of the university's Gower Street observatory domes to peer at the moon and stars. Woolf recorded that she was unable to see the moon, presumably as a result of bad weather (*D5*: 190). As Judith Killen notes, that same year Woolf obtained her own telescope, actually from Williamson, and had it set up at Monks House, the Woolfs' summer home (*D5*: 109; Killen 195–6).[14] Virginia recorded Leonard's "brilliant idea of converting half the library into an open air verandah with glass doors, in which we can sit on a hot night & survey the stars" (*D5*: 159). From this "makeshift Monks House observatory," she and Leonard viewed "Jupiter minus the waiting women: & a plaster cast of the moon," as well as the "cardboard collar" rings of Saturn (Killen 195–6; *D5*: 109, 110). Even in the final months of her life, Woolf recorded her and Leonard's astronomical observations. On a moonlit night in 1941, she jotted in her diary: "L[eonard]. looking at the comet. Rather a strong moon, & so cant identify the constellation" (*D5*: 351).

The allure of telescopic technologies for Woolf was indicative of the larger, pervasive public interest in astronomy and cosmology. As noted in Chapter One, astronomical telescopes like the 100-inch at Mount Wilson, used in combination with advanced photographic technologies, brought into the purview of popular audiences for the first time new vistas of intergalactic space. In addition, popular science writers like James Jeans had captivated the nation's and Woolf's imagination. In constant demand as a lecturer and broadcaster, Jeans had by 1930 acquired in Britain a popular omnipresence. His non-technical publications on astronomy and the new physics helped formulate those issues central to the popular response to Hubble's findings. As Jeans outlined them, those issues concerned 1) a re-scaling of humans within the inconceivable vastness of intergalactic space; 2) the recent emergence of humans in comparison to the cosmological eons; and 3) a heightened sense of the rarity of life within a cold and indifferent universe. Jeans had emphasized the human decentering and re-scaling produced by the new astronomical vistas. "To the question, 'where does man stand in the universe?'" Jeans wrote, "the first attempt at an answer at any rate in recent times, was provided by the astronomy of Ptolemy: 'at the centre.' Galileo's telescope provided the next, and incomparably better, approximation: 'man's home in space is only one of a number of small bodies revolving round a huge central sun'" (*The Universe Around Us* 8). In the nineteenth century, such a human decentering had been imputed to Darwin and theories of evolution, as well as to advances in geological dating of the earth's sediments. Yet even prior to Darwin, the "island universe" theory had suggested that nebulae were "other Milky Ways," and presupposed that galaxies were ancient yet evolving, and in various stages of evolution.[15] The island universe theory, given its evolutional paradigm, implied humans' late emergence within the vast ages of cosmological time. Hubble's findings with the 100-inch telescope at Mount Wilson only further demonstrated earth's insignificant position within the unimaginable depths of intergalactic space, and had pointed up the relative brevity of human existence. "For all but a 500th part of its long journey, the light by which we see th[e] remotest of visible nebulae travelled towards an earth uninhabited by man," wrote Jeans; "Just as it was about to arrive, man came into being on earth, and built telescopes to receive it" (*The Universe Around Us* 67).

Woolf was a particularly close and careful reader of Jeans. Passages taken nearly verbatim from Jeans's non-technical astronomy books appear in her novels *The Waves* (1931) and *The Years* (1937). Woolf explicitly mentioned Jeans in *Between the Acts* (1941) when Isa Oliver wanders into the Pointz Hall library looking for a book that will provide a "remedy" for the century, and considers "Eddington, Darwin, or Jeans" (Killen 161; *BA* 11).[16] In that novel, as Gillian Beer has noted, "Einstein and Eddington are scattered in among other ideas in the gossip" of the villagers.[17] Telescopes or telescopic devices, moreover, appear either literally or metaphorically in six of Woolf's nine novels, and in multiple essays and short stories. In *Night and Day* (1919), for instance, Katharine Hilbery who dreams of being an astronomer, at night secretly works out equations in her bedroom. Katharine defends her quirky behavior in an imaginary conversation with her cousin Henry, in which she explains how she wished "to study mathematics – to know about the stars" and to "calculate things, and use a telescope" (*ND* 203). In one scene, as Katharine walks along the Embankment with Denham, she imagines looking at the moon through a telescope: "all the time she was in fancy looking up through a telescope at white shadow-cleft disks which were other worlds, until she felt herself possessed of two bodies, one walking by the river with Denham, the other concentrated to a silver globe aloft in the fine blue space above the scum of vapours that was covering the visible world" (*ND* 317).

Likewise, in Woolf's novel *Jacob's Room* (1922), the deaf Mr. Clutterbuck invites the women of Mrs. Durrant's dinner party to peer through his telescope at stars and constellations, including Andromeda, the crucial nebula for Hubble's researches of the early 1920s (48). Telescopic devices also figure prominently in *A Voyage Out*. As the *Euphrosyne* makes its way for a South American island, it is viewed "from the decks of great liners" through "strong glasses" or binoculars, which, instead of magnifying the crew on board, miniaturizes them into mere insects and "lumps on the rigging" (*VO* 78). It may be no accident that the ship in the novel is named the *Euphrosyne*. Benjamin Martin, a British manufacturer of optical devices and popularizer of science, in the 1750s published for women interested in astronomy a serialized text titled *The Young Gentleman's and Lady's Philosophy*. One of its main characters is a young woman named Euphrosyne. Written as an instructional narrative, the text recounts how Euphrosyne's brother, Cleonicus, teaches her about the natural sciences and the use of visualization devices – particularly the telescope and the microscope. The frontispiece to this volume depicted Euphrosyne in a study learning about astronomy. "At her shoulder is a telescope, in her lap is a book, and nearby there is a large globe of the heavens" (Meyer, *The Scientific Lady in England 1650–1760* 38).

Other examples include Mrs. McNab's vision of the Ramsays in the "Time Passes" section of *To the Lighthouse*, which is narrated as if viewed through a telescope. In one scene, Mrs. McNab recalls an image of Mrs. Ramsay as if glimpsed in "the circle at the end of a telescope (*TTL* 136). In another scene, the narrator reports: "Once more . . . the telescope fitted itself to Mrs. McNab's eyes, and in a ring of light she saw the old gentleman [Mr. Ramsay] . . . talking to himself, she supposed, on the lawn" (*TTL* 140).[18]

"SEEING STRANGE, GRIM PICTURES"

The argument of this chapter, that Woolf valued the telescope as a structuring device for her own narrative strategies, is evidenced by her 1928 review of Florence Emily Hardy's biography of her husband, *The Early Life of Thomas Hardy*. In that review Woolf contended that the telescope had a shaping effect on Thomas Hardy's aesthetic vision: "It was by chance that he saw things, not by design.... He put the brass telescope to his eye and saw the strangest things."[19] Celebrating Hardy's "faculty for putting the telescope to his eye and seeing strange, grim pictures," Woolf, in turn, would deploy a similar strategy in another of her short stories titled "The Symbol."[20] Written as she revised her telescope story, "The Symbol" evokes a telescopic glimpse of the end, rather than the beginnings of a human life. The suggestive counterpoint between "The Searchlight" and "The Symbol," when read together, further demonstrates Woolf's use of her narrative scoping strategies. Whereas one story provides a glimpse of life's potential (as in the case of Mrs. Ivimey's view of the beginnings of her life), the other reveals life's fragility and uncertainty. Both stories gesture toward humanity's precarious position in a cold and indifferent universe.

In fact, Woolf may have first conceived of "The Symbol," a short story that recounts a mountain climbing accident, only a year after she began her telescope story. In an August 1930 diary entry, she recorded the news of a fatal climbing accident suffered by a tutor hired by Harold Nicolson and Vita Sackville-West. The tutor, "a nice young man with blue eyes white teeth & straight nose," and his fiancée had fallen into an alpine crevasse; their bodies apparently were never recovered (*D*3: 314). Woolf had met the tutor at the Nicolson's home and later recorded her reactions upon hearing of the climbing accident:

It is the hottest day of the year: & so it was last year, almost on this day; & I was at Long Barn, & there was the Eton tutor... & he now lies at the bottom of a crevasse in Switzerland–this very hot evening–lies crushed beside his Mary Irving: there are the two bodies for ever. I suppose some ice drips, or shifts: the light is blue, green; or wholly black; nothing stirs round them. Frozen, near together, in their tweeds & hobnail boots there they lie. And I am here; writing in my lodge, looking over the harvest fields. (*D*3: 314)

The poignant element of the entry is Woolf's evocation of the mountain's seeming indifference towards those silent bodies, perhaps best captured in the image of the ice which on occasion "drips, or shifts." Similarly, the setting for "The Symbol" is an Alpine mountain top, described by the story's sole and unnamed character as inhospitable, even extra-terrestrial: "There was a little dent on the top of the mountain like a crater on the moon. It was filled with snow.... There was a scurry of dry particles now and again, covering nothing. It was too high for breathing flesh or fur covered life" ("The Symbol" 282).

Here again, telescopic technology and dramatic narrative are key to the story's depiction of life's ephemerality. The story's main character, another Mrs. Ivimey in some sense, surveys the peak of a mountain through a pair of field glasses or binoculars as she sits on a "balcony overlook[ing] the main street of the Alpine summer resort, like a box at a theatre" ("The Symbol" 282). While watching the mini-dramas that comprise village life, those "preludes, curtain raisers" as they are "acted out in public," the lady pens a letter to her older sister in England ("The Symbol" 282). "The mountain...is a symbol," writes the lady, while she "focussed the lens" of her binoculars on the mountain "as if to see what the symbol was" ("The Symbol" 282). To some extent, the mountain becomes a symbol for the fragility and ephemerality of human life. Its ominous "landslides and avalanches," the lady is told by the resort proprietor, "have been known... to blot out a whole village" ("The Symbol" 282, 284). Indeed, the "graves in the churchyard near the hotel recorded the names of several men who had fallen climbing" and serve as evidence of the mountain's imperviousness to life ("The Symbol" 282).

As the lady writes to her sister, she acknowledges a group of "young men who in the street below were making ready to start [a climb]," and with whom she has "a certain connection" ("The Symbol" 282). One of the young climbers, we are told, had attended school with her daughter. Shortly thereafter, though, like Hardy who saw "strange, grim pictures" when he put the telescope to his eye, the lady witnesses a liminal moment between life and death through her binoculars: "As I write these words, I can see the young men quite plainly on the slopes of the mountain. They are roped together. One I think I told you was at the same school as Margaret. They are now crossing a crevasse...." ("The Symbol" 284). Here the elliptical breaking off of the sentence marks the disappearance of the men, who at that moment had fallen into the crevasse. The space of the ellipses conveys the end of life, or at least its uncertainty: "The pen fell from her hand, and the drop of ink straggled in a zig zag line down the page" ("The Symbol" 284). Juxtaposed to the earlier drama of the street scenes, the zig zag line and final ellipses, like a flatline on a cardiac monitor, depict the end of life. Dean Baldwin has commented, "It is difficult to accept...that the woman could have seen the climbers disappear, but this is the only false note in an otherwise artful story" (*Virginia Woolf: A Study in Short Fiction* 71). Yet, it is precisely that the lady witnesses the loss of life through her binoculars that produces the story's tension. Woolf's story of the climbers' death witnessed through field glasses echoes British climber Edward Whymper's account of a tragic accident that occurred on the first ascent of the Matterhorn. In July 1865, a team of men, led by Whymper, achieved the summit of the

Matterhorn, but upon beginning their descent, one member of the team slipped, a safety rope broke, and four climbers plummeted 4,000 feet onto a glacier below. Whymper, who held on to the mountain face, later recorded the search party's reactions when the bodies of the victims were sighted from an impassable ridge: "By 8.30 we had got on to the plateau at the top, and within sight of the corner in which we knew my companions must be. As we saw one weather-beaten man after another raise the telescope, turn deadly pale, and pass it on without a word to the next, we knew that all hope was gone."[21]

Woolf's father Leslie Stephen knew of the incident as he, along with multiple British climbers including Whymper, and Rev. Charles Hudson who died in the Matterhorn accident, were early members of the Alpine Club, a group of British climbers who were acclaimed as first to reach the peaks of many of the Swiss, French and Italian Alps. Having climbed several of the most formidable of the Alps including Mont Blanc and the Jungfrau, Leslie Stephen recorded his sense of insignificance before those mountain peaks: "The mountains represent the indomitable force of nature to which we are forced to adapt ourselves; they speak to man of his *littleness* and his *ephemeral existence*" (*The Playground of Europe* 262; italics mine). Likewise "The Searchlight" and "The Symbol" had gestured toward a modern human re-scaling. Through her narrative scoping strategies, Woolf had captured in microcosm the ephemerality of life on earth, which Jeans described as whirling precariously through a vast and indifferent universe.

Popularizers of astronomy of the 1920s and 1930s had a curious affinity for the rhetoric of theatre and drama. Almost invariably, popular explications of astronomy narrated human existence in terms of the earth as a tiny stage upon which humans' futile and brief struggle for survival is observed. One newspaper reported in 1929, "So vast is stellar creation that if our Milky Way with its millions of heavenly bodies were suddenly blotted out of existence, it would be hundreds of thousands of years before the inhabitants of a world in one of the far away spiral nebulae would observe the change, and then only by the sudden flickering out of a faintly luminous spot seen through a telescope."[22] In that same news article the writer queried, "Why and when did man make his debut on the stage of the cosmic drama and what is his destiny?"[23] Arthur Eddington likewise observed in his widely read *The Expanding Universe* (1933):

We walk the stage of life, performers of a drama for the benefit of the cosmic spectator. As the scenes proceed he notices that the actors are growing smaller and the action quicker. When the last act opens the curtain rises on midget actors rushing through their parts at frantic speed. Smaller and smaller. Faster and faster. One last microscopic blur of intense agitation. And then nothing. (131)

Popular science writers often depicted the drama of humanity's demise as if from the perspective of some distant, and seemingly disinterested cosmic observer. It was a motif drawn from literature. Ann Banfield notes Bertrand Russell's citation of a scene from the Faustus tale in which the story of creation is recounted: "For countless ages the hot nebula whirled aimlessly though space. At length it began to take shape, the central mass threw off planets, the planets cooled…"[24] Eventually humankind evolves, but the Creator watching the drama "sent another sun through the sky, which crashed into Man's sun; and all returned again to nebula. 'Yes,' he murmured, 'it was a good play; I will have it performed again.' "[25] Russell and Eddington's dramatic accounts of humanity's place in the universe resulted from the emerging scientific understanding that, as Russell put it, "all the noonday brightness of human genius [is] destined to extinction in the vast death of the solar system…"[26]

Such dramatic depictions of humans' struggle to survive in future eons heightened public concerns regarding the human re-scaling and decentering that emerging telescopic technologies had effected. Jeans too had queried:

Is this, then, all that life amounts to–to stumble, almost by mistake, into a universe which was clearly not designed for life, and which, to all appearances, is either totally indifferent or definitely hostile to it, to stay clinging on to a fragment of a grain of sand until we are frozen off, *to strut our tiny hour on our tiny stage* with the knowledge that our aspirations are all doomed to final frustration, and that our achievements must perish with our race, leaving the universe as though we had never been? (*The Mysterious Universe* 15–16; italics mine)

H.G. Wells, in his short story "The Star," similarly depicted the futile drama of human existence from a non-terrestrial point of view.[27]

The notion that humans played only a small part in the drama of a universe that was dying out had been taken up in the literature of the nineteenth century. Hardy wrote of it, as did Tennyson.[28] By the nineteenth century, it was understood that the stars were expending their energy at a remarkable rate and that eventually our sun would become a cold cinder. Jeans explained the notion of the heat-death of the universe: "For, independently of all astronomical considerations, the general principle known as the second law of thermodynamics predicts that there can be but one end to the universe – a 'heat-death' in which the total energy of the universe is uniformly distributed, and all the substance of the universe is at the same temperature. This temperature will be so low as to make life impossible" (*The Mysterious Universe* 15). Woolf knew well the notion of the heat-death of the universe and wove it into her novel *Mrs Dalloway*, as the battered woman in Regent's Park sings a song in the "voice of an ancient spring sprouting from the earth" (*MD* 80). Her song evokes the ages of a primordial earth, "when the pavement was grass, when it was swamp, through the age of tusk and mammoth, through the age of silent sunrise" (*MD* 81). She sings of "love which lasted a million years" and of a lover "who had been dead these centuries" (*MD* 81) as if to evoke and mourn past ages of life on the earth. The song laments the passing of humanity, long since extinct, as earth has become a cold cinder in the failing heat of a dying sun. The woman's song recounts how "death's enormous sickle had swept those tremendous hills when at last she laid her hoary and immensely aged head on the earth, now become a mere cinder of ice...which the last rays of the last sun caressed; for then the pageant of the universe would be over" (*MD* 81).

But unlike many scientists and science writers, Woolf was inspired by the ever increasing vistas of intergalactic space and the technologies that had made those vistas accessible to the public. Photographic images of distant stars and galaxies, that evoked in Eddington and Russell a more nihilistic response, proved productive for Woolf's formulation of her narrative scoping strategies. Those images of far flung galaxies reprinted in Jeans's texts afforded Woolf a wide-angled vision that allowed the possibility of positioning her characters against the infinite vistas of the universe, as well as launching in "The Searchlight" a critique of the inanity of human aggression and war.

WAR AGAINST THE BACKDROP OF REMOTE AND LIFELESS WORLDS

Woolf began the final versions of "The Searchlight" in 1939, while England and all of Europe was bracing itself for another outbreak of world war. Her decision in January 1939 to change the title of her telescope story to "The Searchlight" demonstrates Woolf's interest in developing the story as a commentary on the impending war she dreaded would erupt. As J.W. Graham points out, "[T]he frame-story is set in a great metropolis preparing for war and in a social club located in view of the sovereign's official residence."[29] Although the setting of "The Searchlight" is peacetime, the threat of war is seemingly imminent: "It was peace then; the air force was practicing; searching for enemy aircraft in the sky" (*HH* 120). In the story, Woolf found a means of linking the ephemerality of humans produced by a new generation of astronomical telescopes to the threat of human extinction international conflict could exact. She accomplished this by consciously conflating the telescope with the searchlight, another war technology, which too involves a thin beam of light or sight that can be controlled and focused. In one instance, the searchlight functions like a telescope, "sweeping across the sky, pausing here and there to stare at the stars" (*HH* 122). In another, the searchlight focuses menacingly on Mrs. Ivimey: "A shaft of light fell upon Mrs. Ivimey as if someone had focussed the lens of a telescope upon her. (It was the air force, looking for enemy aircraft.)" (*HH* 124). At stake, for Woolf, in the prospect of international conflict was not only the loss of millions of lives, but also the very real threat to human civilization altogether.

Because of their initial, and now more elided, military application, telescopes provided Woolf with a structural and thematic device for her general concerns about human survival in the long eons of cosmological time. From their earliest invention in Europe, it seems, telescopes were designed and used for military purposes.[30] Dutch spectacle maker Hans Lippershey traditionally has been credited with constructing the first telescope in 1609. In October of that year, he apparently offered the scope to representatives of the Netherlands' governing body, the States-General, as a secret military device to aid in Holland's fight for independence from Phillip 11 of Spain (Henry King, *The History of the Telescope* 31). While the instrument was deemed " 'likely to be of utility to the State,' " the States-General wondered " 'whether it would not be possible to improve upon it, so as to enable one to look through it with both eyes' " (qtd. in King 31). The earliest prototypes, then, of both the telescope and of field-glasses or binoculars were conceived in the context of military application. Even the Italian professor of mathematics Galileo Galilei, who learned of the development of "Dutch trunks, perspectives or cylinders" by May of 1609 (King 34), immediately recognized the device's martial significance and allegedly only later explored its potential as an astronomical instrument.[31] According to physicist J.D. Bernal, Galileo readily designed his own versions of the apparatus and "was able to sell his invention of the telescope to the Venetian Signory solely on account of its value in naval warfare" (*The Social Function of Science* 168).[32]

Aware of the historical associations between telescopes and the military, Woolf not only subverted the telescope's martial applications through her narrative scoping strategies, but deployed the device to launch in "The Searchlight" an anti-war argument. Woolf's thinking about the great abysses of intergalactic space contributed to her convictions that humans must ensure their own survival. In the early decades of the twentieth century cosmologists believed, unlike today, the universe to be largely devoid of life. "Of the rare planetary systems in the sky, many must be entirely lifeless," warned Jeans, "and in others life, if it exists at all, is probably limited to a few planets... We can still only guess as to the meaning of this life which, to all appearances, is so rare" (*The Universe Around Us* 323). Woolf weighed the implications of Jeans's claims regarding the rarity and fragility of life in the universe against the very real threat of a second world war. As Nancy Topping Bazin and Jane Hamovit Lauter point out, "From her perspective, war was a chaotic nightmare that had no respect for [human] fragility."[33]

Even in her earliest fiction Woolf had anticipated how telescopic technologies might be implicitly linked with a commentary on war and the threat of human extinction. Included in *Jacob's Room* (1922), a novel in which the main character dies in military service during World War I, is an enigmatic narrative interruption in which Woolf juxtaposes two battle scenes recounted as if viewed through a pair of "field glasses." In one vignette, a battleship sinks on the North Sea, while "[w]ith equal nonchalance a dozen young men in the prime of life descend with composed faces into the depths of the sea; and there impassively (though with perfect machinery) suffocated uncomplainingly together" (*JR* 136). In the other battle scene, infantry soldiers are wounded in a ground attack: "Like blocks of tin soldiers the army covers the cornfield, moves up the hillside, stops, reels slightly this way and that, and falls flat, save that, *through field-glasses*, it can be seen that one or two pieces still agitate up and down like fragments of a broken match-stick" (*JR* 136; italics mine). The passage not only "parodies the kind of dehumanized point of view that makes war possible," but also demonstrates how Woolf reverses the telescopic field of view to comment on the inanity of human aggression.[34] Initially, the narrator focuses on a close-up of the sailors' faces, but then the visual field is reversed and the soldiers of the second vignette are seen as if through the binoculars' opposite end. Suddenly, the "tin soldiers" become miniaturized, scaled down in size to mere "pieces" that "agitate up and down like fragments of a broken match-stick" through the binocular lenses. This re-scaling occurs precisely through the lenses of the field-glasses. Woolf's reversing of the visual field, or scaling from a close-up view to a more distanced view miniaturizes the soldiers only to magnify their fragility.

Scaling from a macro to a micro narrative point of view was a practice that suffused her work, and provided Woolf's readers with the possibility of seeing beyond the rhetorics of nationalism and of the necessity of war. The seemingly disinterested and cosmic view of human civilization evoked in her essay "Flying Over London" (1928) likewise linked telescopic devices to a commentary on social and political aggression.[35] The subject of that essay, which recounts a fictional flight over London, is nothing less than "the whole of civilization spread beneath us, silent, empty, like a demonstration made for our instruction" (*CE*4: 170). Here again Woolf deploys a scoping device, in this case a pair of Zeiss glasses, to peer down at earth. Through those glasses humans appear extremely insignificant, in fact, insect-like. As the imaginary Flight-Lieutenant Hopgood's plane swoops close to earth, "the vast creases of the stuff beneath began moving, and one saw in the creases millions of insects moving. In another second they became men, men of business…" (*CE*4: 170–1).

Even as Albert Einstein in 1917 lamented to a colleague, "What a pity we don't live on Mars so that we could observe the futile activities of human beings only through a telescope" (quoted in Clark, *Einstein* 211), Woolf's aerial depiction of human civilization, embodied in the city of London, brings under scrutiny the artificiality of social class:

And one had to change perpetually air values into land values. There were blocks in the city of traffic sometimes almost a foot long; these had to be translated into eleven or twelve Rolls Royces in a row with city magnates waiting furious; and one had to add up the fury of the magnates; and say – even though it was all silent and the block was only a few inches in length, how scandalous the control of the traffic is in the City of London. (*CE*4: 171)

This humorous telescopic perspective on London's class-conscious society, marked by the Rolls Royces and the fury of city magnates, exposes social class and human civilization in general as based on self-aggrandisement, a motive Woolf blames for the kind of aggression that leads to war. The essay's implicit social critique becomes clear as "Flight-Lieutenant Hopgood flew over the poor quarters, and there through *Zeiss glasses* one could see people looking up," such as the person scrubbing steps who nevertheless was "capable of flight" and who "sent up greetings" (*CE*4: 171; italics mine).[36]

It is, most likely, no accident that Woolf's scoping device in this essay is "a pair of Zeiss glasses" (*CE*4: 171), manufactured by a German optical company known for the extreme acuity and performance of its visualization instruments, including cameras and telescopes.[37] The Zeiss concern, established in the mid-1800s, had flourished in large part due to the World War I. While "the name of Zeiss on an optical instrument was generally taken as a hall-mark of optical and mechanical perfection," by 1919 the Zeiss organization, "owing to World War I, was the largest European centre for optical instruments" (King, *The History of the Telescope* 346). The field-glasses Woolf evokes to suggest the possibility of human decimation were produced by a lens company that greatly expanded the marketability of its products directly as a result of world war. Jessica Burstein's argument that the surge of British popular interest in entomology after World War

I was "bound to the battlefield" finds support in a September 1930 diary entry in which Woolf queries, "What is one's relation to insects?" (*D3*: 315).[38] One answer to Woolf's question can be found in the lesson learned from this imaginary flight, and is aptly summed up in the narrator's exclamation, "Extinction!" (*CE4*: 169).

DISRUPTING DISCOURSES OF WAR

Beyond using literary tactics to disrupt discourses on the necessity of human aggression, Woolf proposed a more viable resistance to war rhetoric in her essay "Thoughts on Peace in an Air Raid" (1940). Another dramatic narrative of searchlights and war, the essay reconstructs a narrator's thoughts, taken from Woolf's personal experiences, "while the guns on the hill go pop pop pop and the searchlights finger the clouds and now and then, sometimes close at hand, sometimes far away, a bomb drops" (*CE4*: 173).[39] The "only efficient air-raid shelter," and most effective weapon against human aggression, the narrator claims, requires "thinking against the current" (*CE4*: 173, 175). "[T]here is another way of fighting for freedom without arms," wrote Woolf, "we can fight with the mind.... But to make ideas effective, we must fire them off" (*CE4*: 173).

Her notion of fighting with the mind may have been inspired in part by Alfred North Whitehead, a Cambridge mathematician and philosopher of science whom Woolf had met at Garsington. Whitehead had concluded in *Science and the Modern World* (1925), "In the history of the world, the prize has not gone to those species which specialised in methods of violence, or even in defensive armour" (206).[40] Scientists could lead social reform, Whitehead claimed, but only if humans resisted aggression and instead engaged in "adventures of thought, adventures of passionate feeling, adventures of aesthetic experience" (*Science and the Modern World* 207). Woolf also may have marshaled her "fight with the mind" partly in response to those scientists whom she knew – such as J.D. Bernal, physiologist J.B.S. Haldane, geneticist Julian Huxley, and zoologist Solly Zuckerman – who "whole-heartedly supported the national war effort from the very onset of the Second World War" (Gary Werskey, *The Visible College* 262, 266). These scientists, along with twenty-three others, anonymously published in 1940 a text titled *Science in War*, which called for scientists to actively use their expertise to support Britain during World War II (*The Visible College* 263).

Edwin Hubble ranked among those scientists who had publicly lobbied for America's involvement in World War II in defense of Britain.[41] Hubble's ties to England included his undergraduate years at Oxford as well as his professional and personal associations with Jeans, Aldous and Julian Huxley, and Eddington. And from 1942 until armistice, Hubble was actively engaged in the war effort. He had accepted an appointment to direct ballistics research at the Aberdeen Proving Ground in Maryland as "chief ballistician, the highest civilian ranking outside Washington" (Christianson, *Edwin Hubble* 293). Hubble was chosen for the position as a result of his expertise with visualization technologies or, as he put it, "because ballistics has a curious affinity with astronomy."[42] Overseeing Aberdeen's supersonic wind tunnels laboratory, he conducted research involving high speed photography of, and trajectory calculation for, missiles and ordnance ranging from bullets to rockets. Hubble, moreover, was no mere administrator. He perfected a safe design of one model of the bazooka, a portable rocket launcher; and under his direction his unit designed high-speed clock cameras to examine the orientation and yaw of missiles and ordinance when propelled from moving launch sites such as airplanes (Christianson, *Edwin Hubble* 287, 288). His service earned him the Medal for Merit awarded to civilians "for outstanding contribution to the war effort."[43]

However, upon the declaration of armistice, Hubble had solemnly reconsidered his position on war. In 1946, during a public lecture in Los Angeles, he called for the "absolute necessity of eliminating warfare" and argued that modern military conflict engaged with missiles and atomic weapons "will be the ruin of civilization as we know it."[44] He reasoned, "Even if against our wishes, we must cooperate successfully in order to survive... War and suicide – we must accept these as synonymous terms, for they amount to that."[45] The "ruin of civilization," a catch phrase for the Bloomsbury group in the 1920s and 1930s, meant, for Woolf as well as for Hubble, the possibility of not just the extinction of aesthetic or literary culture, but of humanity altogether.

Woolf's arguments regarding human aggression and possible extinction were linked to the new telescopic vistas of intergalactic space. It was not an entirely novel idea. During World War I, Bertrand Russell had based his anti-war campaign, in part, on the ever widening vistas of the universe. In an article that appeared in 1919 in the *Athenaeum*, Russell observed:

The universe as astronomy reveals it is very vast. How much there may be beyond what our telescopes show, we cannot tell; but what we can know is of unimaginable immensity. In the visible world the Milky Way is a tiny fragment; within this fragment, the solar system is an infinitesimal speck, and of this speck our planet is a microscopic dot. On this dot, tiny lumps of impure carbon and water, of complicated structure, with somewhat unusual physical and chemical properties, crawl about for a few years, until they are dissolved again into the elements of which they are compounded. They divide their time between labour designed to postpone the moment of dissolution for themselves and frantic struggles to hasten it for others of their kind.... Such is man's life viewed from the outside.[46]

Russell's re-scaling of humans to amoeba-like blobs clinging to a microscopic pebble exposed the folly of large-scale military contrivances in mass dissolution. Like Russell, Woolf too attempted narrative strategies for viewing humanity "from the outside," or to effect a human re-scaling in comparison to the backdrop of intergalactic space, in order to demonstrate the need for rethinking the necessity of war.

In 1940, as German planes dropped bombs near Woolf's country home in Rodmell, the possibility of human extinction once more must have flashed before her. Even as the world seemed to have fallen lifeless in the pale light of the 1927 solar eclipse, so again the world must have appeared on the verge of extinction on a dark evening during a bombing raid when Somerset Maugham watched her walk home alone, "lit up by the flashes of gun-fire, standing in the road and raising her arms to the sky" (Lee, *Virginia Woolf* 740). Aldous Huxley contended that Woolf wrote as "one who is a thousand miles away and has only a telescope to look, remotely, at the world."[47] Indeed the telescope afforded Woolf a structural and thematic device for articulating her general concerns about human survival in an age that had witnessed two world wars, and in a universe Jeans had described as nearly devoid of life. Through her literary scoping experiments, Woolf offered readers alternative perspectives on the necessity of war. "We must look at the world through the wrong end of the telescope as well as the right one, see things inside out and backwards, in bright and dim light" writes Stephen Kern, "In this philosophy spaces proliferate with points of view" (*The Culture of Time and Space 1880–1918* 150). Woolf formulated her narrative scoping strategies so that readers might see their responsibility in ensuring their own survival "in this scratching, clawing, and colding universe,"[48] and as a viable means of securing a more liveable world.

3

Maps, globes, and "solid objects"

"The singular, & intoxicating charm of Stonehenge to me, & to most I think, is that no one in the world can tell you anything about it," wrote Virginia Woolf at age 21, upon the occasion of her first excursion along with her sister Vanessa to Salisbury Plain (*PA* 199). "There are these great blocks of stone; [ ] & what more? Who piled them there & when, & for what purpose, no one in the world – I like to repeat my boast – can tell" (*PA* 199). What appealed to Woolf was the mysterious otherness and complete inexplicability of Stonehenge. No one in the world, she enjoyed repeating, could tell anything about it. Although she had seen pictures of Stonehenge, actually visiting the site of the monoliths was a mesmerizing experience: "I suddenly looked ahead, & saw with the start with which one sees in real life what ones eye has always known in pictures, the famous circle of Stonehenge. . . . I had not realised though that the stones have such a look of purpose & arrangement; it is a recognisable temple, even now" (*PA* 199). Woolf contemplates the thousands of years that have passed since the stones were set in place, and comments that the monoliths "have seen sunrise & moonrise over those identical swells & ridges for – I know not how many thousand years" (*PA* 200).

"I felt as though I had run against the stark remains of an age I cannot otherwise conceive; [a] piece of wreckage washed up from Oblivion. There are theories I know – without end; & we, naturally, made a great many fresh, & indisputable discoveries of our own" (*PA* 199). Those indisputable discoveries that she and Vanessa concocted were easily as viable, Woolf re-alized, as any other theory on the origin and purpose of the monoliths. The structure seemed to her obviously to have been a temple to the sun. "[T]here is a rugged pillar someway out side the circle," she observed, "whose peak makes exactly that point on the rim of the earth where the sun rises in the summer solstice" (*PA* 199). Such evidence affirmed her vivid imagining of "the moment the sun rose [and] the Priest of that savage people slaugh-tered his victim [t]here in honour of the Sun God" (*PA* 199–200). Indeed, she noted, "We certainly saw the dent of his axe in the stone" (*PA* 200). However, such seemingly objective descriptions of material phenomena would always prove too simplistic for Woolf. "Set up the pillars though in some other shape," she noted, "& we have an entirely fresh picture..." (*PA* 200).

Even in her earliest writing, Woolf began investigating the ways narrative shapes how one encounters the material world. Stonehenge might be an ancient temple of death and sun worship – the evidence seemed obvious. Or, those prehistoric monoliths might have been something else altogether. "Set up the pillars in some other shape" or, as Woolf suggests, structure one's narrative in some other way, and the significance of Stonehenge is radically altered. Woolf's account of the Stonehenge excursion offers a point of entry into her engagement with Cambridge mathematicians Bertrand Russell and Alfred North Whitehead and their analyses regarding an articulation of material phenomena.

Woolf's celebration of the incomprehensible otherness of Stonehenge, reflects her interest in the interchange with material phenomena particularly at the core of Russell's investigations. The important interconnections between the work of Russell and Woolf explains in part the reasons for her insistence on what Pamela Caughie calls Woolf's "multiform artwork," or her simultaneous deployment of various literary genres and points of view in a single text. This chapter explores how Woolf's multiform narratives emerged in the context of the Cambridge debates on materialism and the nature of physical phenomena, as well as in relation to her thinking of the earth as a globe in space, and, oddly, the development of orthographic maps that depict the earth as a globe. The image of earth's globe became a productive metaphor for her own modernist art. In fact, Woolf's persistent return to the image of the globe in her fiction and essays reveals the extent to which the globe became for her a touchstone for celebrating alterity and a multiplicity of perspectives.

TOWARD A GLOBAL AESTHETIC VISION

As Woolf glimpsed tiny alien worlds through her telescope, she in turn imagined what earth must look like from the plains of some distant planet. Her thinking about earth in space contributed to her persistent exploration of decentered, alien, even non-human narrative perspectives. Those vistas of strange and unknown worlds, of the moon, Saturn with its rings, and of Jupiter, indelibly impressed upon her a vision that would shape her global aesthetics. This vision built on Virginia's life-long fascination with the view of earth from space, which during her childhood years was part of a shared family mythology. There was, apparently, a "Stephen family story of a young painter's spectacular success, which he could never repeat," supposedly a painting titled, "Earth Rise from the Moon" (*D1*: 190, n. 8). Thus, in September 1919, Woolf recalled an occasion on which she was sitting outdoors, "lying on the side of a hollow… & seeing a red hare loping up the side & thinking suddenly 'This is Earth life'" (*D1*: 190). She imagined how she might appear to that hare, or to any non-human observer. "I seemed to see… myself… as if a moon-visitor saw me… [B]ut I can't recapture the queer impression I had of its being earth life seen from the moon" (*D1*: 190–1).

Her reflections regarding such alien perspectives may have been inspired by the French popularizer of astronomy, Camille Flammarion, whose books she perhaps read in her father's library.[1] The 1881 edition of Flammarion's volume *Astronomie Populaire* included etchings of other worlds glittering above a desiccated lunar surface, and a spectacular imaginary view of earth in space (Figure 3.1). Indeed, Woolf's fascination with the view of earth from the moon may have drawn upon a particularly stunning etching included in that volume. Reminiscent of that Stephen family story of the artist who could never repeat his painting of an earthrise, and interestingly of the Apollo 8 images of earth just above the linear surface, the image is captioned "The Full Earth Seen from the Moon" (Figure 3.2).

Views of earth from the moon had actually been the subject of both art and literature at the time. In 1919, the same year Woolf recorded her comments about seeing the earth from the moon, the frontispiece to an American astronomy textbook consisted of a reprint of a painting by American artist and scientist Howard Russell Butler titled "The Earth as seen from a Crater of the Moon." The textbook, titled *Astronomy: A Revision of Young's Manual of Astronomy*, became, according to historian at Mount Wilson Observatory Don Nicholson, the classic textbook on astronomy in the US. In addition, in 1920, H.G. Wells had published his *Outline of History*, the opening lines of which also evoked images of the earth as a globe in space: "The earth on which we live is a spinning globe. Vast though it seems to us, it is a mere speck of matter in the greater vastness of space" (3). Woolf recorded moments in her diary in which she explicitly had been thinking "about the universe" (*D3*: 63) and the oddity of the human position on the globe of earth: "Then (as I was walking through Russell Sqre last night) I see the mountains in the sky: the great clouds; & the moon which is risen over Persia; I have a great & astonishing sense of something there, which is 'it'…. A sense of my own strangeness, walking on the earth is there too: of the infinite oddity of the human position; trotting along Russell Sqre with the

Figure 3.1 **Illustration of the earth in space.** Published in Camille Flammarion's *Astronomie Populaire* (1881), this illustration depicts with striking accuracy the earth in space, though produced at least seventy years before photographic or satellite imaging of earth was possible.

moon up there, & those mountain clouds. Who am I, what am I, & so on…" (*D*3: 62–3).[2]

Woolf's global aesthetic vision grew out of her keen realization of the earth as a globe whirling through the interstellar depths. In *The Waves*, for instance, the characters or personae think of their lives in relation to the great span of cosmological time and space. Bernard contemplates

Figure 3.2 **"The Full Earth Seen from the Moon."** This illustration from Flammarion's *Astronomie Populaire* (1881), or one similar, may have inspired the Stephen family story regarding a young painter who could never repeat a particular success, a painting titled "Earth Rise from the Moon."

"the nature of human destiny" (70), while Neville declares that he and the others "[o]ppose [them]selves to this illimitable chaos" (*TW* 226) of the intergalactic depths. Susan describes how, in the autumn of the year, "[t]he earth hangs heavy beneath [her]" (*TW* 98), and Bernard observes how at the instant of a solar eclipse, the earth, "hangs pendent" and "swings beneath [his] feet" (*TW* 286).

However, the image of the globe represented for Woolf more than the earth as a planetary body racing through space. At times, she used the globe as a trope by which she defined the scope of a human life. In November 1928 she was contemplating the meaning of life through the metaphor of the globe: "I should like to take the globe in my hands & feel it quietly, round, smooth, heavy.... I will read Proust I think" (*D3*: 209). In *Jacob's Room*, the narrator claims that the trivial minutia of a person's life "lace our days together and make of life a perfect globe" (79). Likewise, in *The Waves*, Bernard imagines his life as if it were a globe of glass in which he observes the events of his life played out. " 'This, for the moment, seems to be my life,' " says Bernard. " 'If it were possible, I would hand it to you entire. I would break it off as one breaks off a bunch of grapes. I would say, 'Take it. This is my life.' But unfortunately, what I see (this globe, full of figures) you do not see' " (*TW* 238). Uncertain about narrating his own autobiography, Bernard comments, " 'Let us again pretend that life is a solid substance, shaped like a globe, which we turn about our fingers. Let us pretend that we can make out a plain and logical story...' " (*TW* 251). The stories Bernard incessantly constructs he recognizes later as only fictions. " 'The crystal, the globe of life as one calls it, far from being hard and cold to the touch, has walls of thinnest air. If I press them all will burst' " (*TW* 256). And again, in one of Woolf's early short stories, "The Journal of Mistress Joan Martyn," the narrator describes the process of reading as having the effect of evoking little holograph characters who act out their parts inside a miniature globe: "I saw them [the stories] as solid globes of crystal; enclosing a round ball of coloured earth and air, in which tiny men and women laboured, as beneath the dome of the sky itself" (*The Complete Shorter Fiction of Virginia Woolf* 58). Elsewhere in her writing, the globe suggested to Woolf the positive possibilities for multiplicity in narrating events or in understanding material phenomena.

BERTRAND RUSSELL AND WOOLF'S "MULTIFORM ARTWORK"

In her short fiction experiments like "Solid Objects," "Kew Gardens," and "The Mark on the Wall," Woolf explored the questions that Russell and

Whitehead were working out in their own theories regarding what can be known of the material world. Ann Banfield, in a carefully researched and comprehensive study of Russell and the Cambridge debates regarding theories of knowledge of the material world, points out that along with G.E. Moore, "Russell and Whitehead define[d] the contours of philosophy as Bloomsbury understood it" (*The Phantom Table* 7). Russell examined the interface between humans, objects and events, and the parameters within which material phenomena might be articulated. Banfield comments, "The theory begins with an analysis of the common-sense world. Objects are reduced to 'sense-data' separable from sensations and observing subjects to 'perspectives' " (*The Phantom Table* 1).

Alfred North Whitehead's *The Concept of Nature*, for instance, included a chapter, titled simply "Objects," in which he theorized what can be known of material phenomena and events. Published in 1920, the same year Woolf published her story "Solid Objects," Whitehead's volume argues that a scientific understanding recognizes the physical world as a network of sense data, which are effects of both the object and a percipient observer. "The constructions of science," wrote Whitehead, "are merely expositions of the character of things perceived" (*The Concept of Nature* 148). However, Whitehead claimed, science could say little about "the ultimate character of reality" (*The Concept of Nature* 151). Phenomena must be understood as dispersed, as a multiplex of relations between an observer and a "perceptual object" in a specific "percipient event" (*The Concept of Nature* 155, 152). Interested in epistemological questions regarding perception and the material world, Russell also contended that material objects are better understood as the interchange between an observer, either human or instrument such as a camera, and some event at the point in space where an object exists. "It follows," writes Russell, "that in one tiny region of physical space there is at every moment a vast multiplicity of occurrences corresponding to all the things that could be seen there by a person or recorded by an instrument" (*My Philosophical Development* 106). Thus, a more responsible scientific articulation of material phenomena would account for multiple perspectives of an object or event. As Banfield observes, Woolf was immersed in the Cambridge debates regarding the nature of physical phenomena and consequently developed a literary art that celebrates a multiplicity of perspectives.

Banfield meticulously traces Russell's investigations into "bridging the gap between matter and mind," and the limits of human understanding of material phenomena, in part to an essay by Leslie Stephen titled "What is Materialism?" (*The Phantom Table* 38). In that essay, Stephen contends that adopting multiple perspectives can be deployed as a means to knowledge. In one example Banfield cites, Stephen recalls how "[Johannes] Kepler constructed the solar system" by imagining from various points of view the planets moving through their orbits: "he [Kepler] supplied the intermediate positions by discovering the curve which passed through all the observed positions" of the planets.[3] Stephen argued that knowledge is not limited by the particular perspective space from which an event or object is observed. We can widen our understanding by "seeing in imagination what we should see through a telescope or a microscope, or should see if we moved to Sirius, or could touch a ray of light; what we should see if we could live a thousand years hence or had lived a thousand years ago; or if we could see the back of our heads as well as what lies in front of us.... We thus obtain formulae which are independent, in a sense, of our particular position" (*An Agnostic's Apology* 87).

Woolf's quasi-story, quasi-essay "Solid Objects" illustrates her own sense of the multiplicity of an object or an event, as well as her participation in the exchange between Russell and Whitehead regarding the multiple perspectives necessary for a more accurate articulation of material phenomena or the non-human. That Woolf responded in her fiction to Russell's work has been demonstrated by several literary scholars, including Banfield, Jaakko Hintikka, Judith Killen, and Joanne Wood.[4] While these scholars have pointed up several of the interconnections between Woolf's fiction and Russell's work, what has not been fully explored is how her story "Solid Objects" traverses Russell's arguments on theories of knowledge of material phenomena.

In an insightful theorizing of Woolf's narrative strategies, Pamela Caughie contends that through her "multiform artwork" Woolf resisted adopting one narrative strategy over another in order to explore how narrative, in various configurations, shapes readers' understanding of natural phenomena, or social and political practices (*Virginia Woolf & Postmodernism* 49). One might argue that Woolf's use of multiple literary genres in a single text resulted from her persistent questioning of seemingly definitive articulations of phenomena. Even as *The Waves* develops as a "playpoem," or *Three Guineas* unfolds as a hybrid of genres including fiction, documentary, news reportage, and political essay, "The Mark on the Wall" is neither simply short story nor only polemical essay (*D*3: 203). What these texts reflect is Woolf's shared interest, particularly with Russell, in deploying multiple perspectives within a single work as a means of shaping other "possible worlds."[5]

EARLY FICTION EXPERIMENTS

In November 1918, Virginia Woolf began sketching a bizarre little story about objects and human perception. She titled it simply "Solid Objects." The story opens with the narrator's observation of a "small black dot" moving along the shore of a distant beach. That dot, the narrator notes, "possessed four legs; and moment by moment it became more unmistakable that it was composed of the persons of two young men" ("Solid Objects," *HH* 79). The men happen to be engaged in a vehement political argument, evidenced by the violence of the discussion "issuing from the tiny mouths of the little round heads" (*HH* 79). "[N]othing," the narrator comments, "was so solid, so living, so hard, red, hirsute and virile as these two bodies for miles and miles of sea and sandhill" (*HH* 79).

Despite the strange re-scaling of humans to the size of a dot, and the telescoping effect from which the reader sees the humans as little more than "tiny mouths," the story maintains a simple plot. The younger of the two men is a promising politician, who becomes obsessed with objects. As the men pause in political debate, the young man sticks his hand into the sand and his fingers close around "a full drop of solid matter" (*HH* 80). "It was a lump of glass so thick as to be almost opaque; the smoothing of the sea had completely worn off any edge or shape, so that it was impossible to say whether it had been bottle, tumbler, or window-pane..." (*HH* 80). The young man gazes through the glass, holds it against his body and alternatively "against the sky" (*HH* 81). Marveling that the glass is "so hard, so concentrated, so definite an object" (*HH* 81), he takes the object home and places it on his mantle.

In time, similar peculiar and seemingly worthless objects attract the young man's attention. He takes to rummaging among alleys and junk heaps, where he finds a discarded "piece of china... resembling a starfish," "broken accidentally, into five irregular but unmistakable points" (*HH* 83). "The colouring," the narrator notes, "was mainly blue..." (*HH* 83). In another instance, the young man uncovers a remarkable star-shaped piece of iron, so "massy and globular, but so cold and heavy, so black and metallic, that it was evidently alien to the earth and had its origin in one of the dead stars or was itself the cinder of a moon" (*HH* 84). This strange and foreign chunk of dead star, or moon cinder, is placed on the mantle next to the other collected objects. "[I]t weighted the mantelpiece down," we are told, "it radiated cold" (*HH* 84). Ultimately, the young man becomes so obsessed with his objects that his promising political career is smashed.

Dean Baldwin locates the genesis of "Solid Objects" in a July 1918 visit by Woolf to the studio of the artist Mark Gertler, a painter whom the Woolfs met at Ottoline Morrell's Garsington salon, and who had been Virginia and Leonard's guest on several occasions that year.[6] Woolf commented on that visit:

I was taken to Gertler's studio & shown his solid 'unrelenting' teapot.... Form obsesses him. He sees a lamp as an imminent dominant overwhelming mass of matter. Ever since he was a child the solidity & the shapes of objects have tortured him. I advised him, for arts sake, to keep sane; to grasp, & not exaggerate, & put sheets of glass between him & his matter. This, so he said, is now his private wish. (*D*1: 175–6)

Woolf's curious recommendation regarding the "sheets of glass" may have stemmed from her familiarity with Russell, who used an analogy of looking at an object through blue glass, or blue spectacles, to pose a series of arguments on the multiplicity of the appearances of an object and its physical materiality. "We can shut one eye, or put on blue spectacles, or look through a microscope. All these operations, in various ways, alter [an object's] visual appearance," Russell argued (*Our Knowledge of the External World* 85).[7] More importantly, at least for Woolf, Russell had conjured forth the blue spectacles analogy to explore the question of how objects might be understood as the interchange between material phenomena and the multiple perspectives of subjective experience.[8] Woolf perhaps had in mind to suggest that Gertler's obsession with form could be managed and converted into art through the altering vision he might obtain by allowing himself alternative perspectives.

In December 1921 Woolf recorded in her diary an engaging exchange with Russell, which possibly took place at Garsington: "So Bertie Russell was attentive, & we struck out like swimmers who knew their waters" (*D*2: 146).[9] She admired Russell for his sharp intellect. His was a "mind on springs," she wrote, so she "got as much out of him as [she] could carry" (*D*2: 147). They found easy agreement on the superfluity of social gatherings like those at Garsington. " 'All of this is mush[,]' " Woolf recalled telling Russell, " '& you can put a telescope to your eye & see through it' " (*D*2: 147). He responded, " 'If you had my brain you would find the world a very thin, colourless place' " (*D*2: 147). Their conversation, Woolf noted, ranged from the literature of Milton to Russell's notion that mathematics "is the most exalted form of art" (*D*2: 147).

Woolf also knew of Russell's work through the literary journal, the *Athenaeum*,[10] in which Russell published essays, and through her added associations with the 1917 Club, a gathering of liberal Cambridge scientists and literary types.[11] Virginia frequented the club, which Leonard Woolf helped found and which was located at 4 Gerrard Street. In January 1918, Woolf wrote to her sister, "The centre of life I should say; is now un-doubtedly the 17 Club" (*L2*: 210).[12] There she and Lytton Strachey mingled with Russell, Cambridge physicist J.D. Bernal, social biologist Lancelot Hogben, and classical archaeologist Jane Harrison (Hussey, *A to Z* 192). Hogben, whom Woolf described as a "youth of genius," wrote popular science books and later published *Mathematics for the Million* (1936) (*L2*: 298 and n. 1). Fredegond Shove, daughter of Woolf's first cousin, as well as Alix Strachey, a psychoanalyst and translator of Freud, and Melanie Klein were also members.

By May 1919, the year Woolf began drafting "Solid Objects," Russell's public lectures had become the rage among 1917 Club members. She reported in her diary that "the touchstone of virtue" among club members, including Lytton, Alix, and James Strachey, "is whether you attend Bertie's lectures or not" (*D1*: 273). The lectures, a series of eight public talks titled 'The Analysis of Mind' were held in Bloomsbury "on Tuesdays in May and June" (*D1*: 270, n. 4), and covered topics such as perception, sensation and mental phenomena.[13] Despite Woolf's claims that she "preferred the songsters of Trafalgar Square" to Russell's talks, she nevertheless had a considerable understanding of, and apparent respect for, Russell's philosophical investigations (*D1*: 270).

Joanne Wood, who has identified elements of Russell's work in Woolf's texts, points out that for Russell "the fundamental reality, in and out of the brain, consists of 'events,' neutral with respect to the physical or the mental."[14] In *Our Knowledge of the External World* (1914), for instance, Russell asserted:

What occurs when I see a star occurs as the result of light-waves impinging on the retina, and causing a process in the optic nerve and brain; therefore the occurrence called "seeing a star" must be in the brain. If we define a piece of matter as a set of events... the sensation of seeing a star will be one of the events which *are* the brain of the percipient at the time of perception.... [F]rom the physical point of view, whatever I see is inside my head. I do not see physical objects; I see effects which they produce in the region where my brain is. (129)

Elsewhere, Russell explained, "[P]erception gives us the most concrete knowledge we possess as to the stuff of the physical world, but what we perceive is part of the stuff of our brains, not part of the stuff of tables and chairs, sun, moon, and stars" (*An Outline of Philosophy* 292).

In "Solid Objects," Woolf explored the implications of Russell's investigations. Regarding those pieces of blue-tinted glass and moon-like rock, the narrator of the story notes, "Looked at again and again half consciously by a mind thinking of something else, any object mixes itself so profoundly with the stuff of thought that it loses its actual form and recomposes itself a little differently in an ideal shape which haunts the brain when we least expect it" ("Solid Objects," *HH* 82). The narrator's "stuff of thought" evokes Russell's comments regarding the "stuff of our brains," even as the star-shaped objects of Woolf's story are suggestive of Russell's many analogies gleaned from astronomy.

Russell frequently formulated his epistemological investigations of the material world on examples drawn from astronomical phenomena. He persistently evoked images of stars and starlight, planets, the sun, eclipses, even planetariums to stage his arguments. This is true for early publications such as *Our Knowledge of the External World* (1914) and *The Analysis of Mind* (1921), as well as later works such as *An Outline of Philosophy* (1927), and *My Philosophical Development* (1959). Russell, like Woolf, was clearly fascinated by astronomy and cosmological phenomena. He commented on his uncle Rollo Russell, who lived in Bertrand's childhood home, and whose conversations with Bertrand "did a great deal to stimulate [his] scientific interests" (*The Autobiography of Bertrand Russell* 1: 21). The Honorable Rollo Russell "was a meteorologist, and did valuable investigations of the effects of the Krakatoa eruption of 1883, which produced in England strange sunsets and even a blue moon" (*Autobiography* 1: 21).[15] At a very young age, Bertrand knew something of the planets. He noted that at about age five or six, he would wake early in the morning to watch Venus rise: "On one occasion I mistook the planet for a lantern in the wood" (*Autobiography* 1: 30). "The world of astronomy," Russell once observed, "dominates my imagination and I am very conscious of the minuteness of our planet in comparison with the systems of galaxies" (*My Philosophical Development* 130).[16] This fascination with the stellar universe would be productive for Russell's philosophical inquiries into the nature and multiplicity of physical phenomena.

To make his point, for instance, that sense-datum do not reveal qualities intrinsic to an object, Russell recreates the scene of an observer looking at "stars" in a planetarium:

The world of astronomy, from the point of view of sight, is a surface. If you were put in a dark room with little holes cut in the ceiling in the pattern of the stars letting light come through, there would be nothing in your immediate visual data to show that you were not 'seeing the stars'. This illustrates what I mean by saying that what you see is *not* 'out there' in the sense of physics.... What you see when you see a star is just as internal as what you feel when you feel a headache. (*An Outline of Philosophy* 145)

In one humorous example used to illustrate how knowledge is premised largely on subjective experience, and not objective data, Russell recounted the occasion of explaining to his son the size of the planet Jupiter:

When my boy was three years old, I showed him Jupiter, and told him that Jupiter was larger than the earth. He insisted that I must be speaking of some other Jupiter, because, as he patiently explained, the one he was seeing was obviously quite small. After some efforts, I had to give it up and leave him unconvinced. (*An Outline of Philosophy* 136)

Thus, Russell contended, both the percipient observer and the event comprise knowledge of an object. According to Russell, an object might be understood as an "entire system of [its] appearances" and the location of a percipient observer.[17] "There is," Russell argued, "no reason to single out one percipient [be it human or photographic camera] as seeing the thing as it is. We cannot, therefore, suppose that the physical thing is what anybody sees" (*My Philosophical Development* 103).

With postmodern insight, Russell asserted that cameras and photographic plates could be just as reliable percipient observers as humans since "[s]ensitivity is not confined to living things" (*An Outline of Philosophy* 62). In support of this he noted, "A photographic plate is sensitive to light, a barometer is sensitive to pressure, a thermometer to temperature, a galvanometer to electric current, and so on" (*An Outline of Philosophy* 62). In order to demonstrate that material objects might be understood as events occurring at multiple sites, Russell later deployed a fascinating analogy in which he theorized what cameras, located in the depths of space, might "observe" of a star. "Any star can be photographed at any place from which it would be visible if a human eye were there. It follows that, at the place where a photographic plate is put, things are happening which are connected with all the different stars that can be photographed there" (*My Philosophical Development* 106). Should it be possible to set up an array of cameras in space, each photograph would capture a different image of a star from a specific point of view, and the phenomena those cameras recorded would be different from what the human or camera eye perceives from the surface of the earth. Or as Joanne Wood observed, "[W]hat we ordinarily think of as one object – in this case a star – is in fact a manifold of innumerable events which are related to and constitute that the star."[18] A scientifically responsible depiction of any given star would have to account for the multiple perspectives from which that star could be photographed.

Woolf too had probed the difficult questions regarding the limits of human knowledge and suggested like Russell that phenomena must be understood only in their multiplicities and not from a single perspective. Especially in "The Mark on the Wall," written three years before "Solid Objects," Woolf called into question a notion which Russell too resisted: that human knowledge is of "cosmic importance" and "that mind has some kind of supremacy over the non-mental universe" (*My Philosophical Development* 16).[19] In her quasi-story, quasi-essay, the narrator sees a mark on a wall, and initially perceives it to be a nail. "I cannot be sure," the narrator says of the mark, "but it seems to cast a perceptible shadow, suggesting that if I ran my finger down that strip of the wall it would, at a certain point, mount, and descend a small tumulus, a smooth tumulus like those barrows on the South Downs which are they say, either tombs or camps" ("The Mark on the Wall," *HH* 42).

That perceptible shadow launches the narrator into a contemplation of what the barrows on the South Downs might contain, and of the scientific uncertainty concerning them. The contents of those barrows, so carefully framed and on display "in the case at the local museum," only demonstrate, the narrator states, that "nothing is proved, nothing is known" (*HH* 43). The passage recalls Woolf's delight in the inability of historians or scientists to definitively determine the origin or purpose of Stonehenge. "[B]ut the thing that remains in ones mind, whatever one does," wrote Woolf of those monoliths, "is the stupendous mystery of it all" (*PA* 200). Likewise, the narrator of "The Mark on the Wall" queries: "And what is knowledge? What are our learned men save the descendants of witches and hermits who crouched in caves and in woods brewing herbs, interrogating shrew-mice and writing down the language of the stars" (*HH* 43). As the story suggests, Woolf preferred more provisional articulations of her world, which she effected through multiple genres and perspectives within a single text.

ON THE SCALE OF THINGS

The widespread popular angst regarding a modern human re-scaling was inspired by not only popular astronomy texts like those by Jeans, but also by advances in cartography and mapping, especially in military mapping, and via the proliferation of orthographic maps in the interwar years. Physiologist J.B.S. Haldane addressed this new sense of the human position in the universe in an essay titled simply "On Scales." Haldane argued that the seemingly dizzying effects of scientific discoveries on cosmological as well as atomic scales might be allayed by considering the kind of human re-scaling necessary in using and reading maps: "The average man complains that he cannot imagine the eighteen billion miles which is the unit in modern astronomy when once we leave the solar system.... But one can think of it, and think of it clearly" (*Possible Worlds* 2).[20] The solution, Haldane suggested, was "map reading" (*Possible Worlds* 2). When "we look at a map of the world on a globe measuring sixteen inches round the equator, we are using a model on a scale of one in a hundred million (10^{-8})," and yet, Haldane asserted, "the average man learns to draw practical information from it" (*Possible Worlds* 2).[21] Thus humans could quite easily negotiate a world of cosmic and atomic phenomena. Woolf too had seen the connection between the kind of imaginative re-scaling of humans that globes and maps require, and a re-scaling of humans in relation to the expanses of the universe. This is perhaps best evidenced in Mrs. Ivimey's tale in "The Searchlight," in which the boy of the story each evening looks out at the stars with a telescope, while he spends his days poring over "old books with maps hanging out from the pages" (*HH* 121).

Maps, which might be conceived of as a kind of visualization technology, were integral to Woolf's formulation of a global aesthetic. She was fascinated by maps and associated them with motoring and with striking out into the unknown. Motoring, she reported, had been "a great opening up" for her and Leonard, allowing them to "expand that curious thing, the map of the world in ones mind" (*D3*: 147). When in 1927 the Woolfs obtained their first car, a second-hand Singer (Hermione Lee 508–9), she wrote:

What I like ... about motoring is the sense it gives one of lighting accidentally, like a voyager who touches another planet with the tip of his toe, upon scenes which would have gone on, have always gone on, will go on, unrecorded, save for this chance glimpse. Then it seems to me I am allowed to see the heart of the world uncovered for a moment. (*D3*: 153)

She also wrote to T.S. Eliot of their motoring excursions: "I'm glad to think that we now have another subject in common – motor cars. Did Leonard tell you how our entire life is spent driving, cleaning, dodging in and out of a shed, measuring miles on maps, planning expeditions, going expeditions..." (*L3*: 412–13).

Even as a teenager, when she and Vanessa would make countryside excursions, like those memorable jaunts to Stonehenge, Virginia would usually take a watch and a map (*PA* 33). Later, in 1904, while planning a trip to Italy with Vanessa, her brothers, and Gerald Duckworth, she wrote, "Great travelling enthusiasm has seized us: we spend our evenings following impossible routes with our fingers across the map – all wish to go different ways" (*L1*: 134). While in Florence in 1909, Woolf noted in her diary, "the scene is very emphatic in Italy, but I forbear to write of something hidden on the other side of the Alps. It is strange how one begins to hold a globe in one's head; I can travel from Florence to Fitzroy Square on solid land all the time" (*PA* 399). The Woolfs traveled the continent fairly frequently as she and Leonard crossed the channel into France for multiple excursions. They traversed Germany, Greece, Italy, and Spain. In March 1931, as the Woolfs were planning a trip abroad, she talked with Elizabeth Williamson and Ethel Smyth about their jaunt to Greece. The conversation was "wildly detailed" and called for pulling out a map (*D4*: 88).

It is significant that Woolf often evoked maps and globes to describe her life. When on one occasion she was feeling disconnected from friends and associates, Woolf commented that her "map of the world lack[ed] rotundity" (*D3*: 315, 316). It was through her colleagues, she claimed, that she broadened her global vision. "I use my friends rather as giglamps: There's another field I see: by your light. Over there's a hill. I widen my landscape" (*D3*: 316). At one point when she was feeling lonely and missing Vita Sackville-West, Woolf wrote to her to say, "Here I sit at Rodmell, with a whole patch of my internal globe extinct" (*L5*: 148). Certainly Vita's travels had afforded Woolf vicarious access to the far corners of the globe. Sackville-West hiked and climbed, in July 1924, through the Italian Dolomites, and had written to Virginia from a mountain village in the Tre Croci pass (5,936 ft.) while working on her manuscript for *Seducers in Ecuador*. She described the village as nestled between "two rocky peaks of uncompromising majesty [which] soar into the sky immediately outside one's window, and where an amphitheatre of mountains encloses one's horizons and one's footsteps."[22] Vita's description of her mountain adventures swells with the romance for climbing that was sparked by the British Alpine Club, a group of mountaineers, many of whom became the first to reach the peaks of the Swiss, French and Italian Alps:[23]

Today I climbed up to the eternal snows, and there found bright yellow poppies braving alike the glacier and the storm; and was ashamed before their courage. Besides, it is said that insects made these peaks, deposit by deposit; though if you could see the peaks in question you would find it hard to believe that any insect, however industrious, had found time to climb so far towards the sky. Consequently, you see, one is made to feel extremely impersonal and extremely insignificant.[24]

Woolf later reworked Vita's account of her trip to these mountains in the short story "The Symbol," which echoes multiple elements of Vita's letter, including the "amphitheatre of mountains" just outside the cottage window, and the brave flowers that survive at incredible heights on the mountain ridges. Like the lady who sits writing on the balcony in Woolf's story, Vita reported how she "contemplate[d] young mountaineers hung with ropes and ice-axes, and [thought] that they alone have understood how to live life."[25] Woolf's story is equally suggestive of Vita's comparison of humans to insects and her comments regarding feeling "extremely insignificant." In fact, many of the themes that this entire investigation explores, such as Woolf's interest in a modern human re-scaling (Chapter One), the ephemerality and fragility of life (Chapter Two), as well as Woolf's fascination with insects (Chapter Five) surface in Vita's letter.

Though delighted by the letter, Woolf replied that she could not be smitten by the magic of Vita's Dolomites: "Wasn't I brought up with alpenstocks in my nursery, and a raised map of the Alps, showing every peak my father had climbed?" (*L3*: 126). That raised map of the Alps served as a reminder of her father's harrowing ventures mountaineering in the Alps. With only simple ropes and hob-nailed boots, Leslie Stephen climbed several of the most formidable of the Swiss Alps, including Mont Blanc (15,771 ft.) and the Jungfrau (7,625 ft.). The first to reach the highest peak of the Schreckhorn (13,387 ft.), he also discovered a previously unknown mountain pass to Zermatt.[26] With the aid of Swiss climbing guides Melchior and Jacob Anderegg, Woolf's father reached the top of the Rothhorn, which crests at 13,855 feet (Leslie Stephen, *The Playground of Europe* 109). Mountaineering in the Alps became easily accessible, Noel Annan reports, in the "1850s when the French railways reached Basel and Geneva, and Switzerland came to be hardly more than a day's journey from London and the fare less than ten pounds" (*Leslie Stephen* 90). Furthermore, climbing was relatively inexpensive; for example, "in 1855 a single climbing expedition with five porters and three guides cost a couple of friends only four pounds each" (*Leslie Stephen* 90). Driven by far more than a passing interest, Stephen made at least twenty-five mountaineering excursions into the Alps (*Leslie Stephen* 90). C. Douglas Milner, commenting on the history of the exploration of the Dolomite Alps, lists Leslie Stephen as the "third great pioneer" to explore those mountains (*The Dolomites* 74).[27] In his account of ascending Mont Blanc, Stephen recorded how his view of earth from such incredible heights afforded him a new sense of the smallness, and ephemerality, of humans in relation to the world and the universe. From the summit of Mont Blanc, he had looked over to see the "grim Matterhorn," which rises to 14,692 feet, take on an "infinitesimal minuteness," while "at [his] feet was lying a vast slice of the map of Europe" (*The Playground of Europe* 271). Stephen's accounts of those climbing excursions suggest his own intimations of a human re-scaling effected by large astronomical telescopes.

MAPPING THE WORLD, TAXONOMIZING THE UNIVERSE

If maps suggested, as Haldane proposed, the new human position in the universe, they also reflected the human tendency to aggression. For Woolf, maps denoted an artificial and even restrictive carving up of the world. Particularly in her polemical writing, she associated maps with practices of taxonomizing and with human aggression. In *A Room of One's Own*, Woolf makes the point that women have not been afforded opportunity to be the world's great explorers, even as she parodies the measuring, scaling, and taxonomizing often carried out in the name of science. Whereas the fictional Professor von X classified women under the heading "Mental, moral and physical inferiority of," Woolf's narrator contends that women have not participated in a similar taxonomizing (*AROO* 29). "One could not go to the map and say Columbus discovered America and Columbus was a woman..." (*AROO* 89). Likewise, Woolf critiqued the sciences for a crass spirit of competition and an unwillingness to allow or accept alien perspectives. She writes, "[I]f an explorer should come back and bring word of other sexes looking through the branches of other trees at other skies, nothing would be of greater service to humanity; and we should have the immense pleasure...of watching Professor X rush for his measuring-rods to prove himself superior" (*AROO* 92). In *Three Guineas*, Woolf specifically associated maps with human aggression and war. She indicted fascist militants as being "childishly intent upon scoring the floor of the earth with chalk marks, within whose mystic boundaries human beings are penned, rigidly, separately, artificially" (*TG* 105). It was a viewpoint she shared with novelist Olaf Stapledon who, in his novel *Star Maker*, derided imperialist ideologies and the "old psychology...wakened in modern Europeans by ancient maps which distort the countries of the world almost beyond recognition" (321).[28]

Even the average person on the street associated maps with human aggression and war, as is evidenced by the escalation in map-selling during the interwar years. Sue Roe has noted that "mapsellers' business boomed at the end of the summer of 1914, as large-scale maps of Europe sold to an anxious public."[29] Indeed, in the US during World War II, the Council on Books in War Time had published *A War Atlas For Americans* (1944) so that "the citizen at home" might follow the American troops' "travels and battles."[30] This comprehensive volume included mostly orthographic maps of the major Allied military fronts and various supply lines. Drawn as if from earth's orbit, orthographic maps display the world as a globe supposedly from the perspective of a "cameraman...suspend[ed]...in outer space thousands of miles above the earth."[31] As the anonymous author(s) of this volume pointed out, during World War II, orthographic maps became the map of choice as "no flat map [could] show accurately the geographical relationship of...the scattered theatres of this global war."[32]

The National Geographic Society, which provided the official maps for US military intelligence, also developed orthographic maps during World War II. In a special volume on cartographic developments titled, *The Round Earth on Flat Paper* (1950), the Society pointed out that orthographic maps found a "modern rebirth in Germany with the growth of the Nazi Party" (55).[33] Wellman Chamberlin claimed that Major General Karl Haushofer, founder of the Geopolitical Institute at Munich, established orthographic representation as the standard for map production in Germany and took as his "keynote... the term 'global' " (*The Round Earth on Flat Paper* 55).

Beyond simply detailing how maps are made, *The Round Earth* boasted of National Geographic's extensive involvement in supplying maps used in launching US offensives against the Germans and the Axis powers: "In the seven years which encompassed World War II, 1939–1945, the National Geographic Society supplied its members and the armed services with more than 37,400,000 large ten-color maps" (15). Society maps also were reprinted in *Yank*, the Army's weekly publication, a single issue of which "had a circulation of nearly 3,000,000 copies" and was distributed in "thirty different active Army areas throughout the World."[34] As *The Round Earth* testifies, innovation in twentieth century cartography was driven largely by world war.

Thus, representations of earth developed in orthographic mapping helped shape a renewed public sense of the earth as a globe in space. While Woolf's global aesthetic was linked to the dramatic shift in a popular understanding of earth's size in relation to the universe Hubble had so radically reconfigured, it is also the case that her narrative strategies were grounded in emerging cartographic technologies of the early twentieth century. For her, the globe would become an infinitely suggestive metaphor. She preferred the image of the globe over the flat map, in that the globe inevitably maintains a side that is always hidden, and thus suggests the potential for re-inscribing, to borrow a phrase from Russell, "the world as it can be made."[35]

ALIEN PERSPECTIVES AND POSSIBLE WORLDS

In a well-received essay "Possible Worlds," J.B.S. Haldane asserted: "And one day man will be able to... look at existence from the point of view of non-human minds.... Our only hope of understanding the universe is to look at it from as many different points of view as possible" (*Possible Worlds* 285). Haldane explored, as Susan Squier has noted, how sensory data appear from other frames of references such as that of a dog, an insect, or a barnacle.[36] In the quasi-parable that unfolds in "Possible Worlds,"

Haldane compared humans living on the globe of earth with barnacles, stuck to a rock, who have convinced themselves that "real object[s]" comprise only that which enters the "visual space" of the rock (*Possible Worlds* 279, 278). "Man is after all," Haldane concluded, "only a little freer than a barnacle" (*Possible Worlds* 279). While some barnacles imagine a three dimensional reality and thus ponder what might exist "on the other side of the surface of the rock," most barnacles simply accept the notion that "the surface of the rock is the end of space" (*Possible Worlds* 279). The parable not only illustrates how cultural, political, and scientific discourses shape and define what counts as acceptable reality, but also develops as a reproach of those who fail to accommodate multiple and more global perspectives.

Woolf's own interest in multiple and alien perspectives, and in exploring uncharted narrative strategies in hybrid genres, emerged out of an eagerness to discover what other material realities alternative forms of fiction could make possible. "Woolf tests out various narrative possibilities that allow for different conceptions of self and world," argues Caughie, "Her fiction works on the assumption that narrative activity precedes any understanding of self and world" (*Virginia Woolf & Postmodernism* 67). And as Banfield comments, "The method of multiple perspectives is the novelist's route to wider knowledge" (*The Phantom Table* 312). Woolf's strategy of adopting multiple perspectives, as Banfield points out, was learned in part from her father's story about Kepler imagining the positions of the planets to construct a model of the solar system, and from Russell's epistemological investigations of physical phenomena. Indeed, Woolf's story, "The Mark on the Wall," becomes a site for exploring a multiplex of positionalities, even, interestingly, the non-human perspective of an insect. There is, for instance, that bizarre disruption in which the narrator, from the perspective of an insect among the leaves of grass, considers "[t]he slow pulling down of thick green stalks so the cup of the flower, as it turns over, deluges one with purple and red light. Why, after all, should one not be born there [among insects] as one is born here [among humans], helpless, speechless, unable to focus one's eyesight, groping at the roots of the grass, at the toes of the Giants?" (*HH* 39).

The new vistas of space contributed to her experiments with narrative, particularly her narrative re-scaling from a microscopic to a macroscopic point of view. Woolf linked a dramatic shift in the popular understanding of earth's size in relation to the universe Hubble had unveiled to her own experiments in narrative perspective, as for instance, in "Kew Gardens" (1919) in which the narrator's view scales from the minutia of insects, struggling to cross under the dome of a leaf, to the world of the garden, to the city and cosmos beyond. "Kew Gardens" repeatedly re-positions the reader to observe both the events that take place in the park, and the tiny occurrences on the floor of a flower bed. If beginnings are a place for emphasis in fiction, then "Kew Gardens" highlights the question of whose frame of reference determines the setting of the story: a snail's or that of the humans that stroll through the garden. The story opens with the narrator's observation of the "objects" of the snail's world in which slivers of grass become as large and substantial as trees and a few raindrops caught on a leaf form a lake:

It [the snail] appeared to have a definite goal in front of it, differing in this respect from the singular high stepping angular green insect who attempted to cross in front of it, and waited for a second with its antennae trembling as if in deliberation, and then stepped off as rapidly and strangely in the opposite direction. Brown cliffs with deep green lakes in the hollows, flat, blade-like trees that waved from root to tip, round boulders of grey stone, vast crumpled surfaces of a thin crackling texture – all these objects lay across the snail's progress between one stalk and another to his goal. (*HH* 30)

Woolf's penchant for observing the world from non-anthropocentric or alien perspectives provided her a means of celebrating the multiplicity and complexity of the material world. Re-inscribing the material world from the perspective of a mollusc or snail, suggested, as Haldane inferred, "that the universe is not only queerer that we suppose, but queerer than we *can* suppose" (*Possible Worlds* 286).

THE POSITIVE POSSIBILITIES OF A GLOBAL AESTHETIC

Woolf's phrase, "solid objects in a solid universe," has been cited by modernist scholars in relation to her interest in physics. But the phrase actually appears in a 1929 series of essays, titled "Phases of Fiction." In one of those essays titled "The Psychologists," Woolf explores narrative strategies writers have deployed over the past two centuries. She praised Swift and Trollope, and especially Defoe, for their ability to imbue their narratives with such detail and certainty that readers "seem wedged among solid objects in a solid universe" ("Phases of Fiction" *GR* 95). She claimed that Thomas Peacock resisted realist fiction's "huge burden of facts ... based upon a firm foundation of dinner, luncheon, bed and breakfast," and offered instead a "version of the world, which ignores so much, simplifies so much, and gives the old globe a spin and shows another fact of it on the other side" (*GR* 132). Tracy Seeley, in an essay on Woolf's spatial aesthetics, contends that the globe, with its side that is always hidden, suggested to Woolf a creative liberation from a more "fact-obsessed prose."[37] Woolf evoked the image of the globe to celebrate narrative strategies that refused to limit or control the reading process. The importance of the globe to Woolf's aesthetic practice becomes clear in her praise of Marcel Proust's strategy of scaling from a micro-view, or a "fanatically precise observation" of an object, to a macro-view of the same object from "a station high up" (*GR* 125). "This dual vision," wrote Woolf, "makes the great characters in Proust and the whole world from which they spring more like a globe, of which one side is always hidden, than a scene laid flat before us" as, for instance, in a map (*GR* 126). The passage incarnates precisely the global vision and the re-scaling that I've located, especially in Chapter Two, in Woolf's narrative strategies.

Woolf further argued that Proust's narrative re-scaling exposed the multiple dimensions of an object, and resisted claims that "one [vision or narrative] is right and the other wrong" (*GR* 125). It was Proust's ability to scale between a micro and a macro point of view that suggested to Woolf narrative strategies that could offer more global perspectives – not a god's eye view, but multiple and complex perspectives. "Every way is thrown open without reserve and without prejudice" (*GR* 125). Thus Woolf embraced the image of the globe, in comparison to the analogy of the flat map, for its side that is always hidden and thus not subject to a definitive articulation.

Malcolm Bowie comments that Proust's strategy of zooming "with assured step between microcosm and macrocosm" revealed his "strong liking for physics" (*Proust Among the Stars* 18). In his *In Search of Lost Time*, Proust lamented the artist's difficulties in escaping a human point of view: "A pair of wings, a different respiratory system, which enabled us to travel through space, would in no way help us, for if we visited Mars or Venus while keeping the same senses, they would clothe everything we could see in the same aspect as the things of Earth. The only true voyage . . . would be not to visit strange lands but to possess other eyes, to see the universe though the eyes of another, of a hundred others, to see the hundred universes that each of them sees . . . really fly from star to star" (qtd. in Bowie, *Proust Among the Stars* 19). This is exactly what Woolf attempts within her own art. Through deploying a multiplicity of perspectives Woolf forged new and alternative possibilities for her modernist art, and for inhabiting the world. In May 1933 while sketching out a plan for "The Pargiters," Woolf noted, "The thing is to be adventurous, bold, to make every possible fence. One might introduce plays, poems, letters, dialogues: must get the round, not only the flat" (*D4*: 161). Those experiments in constructing her texts from a variety of genres simultaneously developed out of a commitment to explore uncharted ground for modernist fiction, and to make possible alternative, non-human, even alien perspectives that more responsibly account for the material world.

4

"The riddle of the universe" in The Waves

As Virginia Woolf completed writing and revising her novel *The Waves* between 1930 and 1931, she made several references in letters and diary entries to her reading of James Jeans's popular astronomy texts. On 18 December 1930, Woolf recorded in her diary a conversation of the evening before with Lytton Strachey and Clive Bell: "Talk about the riddle of the universe (Jeans' book) whether it will be known; not by us..." (*D3*: 337). Her speculations on the limits of human comprehension of stars and galaxies flung across the far reaches of the universe were probably inspired by Jeans's *The Mysterious Universe*, published the previous month. Several days later, on a rainy 27 December, Woolf wrote to her good friend Ethel Smyth of her novel *The Waves*, and commented that she had been reading about astronomy: "I read about the Stars, and try to imagine what is meant by space bending back. Eliz [Williamson]: must take me to her telescope" (*L4*: 266).[1] That same day, Woolf noted in her diary that she had been working on *The Waves* and reading Jeans: "I moon torpidly through book after book Defoe's Tour...Jeans; in the familiar way" (*D3*: 340).[2] She was paging through either Jeans's earlier popular book on astronomy *The Universe Around Us* (1929), or *The Mysterious Universe* (1930) (*D3*: 340, n. 17).

In the sensational final chapter to *The Mysterious Universe*, titled "Into the Deep Waters," Jeans characterized the cosmologist as a cinematographer who produces a kind of mathematical motion-picture film of the universe, as a means of narrating how the universe has evolved. E.A. Milne, Jeans's biographer, noted that this chapter, based on the Rede Lecture Jeans gave at Cambridge, "created a sensation in the Press the morning after the lecture" (*Sir James Jeans: A Biography* 62). The public interest stemmed from Jeans's quasi-theological claims that structure in the universe implied the universe was formed by a creator-mathematician. That final chapter to *The Mysterious Universe* would have appealed to Woolf as well due to the parallels Jeans at times drew between the work of scientists and artists.

Mathematics, Jeans assured, provided the most viable "extraneous standards" by which physical or astronomical phenomena might be understood (*The Mysterious Universe* 155). Mathematics served as a kind of blank photographic plate or motion picture screen on which scientists might project their pictures. "[T]he phenomenal universe," asserted Jeans, "would never make sense until it was projected on to a screen of pure mathematics…" (*The Mysterious Universe* 158–9). Jeans concluded that "the final truth about a phenomenon resides in a mathematical description of it" (*The Mysterious Universe* 176), by which he meant to point up the kind of difficulties Bertrand Russell had traced in his arguments regarding attempts to articulate material phenomena. In both his popular and technical publications, Jeans used his analogy of the cosmologist as an artist or cinematographer whose mathematical pictures or "cinematographs" offered scientifically responsible accounts of the material universe. For instance, in *Astronomy and Cosmogony*, his last technical publication, Jeans commented on the "cinematograph film which we [astronomers and cosmologists] set out to construct" as a means of "exhibit[ing] the universe" (421). However, Jeans warned, "The making of models or pictures to explain mathematical formulae and the phenomena they describe, is not a step towards, but a step away from, reality…" (*The Mysterious Universe* 176).

JEANS'S POPULAR ASTRONOMY LECTURES

As a cosmologist, Jeans delighted in photos of stars and nebulae whirling in the depths of space. In compiling both his technical and popular astronomy books he would write to Mount Wilson Observatory, as noted in Chapter One, to obtain stunning photographs of star clusters and nebulae. He also illustrated his public lectures with photographic slides of star clusters and whirling galaxies, using as many as thirty-some slides per presentation. A single page from his notes for a public lecture in a series titled "Through Space and Time," given in 1933, reveals not only the number of slides he had planned for one talk, but also his repeated use of the analogy of the scientist as a cinematographer who creates pictures of the universe.[3] On the left of the note page (Figure 4.1), Jeans listed the number of slides he had selected for his presentation. His notation, "Fly walking on earth," most likely refers to his claim in *The Mysterious Universe* that human comprehension of the universe is limited in the same way that the vision of a fly is restricted to its tiny world (142). Another notation, "Space contains 10^{14} nebulae; perhaps 10^{22} stars – grains of sand," refers to Jeans's repeated comparisons of the number of stars in the universe to the number of grains

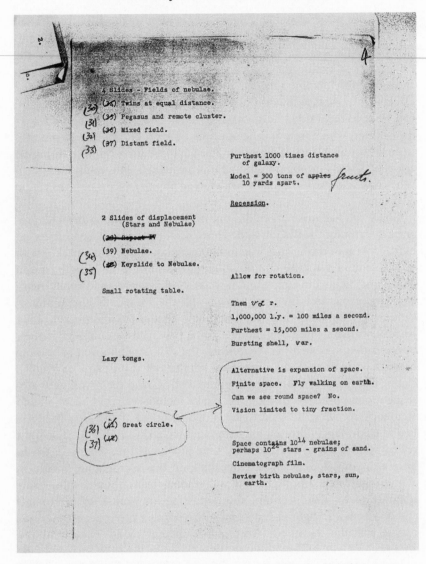

Figure 4.1 **Note page from a talk by James Jeans.** Jeans planned as least thirty-seven slides for a single presentation that he gave as part of the Royal Institution's Christmas Lectures in December 1933. Courtesy of The Royal Society and Christopher Jeans.

of sand on earth.[4] In the bottom right column, he made a note to himself to comment on his "Cinematograph film" analogy, or his notion of cosmologists as cinematographers, an idea Jeans had been contemplating since at least 1929.

With the surge of public interest in astronomy, the BBC by the fall of 1928 invited Jeans to offer a series of wireless talks on the composition of stars and the structure of the universe. Hilda Matheson, the BBC's first talks director, aggressively recruited Jeans for programming, and apparently became a regular guest at Jeans's home.[5] In November and December of 1930, as Woolf was writing *The Waves*, Jeans delivered eight, half-hour lectures titled "The Stars in Their Courses." Public interest in the lectures, which were broadcast prime time on Fridays at 8:30 pm, was so great that Sir Henry Lyons of the Science Museum in South Kensington arranged for an exhibit to accompany the talks.[6] The exhibit attracted large crowds, demonstrating the widespread popular appeal of Jeans's radio talks.

Charles A. Siepmann, then director of Regional Relations and later program director for the BBC, wrote to Jeans on the success of the museum exhibit: "I went to the Science Museum on Sunday, and found it packed with people around the show-case illustrating your talks."[7] As Maggie Humm points out, Siepmann ranked among those close associates and family members whose pictures "in comfy chairs" fill the Monk's House Albums.[8] Besides the likelihood that Woolf may have chatted with Siepmann about Jeans or heard his wireless talks, she also may have read the published lectures by Jeans that appeared in *The Listener*, the BBC's publication of selected broadcasts. In fact, in the spring and summer of 1930, many of Woolf's closest associates were broadcasting for the BBC and their work was subsequently published in this journal. These included Harold Nicolson and Vita Sackville-West; George Rylands, who worked at the Hogarth Press in the mid-1920s; Clive Bell; Desmond McCarthy, and T.S. Eliot. In a review of *The Mysterious Universe*, Vita encouraged readers to "listen to Sir James yourselves when he is speaking on the microphone."[9] Thus as Woolf completed *The Waves*, she was reading Jeans's books, most likely listening to his BBC lectures, and discussing his work with her friends and colleagues. In light of Jeans's pervasive popular presence, it is not surprising that the scientist-as-artist analogy figures so significantly in *The Waves*.

Jean Alexander cites Jeans as one of the scientists whose work "enumerates problems with which Woolf's fiction grapples" (*The Venture of Form* 6). One problem, of course, which Jeans engaged was the question concerning the accuracy and objectivity of cosmologists's claims about the universe. A writer aware of his own metaphors, Jeans clearly understood the disjunction between mathematical articulations of cosmic phenomena, and the phenomena itself. Admittedly, Jeans noted, "*all* the pictures which science now draws of nature, and which alone seem capable of according with observational fact, are *mathematical* pictures" (*The Mysterious Universe* 150). Cosmologists know, Jeans commented, that their mathematical descriptions of the universe bear no direct relation to material phenomena. Narratives of the universe's evolution must be recognized as mathematical constructions, mere fictions not to be confused with the phenomena they describe. "Most scientists would agree," wrote Jeans, "that they are nothing more than pictures – fictions if you like, if by fiction you mean that science is not yet in contact with ultimate reality" (*The Mysterious Universe* 150). He was acutely aware that scientists' methods invariably determine their interpretations of phenomena. In what appears to be an allusion to Russell's analogy of the blue spectacles which alter one's perception of phenomena, Jeans points out, "We may be reminded that Kant discussing the various modes of perception by which the human mind apprehends nature, concluded that it is specially prone to see nature through mathematical spectacles. Just as a man wearing blue spectacles would see only a blue world, so Kant thought that, with our mental bias, we tend to see only a mathematical world" (*The Mysterious Universe* 157).

However, Jeans argued, "The new mathematical interpretation of nature cannot all be in our spectacles – in our subjective way of regarding the external world..." (*The Mysterious Universe* 157). Despite his awareness of the fictitious nature of a mathematical description of the material universe, Jeans nevertheless was convinced that there was something inherently mathematical about the universe, that in fact, "mathematics enters the universe from above instead of from below" or from human observation (*The Mysterious Universe* 159). "Modern scientific theory compels us," Jeans posited, "to think of the creator as working outside time and space, which are part of his creation, just as the artist is outside his canvas" (*The Mysterious Universe* 182). Jeans thus suggested not only that a creator-mathematician had formed the universe, but also that scientists might retain a detached position outside of their work.

Reviewers of *The Mysterious Universe* contended that Jeans's controversial assertion that "the Great Architect of the Universe now begins to appear as a pure mathematician" compromised his own position as an objective observer of the universe (*The Mysterious Universe* 165). In the moment that he made such a claim, Jeans, himself a mathematician and lecturer at Cambridge from 1904 to 1912, became implicated *within* the frame of his own mathematical picture of the universe. His assertion that mathematics appears to be inherent in physical phenomena and not simply imposed through scientific observation opened him to criticisms that his was an anthropocentric point of view. L. Susan Stebbing complained in 1937:

[T]he anthropomorphic fallacy is very obvious in the conclusion that the Great Architect is a super-mathematician, in short, a Being well fitted to become President of the Royal Society – a colleague of Jeans himself.... Can Jeans suppose that such projection of his own personality is scientifically permissible...? (*Philosophy and the Physicist* 15)

Despite the fact that Jeans carefully explained that mathematical represen-tations of the universe have nothing to do with material phenomena, his claims of a creator-mathematician sparked strong criticism in the reviews of *The Mysterious Universe*. While Vita Sackville-West praised "the beautiful lucidity of Sir James Jeans' prose and the simplicity of his images," Sylva Norman writing for the *Nation & Athenaeum* commented, "In vulgar par-lance, he has fairly put his foot in it."[10] Hugh Sykes Davies argued, "The idea that nature may be completely beyond our reason, or, at least, more complicated than we should like her to be, never seems to have entered Sir James's head for serious consideration."[11] Geoffrey Sainsbury claimed that the book "gives itself an air of 'pure objectivity' " and yet the reader "finds that the creator is a kind of remote colleague" of Jeans's.[12]

This chapter examines Woolf's development in *The Waves* of a somewhat similar critique of the complicity between writers and the narratives they produce. Particularly in *The Waves*, Woolf engaged Jeans's analogy of the scientist as artist whose project is to *frame* natural phenomena and then tell its mathematical narrative. Both Woolf's diary entries on *The Waves*, and the text itself, reveal her skepticism regarding notions of the artist remaining outside his or her canvas. In opposition to the creator-mathematician Jeans evoked, who remains outside the canvas of the universe, and to a modernist desire for aesthetic objectivity as suggested by art critic Roger Fry, Woolf instead proffered a decentered aesthetic practice that invariably inserts the artist, writer or scientist within the frame of their own narratives.

ROGER FRY ON AESTHETIC OBJECTIVITY

The associations between art and science emerged as a topic of multiple es-says that appeared in the *Athenaeum* between 1919 and 1920. Roger Fry and J.W.N. Sullivan published in the journal a series of essays that examined the relationship between art and science.[13] Fry's first article, titled simply "Art and Science," suggested that the two disciplines have a shared interest in creating a unified vision of its subject: "[T]he highest pleasure in art is identical with the highest pleasure in scientific theory," wrote Fry, "The emotion which accompanies the clear recognition of unity in a complex seems to be so similar in art and in science that it is difficult not to suppose that they are psychologically the same."[14] A month later, Fry published another *Athenaeum* article on the modernist artist's need for a "disinterested vision" in "apprehending the relation of forms and colour ... as they cohere within the object."[15] For Fry "aesthetic vision" results as one becomes "detached from the passions of the instinctive life": in the "aesthetic apprehension of an object of art," Fry claimed, "no reference to actual life, comes in; our apprehension is unconditioned by considerations of space or time; it is irrelevant to us to know whether [a] bowl was made seven hundred years ago in China or in New York yesterday."[16] In the course of this exchange, Sullivan claimed that science had contributed to society "a large store of aesthetic objects," and that a scientific theory was just as much an "object of surpassing beauty" as a poem: "The fact that the history of a big scientific investigation, such as the Electro-magnetic Theory or Einstein's Theory of Relativity, is not generally regarded as a poem is due merely to an accident of language and education."[17] "[I]ndeed," wrote Sullivan, "there are a number of mathematicians who have felt impelled to write of their science in a kind of prose-poetry ..."[18] Mathematics, according to Sullivan, was capable of describing the material universe in a hybrid genre, the prose poem.[19] The term prose-poetry is exactly the phrase Woolf adopted in descriptions of her own fiction "experiments," especially *The Waves* (*L4*: 378).[20] In both her essay "The Narrow Bridge of Art" (1927), as well as in diary entries about *The Waves*, Woolf investigated how the "prose poem" or "play-poem" might provide a viable aesthetic form for the modern age (*GR* 20; *D3*: 203). Her own concerns regarding how art might evoke what she and Roger Fry called "life itself" traverses this discourse between scientists and artists.

Ann Banfield observes that mutually "Fry and Woolf felt the imaginative power of the 'scientific outlook' ..." (*The Phantom Table* 250).[21] Fry had studied the natural sciences at King's College, Cambridge, and apparently specialized in botany.[22] While Woolf was fascinated, like Fry, with the correlation between the sciences and the arts, she nevertheless was skeptical of Fry's notion of a disinterested and unified aesthetic vision. Leonard Woolf claimed that "in conversation" Virginia was "very much opposed to many of the theories of Roger Fry with regard to literature."[23] Given that she apparently relished a good "argument in person" with Roger, it is likely that she and Fry exchanged ideas on the interconnections between the nature of scientific and aesthetic objectivity (*L3*: 386).

Even after unexpectedly turning his attention to art, Fry remained fascinated with the similarities between the disciplines of the arts and sciences.
In *Vision and Design*, a collection of art criticism essays that Woolf read
in 1920, Fry argued that artists and scientists use similar critical methods.
Like the scientist, he maintained, the artist seeks "accurate observation and
recognition of the variety and distinctness of characters, but... also seeks to
construe these distinct forms into such a coherent whole as will satisfy the
aesthetic desire for unity" (*Vision and Design* 125). A unified artistic vision
might be developed, he claimed, by considering the technology of motion
picture film or the "cinematograph" (*Vision and Design* 14). According to
Fry, a moving film of events taking place on a street would function like a
mirror held up to a street scene: it would frame the events so that observers
of the scene would "abstract [them]selves completely and look upon the
changing scene as a whole" (*Vision and Design* 14). Through such analogies
Fry attempted to preserve an objective ground from which the artist might
obtain a detached yet unified "artistic vision" of "life itself" (*Vision and
Design* 15, 14).

Woolf, too, especially in writing *The Waves*, was concerned with cap-
turing what she called "life itself going on" (*D3*: 229). However, in an
inversion of Fry's street scene captured in the frame of a mirror, Woolf suggested narrative strategies that refused a unified vision or a privileging of a
particular point of view. In "The Mark on the Wall," for instance, Woolf
had held a mirror up to a street scene, but she had inverted the scene to the
underground, and additionally displaced the scene to the omnibus:

As we face each other in omnibuses and underground railways we are looking into
the mirror; that accounts for the vagueness, the gleam of glassiness, in our eyes.
And the novelists in future will realize more and more the importance of these
reflections, for of course there is not one reflection but an almost infinite number;
those are the depths [future novelists] will explore...leaving the description of
reality more and more out of their stories.... (*HH* 41)

Novelists of the future not only see themselves within the mirror of their
work and are thus always implicated within the frame of their own pictures
or narratives, but also recognize that "there is not one reflection" or unified
and objective vision, "but an almost infinite number of reflections."

THE ARTIST AS SCIENTIST IN *THE WAVES*

Several scholars have commented that *The Waves*, in particular, demonstrates Woolf's engagement with popular science writing, radio broadcasts

of science lectures, and popular media expositions on science-related topics. Jane Marcus has noted Woolf's allusions in *The Waves* to Einsteinian
relativity and the new physics: "The monologues are full of waves and
loops, literary versions of the new science of her time, as she heard it on
the radio."[24] Not only does the diction of Jeans's sciences, astronomy and
mathematics, permeate *The Waves*, but Woolf's six non-characters, or personae, frequently refer to the vastness of the universe and the roar of earth
whirring "through abysses of infinite space" (*TW* 225).[25] Both Bernard and
Louis echo several of the persistent themes of Jeans's popular texts and BBC
lectures, which emphasized the brevity of human existence in relation to
the long cosmological ages, and to a universe indifferent, even hostile, to
life. In another instance, Bernard recounts Jeans's theories of the formation
of the earth: "I reflect now that the earth is only a pebble flicked off accidentally from the face of the sun and that there is no life anywhere in the
abysses of space."[26]

The novel also takes as its theme the question of the artist or scientist's
ability to maintain an objective ground exterior to the picture or narrative
she or he creates. Through the persona of Bernard, Woolf tests the possibilities for an aesthetic or scientific objectivity. This is perhaps best evidenced
by the fact that Bernard thinks of himself as both writer and scientist. He
uses the diction of mathematics and astronomy to describe his attempts to
write a memoir of the novel's other personae. In one holograph draft of
The Waves, Bernard explicitly compares himself to a mathematician and an
astronomer:

Now do you think I understood something about life? . . . What interpretation
should I put on it? Am I justified in taking a sheet of paper & writing this down?
Have I any of the certainty that a mathematician has when his calculation . . . works
out, or the planet appears, timed right to the fraction of a second?[27]

Indeed, as Woolf reworked the drafts of The Moths, an early title for the
novel, she remained skeptical about her own artistic objectivity.

Suspecting her novel of becoming "[a]utobiography" (*D3*: 229), Woolf
questioned whether she was not intimately implicated within the text. In a
September 1929 diary entry she noted: "Yesterday morning I made another
start on The Moths. . . & several problems cry out at once to be solved.
Who thinks it? And am I outside the thinker?" (*D3*: 257). To some extent
Woolf appears within the novel's frame, particularly in that surreal scene in
which Rhoda is unable to cross a puddle because "[i]dentity failed [her]"
(*TW* 64). The scene resonates strikingly of a diary entry from three years
earlier in which Woolf had written: "[C]ouldn't step across a puddle once

I remember, for thinking, how strange – what am I?"(*D3*: 113). Her authorial introspection and the inclusion of the Rhoda scene suggests that, for Woolf, artists are always inevitably implicated within the frame of the pictures or narratives they create.

BERNARD'S "DOZEN PICTURES"

To a large extent, *The Waves* unfolds as a commentary on how narrative shapes what Woolf often referred to as "life itself." Particularly in 1928 and 1929, Woolf's diary reveals her preoccupation with how artists construct the world through narrative. "[G]ot then to a consciousness of what I call 'reality': a thing I see before me; something abstract; but residing in the downs or sky; beside which nothing matters . . . Reality I call it . . . How difficult not to go making 'reality' this & that, whereas it is one thing" (*D3*: 196). Woolf remained leery of the result "once one takes a pen & writes" (*D3*: 196). Bernard, like Woolf who once noted that she "should like to be able to take scientific notes of [human] reactions," attempts to inscribe "life itself" in the notebook he persistently carries (*D5*: 306). But such a taxonomizing leads only to his own questioning of the validity of any narrative framing. He imagines momentarily a biographer's description of himself as "the man who kept a book in his pocket in which he made notes – phrases for the moon, notes of features; how people looked, turned, dropped their cigarette ends; under B, butterfly powder, under D, ways of naming death" (*TW* 291). Realizing the partial and forced nature of the writer's practices, Bernard asks: "What is the phrase for the moon? . . . By what name are we to call death? I do not know" (*TW* 295).

Bernard might even be conceived of as the projectionist of his fictionalized world. Like Jeans, he compares his stories to the making of fictitious pictures: "I could make a dozen stories of what he said, of what she said – I can see a dozen pictures. But what are stories? Toys I twist, bubbles I blow . . ." (*TW* 144). During his conversation with the unnamed dinner guest at the close of the novel, Bernard again compares his narratives to the work of a photographer: "But meanwhile, while we eat, let us turn over these scenes as children turn over the pages of a *picture-book* . . . and I will add, for your amusement, a comment in the margin" (*TW* 239; italics mine). Bernard knows that his fragmentary and marginal notes offer only an artificial ordering of "life itself." Even as Louis, the accountant, persists unsuccessfully in attempting to "ad[d] . . . up [the other personae] like insignificant items in some grand total," Bernard finally must concede that he cannot "sum up" for his nameless dinner guest the "meaning of [his] life" (*TW* 92, 238). "[T]o give you my life," claims Bernard, "I must tell you a story — and there are so many, and so many — stories of childhood, stories of school, love, marriage, death, and so on; and none of them are true" (*TW* 238). Bernard's investigations into a unified aesthetic vision such as Fry proposed results only in his own awareness of the structuring possibilities of narrative. "I have made up thousands of stories; I have filled innumerable notebooks with phrases to be used when I have found the true story.... And I begin to ask are there stories?" (*TW* 118). His recognition of the artificial structuring effected by narrative subverts Fry's notion of an objective and detached view that might produce aesthetic unity, or Jeans's assumption that artists can somehow remain outside the frame of their own pictures. In Woolf's aesthetic vision, the ordering function of narrative is decentered or dispersed. Any number of narratives might be deployed. "But why impose my arbitrary design?" (*TW* 188). Elsewhere Bernard asserts, "To speak of knowledge is futile. All is experiment and adventure" (*TW* 118).

WINIFRED HOLTBY ON WOOLF'S CINEMATIC STYLE

The cinematograph became a favored metaphor for Fry, Jeans, and Russell as each had theorized its relevance in relation to the possibility of objective scientific or aesthetic descriptions of phenomena. If the camera is an objective observer, for Russell it had also illustrated the fallacy of any single correct perspective. In a particularly fascinating analogy, Russell imagined a theatre of "cine-cameras" replacing a human audience and recording the scenes of a play being performed. Each camera, Russell pointed out, would record a slightly different play depending on "perspective and according to [its] distance from the stage" (*My Philosophical Development* 19). Thus, no single perspective could be claimed as more accurate. All camera angles would be necessary for a complete recounting of the play. Woolf too considered visualization technologies, especially the camera, as she engaged discourses regarding a scientific or aesthetic objectivity.

The first literary critic to recognize Woolf's cinematic imagination and literary style was probably Winifred Holtby. "Mrs. Woolf had discovered cinema," wrote Holtby in reference to Woolf's short fiction selections "Kew Gardens" and "The Mark on the Wall" (*Virginia Woolf* 111). Woolf's narrative strategies, Holtby pointed out, included "the tricks of the cinema": "In *Kew Gardens* the external figures appear and disappear with such brilliant clarity that we could almost photograph them from the words" (*Virginia Woolf* 111). In her biography of Woolf, Holtby dedicated an entire chapter, titled simply "Cinematograph," to an elaboration of Woolf's cinematic method. "In *Jacob's Room* Mrs. Woolf built for the first time a complete novel with her new tools," wrote Holtby, "and chose for it the technique tried out in *Kew Gardens*. Almost any page in the book could be transferred straight on to a film" (*Virginia Woolf* 117). In that chapter, Holtby in essence transcribes *Jacob's Room* into a motion picture film script, replete with notes on camera angles. The opening scene of *Jacob's Room*, with Betty Flanders sitting on the beach, as narrated by Holtby, unfolds as if it were a movie script: "[Woolf] shows us . . . the complete figure of the woman pressing her heels deeper in the sand to give her matronly body a firmer seat; then there is a close up of her face. . . . The camera swings round then to photograph the entire bay . . ." (*Virginia Woolf* 118).

Woolf gleaned her cinematic style in part, Holtby argued, from Henri Bergson, who also deployed the cinematograph as a metaphor for describing the human encounter with physical phenomena or the non-human. In *Creative Evolution*, Bergson argued that the "mechanism of our ordinary knowledge is of a cinematographical kind" (332). According to Bergson, "We take snapshots, as it were, of the passing reality" that are then stored or "situated at the back of the apparatus of knowledge," the human brain (*Creative Evolution* 332). Processes of thinking, expression and perception, claimed Bergson, "set going a kind of cinematograph inside us" (*Creative Evolution* 332).

Evidence that Woolf had photographs or cinema in mind as she wrote *The Waves* surfaces in descriptions of her work in progress. "I shall attack this angular shape in my mind. I think the Moths . . . will be very sharply cornered. I am not satisfied though with the frame" (*D*3: 219). In addition, Bernard refers to his own mind operating like a camera as he attempts to makes sense of Percival's death: "The little apparatus of observation is unhinged" (*TW* 243). Even Leonard Woolf deployed the camera as an analogy for the mind. In a comment that recalls J.B.S. Haldane's parable of the barnacles stuck to the rock in "Possible Worlds," Leonard Woolf noted[28]:

Your mind thus develops a curiously feverish habit of regular and ephemeral opening and shutting. You become like a shell fish or a camera, but, unlike them, you soon delude yourself into thinking that the opening and shutting of your mind and the contents of the mollusc or camera are of immense importance. (*Beginning Again 132*)

Virginia, by linking visualization technologies such as the camera or the cinematograph to questions regarding scientific and artistic objectivity, had engaged in a major modernist rethinking of how visualization technologies could have a shaping effect on the development of fiction.

She was aware of the ways the camera both produced and subverted the aggressive visualization practices that, according to Martin Heidegger, were central to modernity. Heidegger contended, "The fundamental event of the modern age is the conquest of the world as picture."[29] Humans have come to perceive of themselves, Heidegger asserted, as the objective observers and framers of natural phenomena, specifically as a result of advances in photographic technologies. A scientific conception of the universe, claimed Heidegger, attempts to place humans as the "relational center of that which is," so that humans might "give the measure and dra[w] up the guidelines for everything that is."[30] What humans have learned from photographic technologies, Heidegger insisted, were strategies for taxonomizing physical phenomena in an aggressive imposition of human-centered paradigms: "As soon as the world becomes picture, the position of man is conceived as a world view."[31] It is this sort of aggression that Woolf's decentered or dispersed narrative practices resisted.

The composition of *The Waves*, with its syncopation of interludes and soliloquies in lieu of an omniscient narrator, and its reinscription of conventional plot and character, demonstrates an attempt to move away from a literary unity either in structure or point of view. The novel's structure as a "playpoem" further suggests her interest in developing more viable, hybrid genres that might better account for "life itself." Her notion that material phenomena always exceed or resist a human articulation is suggested in that detached scene in which Bernard states, "And the light of the stars falling, as it falls now, on my hand after travelling for millions upon millions of years – I could get a cold shock from that for a moment – not more, my imagination is too feeble" (*TW* 267–8). In the moment Bernard contemplates the star's light on his hand he attempts to think his own alterity and to take on a decentered artistic vision. Dislocated within the larger matrix of a universe Jeans had described as finite yet expanding beyond human imagination, Bernard says, "I, who had been thinking myself so vast...a whole universe...am now nothing but what you see – an elderly man, rather heavy, grey above the ears..." (*TW* 292).

DEVELOPING A DECENTERED AESTHETIC VISION

Pamela Caughie has eloquently argued that "Woolf relinquishes in [*The Waves*]...the belief that art has a center of vision, that it can reveal some truth or effect some 'ultimate synthesis' " (*Virginia Woolf & Postmodernism* 50). Certainly, Woolf deployed in *The Waves* a multiplicity of perspectives that demonstrates the situatedness of any narrator, observer or artist. Thus, she anticipated the work of feminist theorists like Donna Haraway, who advocates knowledges that are always partial, and "differential" and who calls for a feminist scientific inquiry "ruled by partial sight and limited voice."[32] Woolf created in her novel personae or characters whose knowledge of themselves and of their world is always local, contingent, and situated. In an eloquent analysis of the proliferation of perspectives in Woolf's texts, Banfield notes that Woolf produces a "multiplication and assemblage of perspectives" through the dispersion of the author: "Such is the condition of all seeing, to have a partial view" (*The Phantom Table* 343). Woolf's decentered aesthetic vision traversed the discourses of both the sciences and the arts and responded in part to Fry's theory of an aesthetic unity, and, perhaps, to those reviews of *The Mysterious Universe* which claimed Jeans's complicity with his own cosmological pictures.

Modernist writers, Woolf observed, wrote under the pressure of "monstrous, hybrid, unmanageable emotions" in an "age when we are not fast anchored," and in which emerging visualization technologies and advances in astronomy and geology enabled a re-calculation of the scope and age of the universe.[33] The Woolf's owned Arthur Holmes' volume, *The Age of the Earth*, (1927) in which Holmes, a professor of geology at the University of Durham, reported that radioactive dating demonstrated the earth was at least two billion years old.[34] In the introduction to that text, Holmes pointed out how a calculation of the earth's age might be revealed by astronomy: "The oldest meteorites, representing material from beyond the earth and, at least in part, from beyond the solar system, also date back some 2,000 million years" (*The Age of the Earth* vi). Likewise, Hubble's theories regarding the expansion of the universe and the formation of spiral nebulae supported the idea that if nebulae or galaxies represented large coagulations of stellar material then the scale on which these organized structures had evolved into neat spirals must be on the order of billions of years (Holmes, *The Age of the Earth* vi).

The long ages of the universe had, Woolf reasoned, effectively made defunct the realist novel as well as traditional poetic forms. In her essay "The Narrow Bridge of Art" (1927), Woolf considered the brevity of human existence in relation to the billions of years of cosmological time and claimed that contemporary aesthetic forms were inadequate in light of that disparity:

That the age of the earth is 3,000,000,000 years; that human life lasts but a second [...] it is in this atmosphere of doubt and conflict that writers have now to create, and the fine fabric of a lyric is no more fitted to contain this point of view than a rose leaf to envelop the rugged immensity of a rock. (*GR* 12)

Having become deeply skeptical of traditional literary conventions, she denigrated the "appalling narrative business of the realist" as "false, unreal, merely conventional" (*D3*: 209). She argued that writers needed to rework literary genres to forge more appropriate means of articulating human existence. The "Narrow Bridge" essay prefigures her deployment of a different sort of novel, and marks her interest in pushing beyond what she saw as the insipid "getting on from lunch to dinner" of realist fiction (*D3*: 209). As she was planning *The Waves*, one literary critic complained in November 1928 of Woolf's "crisis in the matter of style" which was denounced as being "so fluent & fluid that it runs through the mind like water" (*D3*: 203). Woolf's response was to develop *The Waves* as a compilation of "a variety of styles": as such, she decided, her novel would become a "playpoem" (*D3*: 203). "We shall be forced to invent new names for the different books which masquerade under this one heading [i.e., the genre of the novel]," wrote Woolf, "And it is possible that there will be among the so-called novels one which we shall scarcely know how to christen. It will be written in prose, but in prose which has many of the characteristics of poetry."[35] Her "prose poem," *The Waves*, suggests Woolf's investment in that *Athenaeum* exchange between Roger Fry and J.W.N. Sullivan regarding the interconnections of art and science. She knew, and most likely hoped, that her "experiment," her "prose poem," would interfere with, and disrupt, critical discourses on aesthetic unity and scientific objectivity. Throughout her writing career Woolf actively sought out "a new method" (*D5*: 340), hybrid genres, and alternative narrative strategies capable of sustaining a dispersed aesthetic vision, one that could account for the de-centering of humans produced by contemporary scientific and technological developments. A reading of *The Waves* as it intersects with the work of Jeans, Fry, and Russell points up Woolf's exploration of the positive possibilities for a decentered aesthetic vision that might demystify the pictures artists and scientists create. For Woolf there are no objective positions from which artists or scientists narrate their stories, even as Bernard cannot definitively sum up his life and must concede to focus on "the panorama of life, seen not from the roof, but from the third story window" (*TW* 242). An experiment in thinking the alterity of realist fiction, her "prose poem" *The Waves* inscribes the opposition to a seemingly objective articulation of the world as picture.

5

Woolf and Stapledon envision new worlds

The brilliant blue earth rising over the moon's craggy and desiccated plains magnified the Apollo astronauts' sense of our planet as a tiny oasis in a vast and trackless expanse. Those first human glimpses of earth from the moon, as multiple astronauts have noted, made tangible our planet's delicate existence in the hostile vacuum of space. For the Apollo astronauts especially, the earth appeared "so small and so fragile and such a precious little spot in th[e] universe," as astronaut Russell Schweickart observed: "[Y]ou realize on that small spot, that little blue and white thing, is everything that means anything to you – all of history and music and poetry and art...all of it on that little spot out there that you can cover with your thumb."[1] Views of earth from space first achieved during the early Vostok, Mercury, and Gemini missions helped ease nationalist barriers between astronauts and cosmonauts, despite the cold war that raged between the two nations that first sent humans into space. Schweickart explains:

When you go around the Earth in an hour and a half, you begin to recognize that your identity is with that whole thing. That makes a change. You look down there and you can't imagine how many borders and boundaries you cross, again and again and again, and you don't even see them. There you are–hundreds of people in the Mideast killing each other over some imaginary line that you're not even aware of and that you can't see.[2]

Space historian Frank White has argued that the earliest views of earth from orbit irreversibly altered how we perceive of our planet and demonstrated the need for peaceful conflict resolution if humans hope to survive eons into future. "The pity of it is," astronaut Michael Collins poignantly has noted, "that so far the view from 100,000 miles has been the exclusive property of a handful of test pilots, rather than the world leaders who need this new perspective, or the poets who might communicate it to them."[3] British authors Virginia Woolf and William Olaf Stapledon could easily have been the "poets" Collins imagined who could articulate the significance of such a vision. Both writers forged literary images of earth in space as a means of launching a critique of human aggression and war.

While Chapters Two and Four of this study demonstrated how telescopic views of other worlds indelibly impressed upon Woolf a global aesthetic vision, this chapter explores the cultural milieu within which Woolf developed her social and political vision for what Stapledon imagined as a "future global community" (Robert Crossley, *Olaf Stapledon* 208). Woolf and Stapledon's fascination with the image of earth in space, I argue, helped shape their pacifist politics. In support of this claim, this chapter offers a comparison of their novels *The Years* and *Star Maker*, published in 1937 by Woolf and Stapledon respectively. While Woolf's novel spans five decades of the Pargiter family, as the main character Eleanor considers the future of human existence and dreams of a "new world" free of military aggression, Stapledon's novel, *Star Maker*, offers a sweeping vision of the universe and the possibilities for long-term survival of the human species.[4] The interconnections between these two novels demonstrate Woolf and Stapledon's concerns regarding the future of humanity, as well as preoccupations at work within British popular culture in the interwar years. The chapter traces how advances in astronomy not only served these two modernist writers in their articulation of a pacifist politics, but also catalyzed a new sense of the human position in the universe that explains a curious and seemingly unrelated popular interest in insects.

IMAGINING EARTH AS SEEN FROM SPACE

By the 1930s, the world's largest telescopes had revealed other worlds scattered across the depths of space, a new planet within our own solar system, as well as innumerable galaxies beyond the limits of the Milky Way. The decade prior to that had unveiled millions of galaxies within the observable universe. There is no doubt that Woolf and Stapledon were inspired by the vistas of space made possible by the new telescopic technologies. Though actual images of earth from orbit were not yet possible in the early decades of the twentieth century, both writers included in their fiction and essays descriptions of earth's globe adrift in the abyss of space.[5] The narrator of Woolf's story, "The Mark on the Wall," imagines earth as a space-faring vessel, hurtling through the interplanetary void with a lone tree serving as a kind of ship's mast: "I like to think of [the tree] too, on winter's nights standing in the empty field with all leaves close-furled, nothing tender exposed to the iron bullets of the moon, a naked mast upon an earth that goes tumbling, tumbling all night long" (*HH* 45). Likewise, in her novel *Between the Acts* there is a description of the "black blue" of that part of the sky which extends far above the clouds. The black of outer space, the narrator suggests, "disregarded the little coloured ball of earth entirely" (*BTA* 13).

Stapledon, who published his first novel at age 44, maintained throughout his life a deep interest in astronomy and cosmology. "Almost from the time he learned to use pen and paper," biographer Robert Crossley notes, "Olaf could not help writing about the stars – in youthful diary passages and in the poems of *Latter-Day Psalms*, in reports from his ambulance post during the war and in his verses of the twenties" (*Olaf Stapledon* 229). Even as a youth as he gazed through his father's telescope, Olaf peered at the mountains of the moon, and eventually began to conceive what earth must look like from space (Crossley, *Olaf Stapledon* 228).

One of Stapledon's most vivid literary sketches of earth's globe appears in the novel "he had been rehearsing all his life" (Crossley, *Olaf Stapledon* 228). *Star Maker* presents a sweeping imaginary vision of the life span of the universe, and considers the possibilities for human survival eons into the future. In the opening scene, as the narrator gazes out at the stars, he suddenly has a vision of being whisked into earth's orbit:

The Earth appeared now as a great bright orb hundreds of times larger than the full moon. In its centre a dazzling patch of light was the sun's image reflected in the ocean. The planet's circumference was an indefinite breadth of luminous haze, fading into the surrounding blackness of space. Much of the northern hemisphere, tilted somewhat toward me, was an expanse of snow and cloud-tops. I could trace parts of the outlines of Japan and China, their vague browns and greens indenting the vague blues and greys of the ocean.... A little whirl of brilliant cloud was perhaps the upper surface of a hurricane. The Philippines and New Guinea were precisely mapped. Australia faded into the hazy southern limb... [T]he sheer beauty of our planet surprised me. It was a huge pearl, set in spangled ebony. It was nacreous, it was an opal... It displayed the delicacy and brilliance, the intricacy and harmony of a live thing. (*Star Maker* 234)

Written roughly twenty years before space flight had become a reality, Stapledon's depiction of earth as seen from low earth orbit is uncannily accurate excepting only, according to NASA payload specialist James Pawelczyk, that his colors are too muted.[6]

In the summer of 1937, while Woolf was thumbing her way through Stapledon's *Star Maker*, he in turn was devouring Woolf's novel, *The Years*. That summer Stapledon and Woolf exchanged a series of letters regarding their mutual appreciation for each other's work. Upon receiving in June a copy of *Star Maker*, Woolf noted in her diary: "Olaf Stapledon has sent me his new book: wh[ich] flatters me, as 3 papers say it's a masterpiece...."

(*D5*: 99). Fascinated by Woolf's artistic style, Stapledon wrote to Virginia in July: "I have recently read 'The Years' with delight, and also with despair at the thought of the contrast between your art and my own pedestrian method."[7] Virginia cherished the praise: "Last year of course I was carefully drawing my poor limp horns in," she noted in her diary, "And now Elizabeth Bowen thinks The Years – oh, all I wanted it to be. And Olaf Stapledon also, & so on" (*D5*: 103).

Although it is unclear whether they ever met, Woolf and Stapledon would have known each other's work through the *London Mercury*, for which they both wrote reviews and essays. By the mid-1930s, Stapledon was writing reviews for this eclectic literary journal, which also published essays on popular science topics and to which both Virginia and Leonard contributed. A review of *The Years*, for instance, appeared in the journal's April 1937 issue while Bertrand Russell's praise of Stapledon's "cosmological imagination" in a review of *Star Maker* was published in the July issue that same year.[8] Stapledon in addition had come to know some of the most prominent scientists and science popularizers in Britain. His first novel *Last and First Men* (1930), a futuristic vision of the evolution of humans as they move out into the solar system and develop off-earth settlements, was read by Bertrand Russell and Arthur Eddington. By the 1930s, Stapledon was closely acquainted with J.B.S. Haldane, science writers J.W.N. Sullivan and Gerald Heard, as well as novelist H.G. Wells; he also had read Julian Huxley's work and may have known Huxley along with Harold Nicolson through his years at Balliol College at Oxford (*Olaf Stapledon* 268; 69). Thus while Stapledon remained at the periphery of Bloomsbury, he socialized with, or at least read, many of the same scientists and writers who were close to Woolf. They, in turn, read him, which reveals the shared interest in astronomy and cosmology between Stapledon and Woolf's colleagues and associates.

TO "CALL IN ALL THE COSMIC IMMENSITIES"

In writing *The Years*, Woolf noted in her diary that she attempted to "call in all the cosmic immensities" (*D5*: 135).[9] Indeed, scattered across the novel's pages are multiple references to the moon and stars, and the far reaches of intergalactic space. Several characters including Eleanor, her first cousin Sara, as well as their niece Peggy, gaze skyward and ponder their own relation to the stars. In one scene Sara imagines the moon's cold and alien terrain with its mountains and "icy hollows" (*TY* 115). Lying in bed, she contemplates "engravings chased over the [moon's] white disc. What were they, she wondered – mountains? valleys? And if valleys, she said to herself half closing her eyes, then white trees..." (*TY* 115). This scene which opens with Sara returning from a party, and then lying in bed to look out at the moon, is a reworking of two short autobiographical essays by Woolf dated 1903. In the first Woolf recalls lying in bed listening to the sounds of a nearby party: "I lie in the cool & look out through my open window. In a moment if I choose, I need think no more of the dancers – I am looking into the awful night sky.... The same sky stretches round the world, I think –" (*PA* 165). In the other essay, Woolf again recounts the events of an evening party she has just attended. The essay concludes: "Now I open my book of astronomy, dream of the stars a little, & so to sleep –" (*PA* 172). That astronomy book may have been Camille Flammarion's *Astronomie Populaire*, in which Flammarion speculated whether the surface of the moon sustained frozen water and plant life, and how the extreme cold and heat might tint the color of lunar vegetation.[10] Sara, like Flammarion, imagines a lunar landscape of frozen trees in icy hollows.

Likewise Peggy, in a moment of escape from her aunt Delia's crowded dinner party, looks out from the window of Delia's London home, and tries to comprehend the immensity of interstellar space:

There were the stars pricked in little holes in the blue-black sky... Inscrutable, eternal, indifferent – those were the words; the right words. But I don't feel it, she said, looking at the stars. So why pretend to? What they're really like, she thought, screwing up her eyes to look at them, is little bits of frosty steel. And the moon – there it was – is a polished dish-cover. But she felt nothing, even when she had reduced moon and stars to that. (*TY* 314)

In fact, the very opening chapter to *The Years*, titled "1880," hints at the "cosmic immensities" Woolf intended the novel to include. The character Kitty Malone reads in *The Times* [London] of British naval experiments with an electric searchlight. "There's been an experiment," Kitty tells her mother as she reads *The Times*, "An experiment with electric light. 'A brilliant light,' she read, 'was seen to shoot forth suddenly shooting out a profound ray across the water to the Rock. Everything was lit up as if by daylight.' She paused. She saw the bright light from the ships on the drawing room chair" (*TY* 68).

Kitty reads from an 1880 *Times* article on maneuvers conducted by the H.M.S. *Agincourt* and *Minotaur* on the bay near the British crown province of Gibraltar and its famous rock.[11] These naval investigations were most likely maneuvers related to using an early model searchlight. In fact, the *Minotaur* was the first Royal Navy vessel to carry a searchlight.[12] The "profound ray" that Kitty imagines "suddenly shooting...out across the water" also evokes American astronomer A.A. Michelson's experiments in the US on the velocity of light. Michelson in 1879, the year before the Navy searchlight experiments, had re-calculated the velocity of light at 186,320 miles per second (Dorothy Livingston, *The Master of Light* 95).[13] Michelson's velocity for light "became the accepted standard for forty-four years" until, through his own later experiments at Mount Wilson Observatory, he determined a more accurate figure (Livingston 96). The significance of Kitty's contemplation of the light ray, in part, is that by the end of the nineteenth century the velocity of light, and the light-year, would become the standard measures for the great cosmological distances.[14]

In December 1920, Michelson stunned the reading public in the US by demonstrating the nearly unimaginable mass and size of red giant stars. Sensational news reports were leaked to the press regarding recent experiments with an interferometer that Michelson, "generally recognized as the foremost authority in the world on the subject of light,"[15] had set up at Mount Wilson Observatory. It was determined that a single star named Betelgeuse, a red supergiant in the Orion constellation, had a diameter of approximately the orbit of Mars, which meant the star was millions of times the size of our sun.[16] Reports of Michelson's findings garnered front-page coverage in the *New York Times*, and shocked both the "press and the public [which] had no notion of the colossal bulk of Betelgeuse" (Livingston 276). "GIANT STAR EQUAL TO 27,000,000 SUNS LIKE OURS: As for Our Little Earth, Betelgeuse Is as Big as Trillions of Globes Like It," read the *New York Times* headline.[17] Illustrations accompanying the news report included a dramatic diagram of Betelgeuse nearly filling the orbit of Mars.[18] What made the announcement regarding Betelgeuse so sensational was the unimaginable scale of cosmic phenomena. The result of such discoveries was that the average person on the street found herself attempting to make sense of the scale of astronomical phenomena in human terms.

In April 1925, when measurements of the star Mira indicated it was larger than the red supergiant Betelgeuse, the *Illustrated London News* included a full-page diagram of several red giant stars showing that each exceeded 150 million miles in diameter (Figure 5.1). The newspaper, known "for its illustrations of the most recent events in exploration, science and archaeology," featured a full-page spread on some of the largest stars known, including Betelgeuse, Aldebaran, and Arcturus (*E*4: 141, n. 1); *The Times* [London] also ran an article on calculations at Mount Wilson Observatory measuring Mira's diameter at 250 million miles.[19]

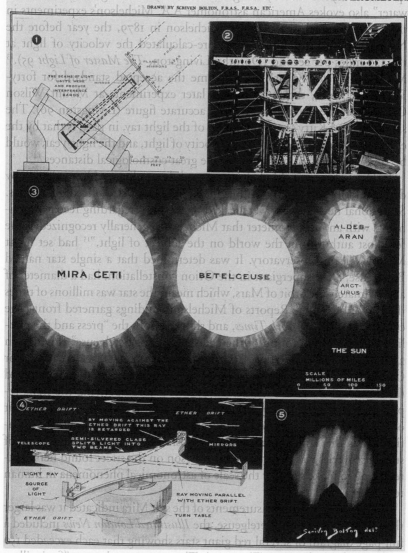

Figure 5.1 **Graphic of giant stars printed in *Illustrated London News*.** An April 1925 issue of the *Illustrated London News* included a full page spread on observations at Mount Wilson Observatory that indicated the star Mira was even larger than Betelgeuse. Here the diameter of these red giant stars is shown to extend to millions of miles. The illustration is one example of the popular appeal news of astronomical discoveries in America had in Britain. Courtesy of the *Illustrated London News* Picture Library.

Vita Sackville-West, who shared with Woolf a passion for astronomy, knew of the colossal size of red giant stars. The stars Betelgeuse and Aldebaran are named in Sackville-West's poem "Full Moon," published in her collection *Orchard and Vineyard* just a year after reports on Betelgeuse appeared in the American press (56). Her poem "From 'A Masque of Youth'" also includes references to "[g]reat, measurable stars," "many coloured moons," comets, and "Saturn within his hoop of shining rings" (*Orchard and Vineyard* 70, 71). Likewise, her poem "Spring," which appeared in *The Land* published a year later in 1926, described the constellation Orion, along with the stars "Betelgeuse, Aldebaran, and brightest Sirius" (*The Land* 51).[20] Even Jeans, awed by the immensity of stars, had launched the opening lines of *The Mysterious Universe* (1930) with a description of the incredible size of the red giants: "A few stars are known which are hardly bigger than the earth, but the majority are so large that hundreds of thousands of earths could be packed inside each and leave room to spare; here and there we come upon a giant star large enough to contain millions of millions of earths" (1).

Woolf too clearly knew of Michelson's findings on the unbelievable size of red giant stars. In both her longer fiction and short stories, her characters refer to the stars and constellations and know them by name. And often the stars her characters mention rank among our sun's largest neighbors, especially Betelgeuse and Aldebaran. Both of these red giants are named in multiple early drafts of Woolf's "The Searchlight," a short story, as noted in Chapter Two, permeated with concerns regarding the human re-scaling that I have been elaborating.[21]

FROM THE ATOM TO THE UNIVERSE

As advances in astronomy headlined the pages of newspapers, so too did discoveries related to the new physics. As a result the popular imagination bounded from the far reaches of space to the infinitesimally small particles of atoms. Eddington claimed that the size of the universe perhaps determined, as Bertrand Russell noted, the size of the atom:

Einstein and others have suggested that the universe has a 'curvature,' so that we could theoretically go all round it . . . in the sort of way in which we go round the earth. All the way round the universe, in that case, must be a certain length, fixed in nature. Eddington suggests that some relation will probably be found between this . . . and the radius of the electron, which is the least length in nature. (*The ABC of Atoms* 156)

Eddington further argued that the atom provided a perfect analog for understanding the structure of the solar system. The size of electrons in relation to the nucleus of an atom could be considered as proportional to "that of the sun and its planetary system," Eddington suggested; "We may thus picture an atom as a miniature solar system."[22] In *Atoms, Men and Stars* (1937), an artifact of an era enraptured with a modernist human re-scaling, Rogers Rusk attributed the solar system-atom analogy to Niels Bohr, who apparently claimed in 1913 that electrons moved in orbits around an atom's nucleus similar to the way planets orbit the sun (40). Rusk noted: "Thus was evolved the idea of the atom as a tiny solar system... Here was revealed a new frontier of knowledge, a whole universe in the minute..." (*Atoms, Men and Stars* 40). As a means of making the new astronomical vistas intelligible, science writers suggested that people simply consider themselves as being somewhere in between these unimaginable extremes. Olaf Stapledon once observed, "Julian Huxley... has pointed out that man's body is approximately half-way in size between an electron and the whole universe"("Interplanetary Man?" *An Olaf Stapledon Reader* 231).

The Years and Star Maker, in particular, traversed this popular milieu and responded to the broad cultural concerns regarding the new vistas of space and the micro-worlds of atoms. In *The Years*, as Judith Killen has shown, the characters are fascinated with far more than looking up at the stars; they find themselves inversely intrigued by the very small. Interspersed throughout the novel are repeated references to atoms and insects. In stark contrast to questions regarding "the nature of the universe," Eleanor, for instance, contemplates the structure of the atom (*TY* 336). "Eleanor formulates in her meditations the questions physicists were asking about the atom – what is an atom? How does it make a world?"[23] In various scenes, Eleanor sketches "a dot with strokes raying out round it" which, Killen convincingly claims, most likely represents an early twentieth century model of the atom: "In 1910, the year the English scientific establishment publicly accepted Planck's radiation theory, Eleanor's 'doodling' is narrated in detail."[24]

By deploying in their novels a movement from the microscopic to the "cosmic immensities," both Woolf and Stapledon tapped into popular concerns regarding the significant relation between the expanses of the universe and humans – those mere atoms by comparison. The opening scene of *Star Maker* takes place on earth, but within a few pages the narrative swells to the broad canvas of a universe populated with multiple alien worlds. By a strange out-of-body experience, the narrator is whisked into earth orbit, and later out into the far reaches of the universe. Transformed thus into a "disembodied view-point," Stapledon's narrator surveys first the galaxy, then explores inhabited extra-solar planets, and investigates the struggle of each planet's inhabitants to survive catastrophes such as cosmic collisions, the supernova of their sun, and military aggression.[25] The narrator also finds that the more evolved alien species, those which have survived the eons of time, chose peaceful coexistence over military annihilation of alien others.

Stapledon's novel resonated to a public angst about a human decentering and re-scaling effected by discoveries regarding the age of the universe. *Star Maker* sketches a universe of myriad worlds on which, the narrator explains, "millions of persons were flashing into existence, one after the other, to drift gropingly about for a few instants of cosmical time before they were extinguished" (*Star Maker* 275). Indeed, the novel's foremost theme emerges as a re-scaling and decentering of humans in a universe in which human history appears as only a flash in the pan before human existence winks out in the long eons of cosmological time. The disembodied narrator, who enumerates his encounters with alien civilizations struggling for future survival, at one point glimpses a panoramic view of the history of the universe in which humankind appears only briefly. "The two-billion-year history of the human race... gets just half a paragraph in *Star Maker*," notes Crossley, "Never before had humanity been so definitively marginalized in a work of fiction" (*Olaf Stapledon* 230–1). Indeed, an appendix to the novel, titled "A Note on Magnitude," includes a chart that depicts the fleeting span of human existence in this fictional, historical overview of the cosmological eons (*Star Maker* 410–12).

WOOLF AND STAPLEDON READING AND RESPONDING TO JAMES JEANS

Woolf and Stapledon's mutual fascination with James Jeans marks another important intersection of their work. Avid readers of Jeans, both authors had subtly incorporated elements of his texts into their creative and nonfiction writing. They read his non-technical books, and Woolf, because she lived in London, would have heard Jeans's BBC broadcasts on the stars and the structure of the universe.[26] References to Jeans and his popular astronomy books permeate *The Years* as well as *Star Maker*. There is, for instance, in *The Years*, Woolf's recurring image of the caravan crossing the desert, which surprisingly has a great deal to do with Jeans. Grace Radin points out that in the holograph to "The Pargiters," an early draft of what became the 1880 chapter of *The Years*, Woolf frequently used the image of "[a] caravan crossing a desert as a metaphor for the [Pargiter] family"(*Virginia Woolf's*

The Years 50). Likewise, in the 1910 chapter of *The Years*, Eleanor recalls Sara's description of the Pargiter family as a "caravan crossing the desert" (149). That memory offers a context for understanding Sara's earlier vision of the Pargiter family "going on and on and on...until they come to a rock" (*TY* 146). In fact, one of the titles Woolf considered for the novel was "The Caravan" (Radin 50, n. 17; *D4*: 274.)

Though Woolf contemplated the image of the caravan crossing a trackless desert as early as 1905, the caravan image in *The Years* may have been in part drawn from Woolf's reading of James Jeans's popular astronomy texts.[27] The stars, Jeans noted, served as guides for human survival in the early days of exploration, and as a means for mankind "to find his way *across the trackless desert, and later, across the trackless ocean*" (*The Universe Around Us* 9; italics mine). For Woolf, the image of a caravan crossing a desert depicted humans' fragile and ephemeral position in a universe Jeans had described as indifferent to life. More importantly though, evidence from her diary indicates that her image of the Pargiter family caravan was meant to represent humanity pitted against the abysses of intergalactic space. "[M]y thoughts turn with excitement to The Pargiters," wrote Woolf, "for I long to feel my sails blow out, & to be careering with Elvira, Maggie & the rest over the whole of human life" (*D4*: 134). In one draft, Elvira (Sara/Sally in *The Years*) reflects on her family's shortcomings and thinks to herself: "I... see the Pargiters crossing the desert; & the stars. [T]his I think is all life taking its way from the end of time: a sort of reverence fills me: helpless, small, tenacious as they are" (quoted in Radin, *Virginia Woolf's The Years* 50). The Pargiters, representing the whole of human existence, are depicted against the backdrop of the long eons of the universe.

The image of humans struggling to survive in a desolate and unforgiving environment may also have been on Woolf's mind during a trip to Greece in May of 1932. The landscape, she noted, was as "the country of the moon... lit by a dead sun" (*D4*: 94). Rambling through those rustic Greek communities afforded her a vision of human civilization just barely clinging to existence. Woolf noted:

Greece... is a land so ancient that it is like wandering in the fields of the moon... The living, these worn down, for ever travelling the roads.... We met them always on the high mountain passes padding along beside their donkeys, so small, existing so painfully, always marching in search of some herb, some root, mastered by the vast distances, unable to do more than dig their heels in... the rock. (*D4*: 94)

Woolf imagined the Greek peasants "wandering in the fields of the moon" and "mastered by the vast distances" even as she envisioned the Pargiter family as "a little caravan bravely crossing the desert, a group of human beings who have banded together for protection against the terrors of isolation and savagery" (Radin 50). As literary motifs, the trackless desert and the vast wastes of ocean were equally compelling for Stapledon, who had envisioned how one day the stars would navigate humans across another trackless desert, that of interplanetary space, the outer reaches of the solar system, and beyond. It was the story he told in his earlier novel, *Last and First Men* (1930), of the settlement of the solar system and of humanity's evolution and eventual demise.

Elsewhere in *The Years*, references to Jeans surface, especially in the air raid scene. Maggie and her husband Renny are hosting Eleanor, Sara, and Sara's friend Nicholas when sirens suddenly blare and the party moves to the cellar. The scene, as Karen Levenback makes clear, was drawn from Woolf's own air raid experiences during World War I (*Virginia Woolf and the Great War* 123). Eventually, the conversation turns to a toast in honor of a "New World," one Eleanor imagines as free of human aggression and international conflict. Sara calls for Nicholas to give a speech (*TY* 256), but just as Nicholas begins, Renny, a munitions maker disgusted with his own contribution to Britain's bomb production, interrupts and indicates the raid has ended and that the group should return upstairs. Sara protests, "And leave this cellar... this cave of mud and dung..." (*TY* 256). At that, Nicholas turns to Eleanor and attempts to pass off the air raid as harmless: "Only children letting off fireworks in the back garden" (*TY* 256).

Radin notes that while "Nicholas' remark sounds facetious and condescending in the context of the air raid... he is actually alluding to his theory of evolution, which posits that man is now in a primitive and infantile stage of development" (*Virginia Woolf's The Years* 142). She further points out that the scene refers to an earlier comment by Sara on future generations that will judge Sara's childhood home as a "cave, this little antre, scooped out of mud and dung" (*TY* 164). Radin, however, does not see the link between Sara's derision of modern existence and Nicholas's comment regarding international war as mere child's play: "Sara's remark immediately precedes Nicholas's comment about the children playing with fireworks, but it would require a very sophisticated reading of the text of *The Years* to see their connection" (*Virginia Woolf's The Years* 142).

Perhaps not. Nicholas's criticism of humanity's infant-like development clarifies Sara's complaint that European culture has barely advanced beyond that of cave-dwellers. One significant connection for Sara and Nicholas's conversation is the work of James Jeans, who often wrote of humanity's only recent emergence in an ancient and perhaps dying universe. In his volume

Eos (1928) the title of which refers to the Greek goddess of the dawn, Jeans frames the text with commentary on humanity's nascent understanding of the universe:

Looked at on the astronomical timescale, humanity is at the very beginning of its existence – a new-born babe.... It has just become conscious of the vast world existing outside itself and its cradle; it is learning to focus its eyes on distant objects [stars and galaxies], and its awakening brain is beginning to wonder... what they are and what purpose they serve. (*Eos* 11–12)

While this passage appeared in a chapter titled "The Position of Man in the Universe," the conclusion of *Eos* again likens humanity to an "infant [who] cannot be very confident of any interpretation it puts on a universe which it discovered only a minute or two ago" (87). Woolf too imagined humans as naïve to a universe far older than previously thought. In fact, she noted having considered "Dawn" as a possible title for *The Years* (*D4*: 241).

The gesture toward Jeans's work in Woolf's novel also becomes clear as Eleanor considers what Nicholas, had he actually given a speech on the "new world," might have proffered. "When, she wanted to ask him, when will this new world come?... When shall we live adventurously, wholly, not like cripples in a cave?" (*TY* 259). Given Eleanor's added reflections that humans exist like "cripples in a cave," the scene is suggestive of Plato's well-known parable of cave dwellers and points directly to James Jeans's popular publications. In his widely read volume *The Mysterious Universe*, Jeans used the cave analogy from Plato's *Republic* to illustrate astronomers' nascent and limited awareness of worlds beyond the Milky Way. In the epigraph to that book, he quoted the passage from Plato regarding those "strange prisoners" who see only "shadows of images" on the cave wall and cannot discern the shadows from the objects that produce them (xi). Again in the closing chapter Jeans repeatedly evoked Plato to characterize the limitations of early twentieth century astronomers and their telescopic technologies:

To speak in terms of Plato's well-known simile, we are still imprisoned in our cave, with our backs to the light, and can only watch the shadows on the wall. At present the only task immediately before science is to study these shadows, to classify them and explain them in the simplest way possible. (*The Mysterious Universe* 151)

Allusions to Jeans surface as well throughout Stapledon's fiction and poetry. Stapledon was an avid reader of Jeans and often incorporated elements of Jeans's texts into his fiction and poetry. In part, Stapledon took his cues on the rarity and fragility of life in the universe from Jeans. In *Star Maker*, for instance, the narrator rehearses Jeans's tidal theory on the rarity of planet formation: "I knew well that the birth of planets was due to the close approach of two or more stars, and that such accidents must be very uncommon" (240). The *Star Maker* narrator also observes in rhetoric like that of Jeans: "I reminded myself that stars with planets must be as rare in the galaxy as gems among the grains of sand on the sea-shore" (240). "And the total number of stars in the universe," Jeans had noted, "is probably something like the total number of grains of sand on all the seashores of the world. Such is the littleness of our home in space when measured up against the total substance of the universe" (*The Mysterious Universe* 1).

In order to illustrate the scale of human existence in such a vast universe, Stapledon developed in his prose and poetry images of humans as tiny insects or as bacteria. He drew his inspiration from Jeans, who claimed that " '[l]ike the animalculae [sic] of the raindrop looking out on to Niagara,' " humans observe " 'the ocean [of intergalactic space] the existence of which we are only just beginning to suspect' " (Crossley, *Olaf Stapledon* 177; 424 n. 43). Stapledon responded to Jeans's assertions through a series of poems that compared the brevity of human existence to the long ages of the universe (Crossley, *Olaf Stapledon* 177). In the first sequence of these poems, originally titled "Astronomical Posters," humans are scaled down to the size of insects in relation to the vast expanse of the cosmos. In one poem, for example, humans are described as mere "[w]ater beetles/skating on the stagnant skin of a backwater," who dream of annexing other worlds as well as entire "island universes" or galaxies.[28] In the poem's final stanza, Stapledon suggests not only that humans eventually will face extinction, but also that human life is as ephemeral as that of an insect: "And long after man the stars/will continually evaporate in radiant energy/to recondense as nebulae/and again stars,/till here and there some new planet/will harbour again insect populations."[29]

In contrast, a second sequence of Stapledon's poems explored the world of the minute and, much like Woolf's "Kew Gardens," imagined the limited cosmology of a snail as a means of commenting on humans' limited understanding of the universe: "Outraged by uncouth contacts, the snail mind, with eyes retracting, subsides within his brittle whorl."[30] Stapledon also incorporated into this poetry sequence Jeans's analogy of humanity's awakening from a nascent understanding of the universe. Crossley comments, "That humanity might just be emerging from its childhood, groping for a first mature understanding of the universe and its own physical and metaphysical status, was the implication of Jeans's [work] and the argument of Stapledon's poetic sequence" (*Olaf Stapledon* 177).

Scenes in *Star Maker* likewise scale from the vast reaches of intergalactic space to worlds populated with civilizations of "insectoids." Indeed, entire communities of these insectoids are nearly obliterated by aggression and "insane warfare" (*Star Maker* 307). As the *Star Maker* narrator bounds from galaxy to galaxy, Stapledon unfolds a pacifist polemic that drew upon the public interest in astronomy and a concurrent and seemingly unrelated popular fascination with insects. One British reporter commented on the relationship between astronomy and entomology: "The result of thinking in millions of years, and in stellar spaces where our earth is but a tiny grain of sand, is to make of mankind the spawn of animalculae, and of its history, its poetry, its religion, its virtues, and its vices nothing more significant than the scurryings of the anthill."[31] Insects, it seems, were another shared preoccupation for Woolf and Stapledon. For both writers insects were linked to the re-evaluation of the human position in the universe catalyzed by astronomical discoveries.

INSECTS IN POPULAR CULTURE

In an engaging essay on the British fascination with insects and the "fantasy of the insect body," Jessica Burstein has examined "[t]he surge in the English appetite for books on bugs" at the turn of the century.[32] Burstein reports that from 1898 to 1905 only nineteen books related to insects had been published in England, but that by 1935 an additional 150 books on insects had appeared in print.[33]

Additional evidence of the popular fascination with insects that pervaded the period was the production of the Čapek brothers' play, "*And so ad infinitum*": *The Life of the Insects*. A Czech writer and playwright, Karel Čapek (1890–1938), along with his brother Josef, garnered public visibility in Britain when this play was translated and directed for the London stage.[34] The Čapeks drew upon Jean Henri Fabre's *La vie des insects* and his *Souvenirs entomologiques* in writing the play, originally titled "From the Life of Insects" (Bohuslava Bradbrook, *Karel Čapek* 52). The year before *The Years* and *Star Maker* were published, the show was produced at London's Little Theatre, in August of 1936, under the title *The Insect Play*. Besides the fact that Karel Čapek was one of Stapledon's favorite authors, both Stapledon and Woolf would have known of this production if by no other means than their association with the *London Mercury*. The journal favorably reviewed the production and the show's costumes designed by Mervyn Peake, and even printed a few of Peake's costume illustrations.[35] Peake's sketch of an armored-looking dictator ant, standing astride what is presumably the earth, illustrates one source Stapledon most likely drew upon in developing in *Star Maker* his own critique of military aggression. The Čapeks' searing commentary on social and political aggrandizement develops with the play's opening scene, which takes place in a wood as a lepidopterist explains that the butterflies he obtains "must be carefully killed, and then carefully pinned, and properly dried"; this is done, he explains, all for the "[l]ove of nature" (*"And so ad infinitum"* 6, 7). By the second act, it becomes clear that humans are not the only aggressors in the wood. A pair of dung beetles guard their dung ball, only to have their stash filched by an ichneumon fly, who later kills the female dung beetle as food for his larva daughter.

In the final act, a clan of worker ants provokes a community of yellow ants to war over an insignificant "road [located] between the two blades of grass" (*"And so ad infinitum"* 53).[36] The worker ants' chief engineer immediately declares himself dictator and claims that war must be waged – both in "the interest of civilization and our military honour" (*"And so ad infinitum"* 56). While the chief engineer ant observes the battle through his telescope, another worker ant chants nationalist pro-war slogans: "War on the world. For a Great Home Country. One, two – a ruthless enemy. Will of the Nation!... Historical claims. Brilliant spirit of the Army" (*"And so ad infinitum"* 57, 56). The irony is that both ant communities conceive of their tiny struggle as having global significance. The worker ants claim that the war will be waged for "World interests" (*"And so ad infinitum"* 48). Yet, the cosmos in which these insects thrive affords no justice. Civilian ants are ruthlessly killed, and prisoners are unhesitatingly eliminated by both warring ant nations. Upon the success of the yellow ants, their leader proclaims himself not simply dictator, or ruler of the world, as the *London Mercury* cartoon caption indicated, but "Ruler of the Universe" (*"And so ad infinitum"* 62) (Figure 5.2). Thus, the play parodies imperialist aggression and the inanity of sacrificing entire populations for no more than a few blades of grass or a "bit of the world from the Birch tree to the Pine tree" (*"And so ad infinitum"* 53).[37] More importantly, the play points up the extreme limitations of human cosmologies. First published in England in 1921, the drama may have inspired Woolf to observe in *Jacob's Room* (1922) that "in Lombard Street and Fetter Lane and Bedford Square – each insect [like each human] carries a globe of the world in his head" (143). Woolf's point in that novel was to demonstrate the minute scale of human endeavors, including military campaigns, in relation to a larger universe.

The Čapek production likewise compares the ephemerality of humans to that of insects as a means of demonstrating the inanity of military aggression and imperialism – especially, in light of the fragility of life in a cold

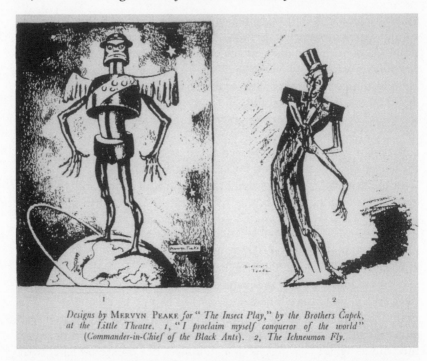

Designs by MERVYN PEAKE for " *The Insect Play,*" by the Brothers Čapek,
at the Little Theatre. 1, " I proclaim myself conqueror of the world"
(Commander-in-Chief of the Black Ants). 2, The Ichneumon Fly.

Figure 5.2 **Mervyn Peake illustration for *The Insect Play*.** These illustrations by Mervyn
Peake depict (on left) the costume for the Commander in Chief of one ant colony in *The
Insect Play*. The commander ant stands on what is presumably the earth, and has
proclaimed itself not simply "conqueror of the world," as the *London Mercury* caption
read, but "Ruler of the Universe." To the right is Peake's costume design for the
self-aggrandizing character of the ichneumon fly. The play demonstrates how, in the
popular imagination, insects had become associated with a re-scaling of humans in the
universe. Courtesy of David Higham Associates.

and indifferent universe. At the play's conclusion, a bevy of moths throw
themselves into a fire while fervently chanting a mantra about eternal life
in death. One chrysalis moth, which throughout the entire drama has attempted to burst forth from its cocoon existence, finally succeeds only to
expire as well in the flames. Even the character of the tramp, who serves
as the sane voice of reason throughout the drama, dies at the end as he
exclaims, "I'm a battered moth, I am..." (*"And so ad infinitum"* 65).

Fascism and military aggression, in many modernist writers' assessment,
had reduced industrialized European societies to little more than an insect
existence. In H.G. Wells's *The First Men in the Moon* (1901), the lunar interior is populated by a species of ant-like moon inhabitants or Selenites,

who live solely in service to their collective. Described as "hunch-backed insects, with very strong arms, short, bandy legs, and crinkled face-masks," the Selenites have converted the moon into "a sort of vast ant-hill" (Wells, *The First Men in the Moon* 226, 232). Life for the lunar insects is far from ideal. The Selenites are physically altered or conditioned from birth so that they can efficiently carry out their assigned tasks. The scientist Cavor, who has traveled to the moon, transmits messages back to earth how he became unnerved by the Selenites' physical conditioning. Cavor observes "a number of young Selenites confined in jars from which only the fore-limbs protruded, who were being compressed to become machine-minders of a special sort" (*The First Men in the Moon* 242). For Cavor, a "wretched-looking hand-tentacle sticking out of its jar" suggested the extreme limitations industrialization could impose on humans (*The First Men in the Moon* 243).

Yet despite the fact that the Selenites are "much more like ants on their hind legs than human beings," their leader, the Grand Lunar, demonstrates the Selenites' superior vision with regard to military aggression and war (*The First Men in the Moon* 141). The Grand Lunar asks his human visitor Cavor, "You mean to say...that you run about over the surface of your world – this world, whose riches you have scarcely begun to scrape – killing one another...?" (*The First Men in the Moon* 259). In the serialized version of the text, Cavor attempts to offer an explanation for such acts of aggression: "You must remember...we are only beginning. Man has scarcely awakened to himself and the universe around him....As yet this is only the dawn of mankind" (qtd. in *The First Men in the Moon* 258, n. 233).

The parallels between human and insect societies, especially ant societies, were commonly elaborated within the Bloomsbury group and associated intellectual circles. T.S. Eliot contended that it was the task of modern poets to rescue society from an intellectual disintegration that would result in humans devolving into nothing more than "a highly perfected race of insects" (*The Varieties of Metaphysical Poetry* 221). Roger Fry as well had theorized "a new idea about the real meaning of civilisation"; humans, Fry argued, "have lost the power to be individuals. They have become social insects like bees and ants" (qtd. in Woolf, *Roger Fry* 272). Similarly, J.B.S. Haldane complained that a view of earth from Venus would expose human society, despite its seeming modernity, "as little more than an ant-heap."[38] Julian Huxley was one of the few who opposed such a future vision for human evolution. In his volume titled *Ants* (1930), Huxley resisted simple analogies of humans as aggressive insects. He claimed the improbability of humans "breed[ing] armoured...soldiers" or of settling for "a mechanized and stable condition of existence" (*Ants* 143). Humans "can create new works of art" and could choose their own destiny, and that, Huxley argued, was "precisely what even the most intelligent ant ... entirely, inevitably, and for ever lacks" (*Ants* 143). But Woolf and Stapledon, like Eliot, cautioned that military aggression represented a kind of human devolution into something closer to an insect existence.

Although insects of all kinds appear throughout her novels and short fiction,[39] Woolf's personal interest in lepidoptera has been well documented. One of the most memorable accounts of Woolf's fascination with insects appears in the autobiographical essay, "Reading," in which she recalls a childhood moth-hunting foray. On an evening in 1899, she and the Stephen siblings ventured into the family garden to capture moths. The essay illustrates Woolf's own associations of insects with a modern human re-scaling effected by visualization technologies. "We waited in a group, and the little circle of forest where we stood became as if we saw it through the lens of a very powerful magnifying glass. Every blade of grass looked larger than by day, and the crevices in the bark much more sharply cut" (*E*3: 150). The circle of light thrown out by their lantern gives the garden and the Stephen children the sense of being small, even microscopic, against the "gloom of the unknown" (*E*3: 150).[40] Conjuring forth the vastness of interstellar space which Jeans had described as indifferent to life, Woolf noted, "The space surrounding us seemed vast.... Somehow, this world of night seemed hostile to us. Cold, alien, and unyielding, as if preoccupied with matters in which human beings could have no part" (*E*3: 151–2).

Woolf recalled how after they placed their lamp on the ground, almost instantly "the grass bent, [as] the insects came scrambling from all quarters, greedy and yet awkward in their desire to partake of the light" (*E*3: 151). She noted her sense of the absolute alien otherness of those insects in the forest. "Just as the eyes grow used to dimness and make out shapes where none were visible before, so sitting on the ground we felt we were surrounded by life, innumerable creatures were stirring among the trees; some creeping through the grass, others roaming through the air" (*E*3: 151–2).

It should be noted that the Stephen siblings took their bug-hunting very seriously. At age 14, Woolf wrote in her journal: "After tea Thoby read the Ent[omological]. Soc, a paper upon the History of the Club. Also a retrospect of 1896 – It was agreed ... that the lectures of the Pres. [Leslie Stephen] etc. should not be entered in the book" (*PA* 5–6). The "Entomological Society" was a Stephen family quasi-publication compiled by Woolf and her siblings. A later diary notation reveals that Virginia associated entomology with her own contemplation of the universe. She recorded highlights of Christmas Day 1897:

> Discussed the Universe!
> Meeting of Entomological Society.
> L[eslie]. S[tephen]. president
> G[eorge]. H[erbert]. D[uckworth]. Librarian
> J[ulian]. T[hoby]. S[tephen]. Larva Groom
> A[deline]. V[irginia]. S[tephen]. Secretary Chairman & Treasurer.
> A[drian]. L[eslie]. S[tephen]. not on the Committee.   (*PA* 134)

Moths, in particular, became a literary motif that Woolf as well as Stapledon would deploy in commentaries on humanity's ephemeral existence in the universe. In the 1911 chapter of *The Years*, Eleanor drops off to sleep one evening as she contemplates "three moths dashing round the ceiling" (*TY* 184). "Things can't go on for ever, she thought. Things pass, things change, she thought, looking up at the ceiling. And where are we going? Where? Where?" (*TY* 185–6). Eleanor's questions have to do with whether humans as a species will survive in future eons. As she clicks off the light to turn to sleep, the narrator starkly reports, "Darkness reigned" (186), powerfully suggesting the very real possibility of a human extinction. Peggy too, during Delia's party, envisions humans as fragile insects "sheltering under a leaf" and desperately clinging to life:

But how can one be "happy"? she asked herself, in a world bursting with misery. On every placard at every street corner was Death; or worse – tyranny; brutality; torture; the fall of civilisation; the end of freedom. We here, she thought, are only sheltering under a leaf, which will be destroyed. (*TY* 339)[41]

In this scene Peggy contemplates the brutality of modern technological societies capable of global war, and the hopelessness of humans surviving in the coming eons of the universe. Just prior to this, Peggy had been reading from a volume "bound in green leather" and decorated with "little gilt stars": " 'La mediocrite de l'univers m'etonne et me revolte,' she read. That was it. Precisely. She read on … 'la pauvrete des etres humains m'aneantit.' She shut the book and put it back on the shelf. Precisely, she said" (*TY* 335).[42]

A reading of Woolf's fascination with insects, alongside her very clear sense of earth as a planet whirling through space, affords the possibility of new interpretations of her often cited essay "The Death of the Moth." Most likely written very late in her career and probably not published in her lifetime, "The Death of the Moth" comments on the brevity of human existence in comparison to the cosmological eons.[43] In that essay, a narrator describes the scene of a moth that flutters against a window pane which constrains and limits its tiny life: "He flew vigorously to one corner of his compartment, and, after waiting there a second, flew across to the other.... That was all he could do, in spite of the size of the downs, and the romantic voice, now and then, of a steamer out at sea" (*DM* 4). Observing the tiny drama, the narrator notes: "[T]he thought of all that life might have been had he been born in any other shape caused one to view his simple activities with a kind of pity" (*DM* 4–5).

As the moth suddenly expires, the narrator reflects on the indifference of the universe to this minute extinction: "[T]he power was there all the same, massed outside indifferent, impersonal, not attending to anything in particular" (*DM* 6). The moth's death represented for Woolf what Jeans had characterized as the universe's cold indifference to humans' meager attempts at survival: "One could only watch the extraordinary efforts made by those tiny legs against an oncoming doom which could, had it chosen, have submerged an entire city, not merely a city, but masses of human beings..." (*DM* 6). The analogy for humans becomes clear: our short-lived existence on our tiny grain of sand, the earth, must be seen in the larger context of the vast expanse, and long eons, of the interstellar wastes.

Such a re-reading of "The Death of the Moth" also offers a radically new understanding of Woolf's quasi-characters or personae in her novel *The Waves*. Originally titled "The Moths," the novel depicts its personae against the backdrop of intergalactic space. Quentin Bell has noted that *The Waves* was actually inspired by an incident recounted by Vanessa Bell, who had written Virginia about an evening on which "some creature tapped so loudly on the pane that Duncan [Grant] said 'Who is that?' 'Only a bat' said Roger [Fry] 'or a bird', but it wasnt man or bird, but a huge moth – half a foot, literally, across" (quoted in Bell, *Virginia Woolf* 2: 126). Woolf wrote back to Vanessa, "By the way, your story of the Moth so fascinates me that I am going to write a story about it" (quoted in Bell, *Virginia Woolf* 2: 126). In June 1927 as she mulled over the plot for the story, she considered including a female character who "might talk, or think, about the age of the earth: the death of humanity..." (*D3*: 139).

Even as the earth-day of the interludes in *The Waves* is juxtaposed to the lifetimes of the novel's personae, Bernard compares the human life span to the billions of years that the universe predates human existence: "[W]hat has permanence?" asks Bernard, "Our lives too stream away, down the unlighted avenues, past the strip of time, unidentified" (*TW* 227). Constructed as a multiplex of monologues often on humans' meager attempts at survival in future cosmological ages, *The Waves* includes images of Earth's globe adrift in space, and the novel's personae are keenly aware of the eventual end to human history. Bernard imagines human civilizations expiring like spent sparks in the dark abyss of the universe:

[W]e felt enlarge itself round us the huge blackness of what is outside us, of what we are not. The wind, the rush of wheels became the roar of time, and we rushed – where? And who were we? We were extinguished for a moment, went out like sparks in burnt paper and the blackness roared. Past time, past history we went. (*TW* 227)

Like Jeans who wrote of humans' "brief past [as] a mere speck of time in the history of the universe" (*The Stars in their Courses* 134), Bernard calculates the limited extent and scope of a human-centered history: " 'But how strange it seems to set against the whirling abysses of infinite space a little figure with a golden teapot on his head. . . . Our English past – one inch of light' " (*TW* 227). Compared to the vast eons of cosmological time measured in light-years, human civilizations have existed for only a mere fraction of time. It was a point Jeans often emphasized. Similarly, Louis envisions all of human history silenced in future eons: " 'But listen,' said Louis, 'to the world moving through the abysses of infinite space. It roars; the lighted strip of history is past our Kings and Queens; we are gone, our civilisation; the Nile; and all life. Our separate drops are dissolved; we are extinct, lost in the abysses of time, in the darkness" (*TW* 225). The Nile, representing for Louis the earliest beginnings of human civilization, also recalls T.S. Eliot's lament in *The Waste Land* over the loss of Alexandria, London, Rome and the great cultural centers of western civilization. Jinny, however, attempts a more defiant tone as she declares: "We have triumphed over the abysses of space, with rouge, with powder, with flimsy pocket-handkerchiefs" (*TW* 228).

It is, perhaps, Bernard who best articulates a sense of human ephemerality when he imagines himself as a tiny bug on the face of the planet: "I feel myself carried round like an insect on top of the earth and could swear that, sitting here, I feel its hardness, its turning movement" (*TW* 185). As he considers the possibility of his own death, Bernard imagines himself "shut . . . in a hot room . . . dashing like a moth from candle to candle" (*TW* 293). Yet Bernard, like Jinny, defies death at the close of the novel, and in so doing he resists far more than simply his own aging and eventual annihilation. Like the entrapped moth of Woolf's essay that makes a last effort "against an oncoming doom," Bernard resists that "splendid unanimity" that "broods" over humanity (*TW* 111). By the novel's close, he decries those processes of evolution that will eventuate in human extinction. And for that brief moment of defiance, the narrator notes, the stars "draw back and are extinguished" (*TW* 296).

In "The Burnt Dancer" (1914), T.S. Eliot had evoked the image of a moth, a "vagrant from a distant star," whose dangerous dance near a candle flame forebodes of an unknown destiny for humankind: "Dance fast dance faster/ . . . The destiny that may be leaning / Toward us from your hidden star / Is grave, but not with human meaning" (*Inventions of the March Hare* 62–3). Stapledon too used the moth-to-flame image in *Star Maker*. His narrator, witnessing the entire history of the universe reeling before him like a film in fast forward mode, describes humankind's struggle to survive after our sun has expanded into a red giant: "Later still, after an aeon that was a sigh in the lifetime of the cosmos, [humankind] fled before the exploding sun to Neptune, there to sink back into mere animality for further aeons again. But then he climbed once more and reached his finest intelligence, only to be burnt up like a *moth in a flame* of irresistible catastrophe" (*Star Maker* 353; italics mine).[44] Like Jeans, Stapledon characterized the universe as indifferent to human extinction: "All this long human story, most passionate and tragic in the living, was but an unimportant, a seemingly barren and negligible effort, lasting only for a few moments in the life of the galaxy" (*Star Maker* 353).

FROM INSECTS TO ATOMS: MAKING A STAND
AGAINST HUMAN AGGRESSION

If humans had been sized down to mere insects in the modernist universe, they certainly couldn't rival the long evolution and survival of insects. Astronomer Harlow Shapley argued in 1929 that insects had demonstrated tremendous resilience in millions of years of survival. Were humans, he queried in a news story on the new astronomical vistas, capable of the same?

It [the human species] has no chance against the stars, of course, but can it long hold its own as a surviving form, or be ancestral to surviving forms, against other organisms, against primitive microbes and advanced insects? There is a fair chance . . . if it were not that man's worst enemy is man.[45]

As Europe faced military arms buildup in the mid and late 1930s, Woolf and Stapledon contemplated humanity's chances for survival against the threat of global war. Insects and atoms represented for both writers far more than merely two instances of the microscopic. By the early 1930s, the possibilities of splitting the atom, and harnessing atomic power in weaponry, were no longer considered the stuff of science fiction.[46] The Woolf's owned George P. Thomson's book *The Atom* (1930), in which Thomson had suggested the potential military applications of fission.[47] And in 1932, as Leonard and Virginia were touring Greece with Margery and Roger Fry, Woolf recorded in her diary a note about Leonard "informing Roger about the break up of the atom" (*D4*: 96; Killen 140).

Woolf and Stapledon tapped into the popular fascination with discoveries in astronomy, and the related public interest in insects, with a specific purpose: to launch a political critique against fascism. In July 1940, Woolf pondered the potential for human survival as German bombing raids over Monks House grew so intense that she and Leonard on one occasion "lay flat on [their] faces, hands behind head," careful not to grit their teeth as nearby bombs shook the windows to their home and Virginia's writing lodge (*D5*: 311). She noted on that occasion that the planes "[h]um & saw & buzz all round" them like insects (*D5*: 311). In much of her private and polemical writing throughout 1940, Woolf equated humans with insects as she described the planes flying over Monks House, and the soldiers constructing military bulwarks near Rodmell. In July, she wrote in her diary of the downing of a Royal Air Force plane, "a little gnat, with red & white & blue bars," the crash site of which she walked to see (*D5*: 300). She contemplated in that same diary entry the futility of "bothering [her]self with Coleridge... when the flies are printing their cold little feet on [her] hands," as the Germans were flying raids nearby (*D5*: 300). Again in August, she scribbled, "Men excavating gun emplacements in the bank. They look like little swarms of busy ants, as I walk. Cementing floors; sand bagging walls.... No one pays any attention – so blasé are we" (*D5*: 310). Other examples include her insect-like dictator of *Three Guineas*, hatched from the egg of fascism and nationalism (*TG* 127). The narrator of her essay "Thoughts on Peace in an Air Raid" (1940) describes the sound of war planes overhead as sawing and buzzing like insects. "The Germans were over this house last night and the night before that. Here they are again. It is a queer experience, lying in the dark and listening to the zoom of a hornet which may at any moment sting you to death" (*DM* 243). Awaiting in dread as she attempts to fall asleep, the "Thoughts" narrator feels like an insect, as if "[a] nail fixed the whole being to one hard board," and comments that from her window "one can see *a little silver insect* [a fighter plane] turning and twisting in the light" (*DM* 247, 248; italics mine). In this essay written for an American audience, Woolf calls for an international effort in ending aggression by suggesting the entire globe is humanity's community with

England lying, presumably as she completed the piece, "in the shadowed half of the world" (*DM* 248).

Stapledon similarly deployed insects in *Star Maker* with the objective of resisting rhetoric on the necessity of human aggression. In this novel, "a species of insectile beings decides to disarm unilaterally when threatened by a bellicose neighboring species" (Crossley, *Olaf Stapledon* 246). However, in another instance, "populations of insect-like creatures" or "insectoids" destroy each other over issues of ethnic difference so that "not one of them was destined to play an important part of the history of the galaxy" (*Star Maker* 308). By the close of *Star Maker*, as the narrator again views earth from orbit, London is scaled down to the size of bacteria as if seen under the lens of a microscope: "Beyond the plains, London, neon-lit, seething, was a microscope-slide drawn from foul water, and crowded with nosing animalcules. Animal-cules! In the stars' view, no doubt, these creatures were mere vermin…" (*Star Maker* 406). The narrator's view then pans across earth's limb to focus on France and Germany in an attempt to make the reader see the nations of the world as part of a single, fragile, yet unfortunately militant global community: "Beyond poplared Normandy spread Paris, with the towers of Notre-Dame tipped slightly, by reason of Earth's curvature" (*Star Maker* 406). In Germany, the "cathedral squares" are filled with "young men ranked together in thousands, exalted, possessed, saluting the flood-lit Führer" (*Star Maker* 406). "Far left-wards again," the narrator continues, "Russia, an appreciably convex segment of our globe, snow-pale in the darkness, spread out under the stars and cloud-tracts. Inevitably I saw the spires of the Kremlin, confronting the Red Square. There Lenin lay, victorious" (*Star Maker* 406). As Stapledon's reader looks closer at earth's globe from space, the future of humanity becomes less assured.

ENVISIONING NEW WORLDS

A social and political assessment of fascist regimes of the 1930s, *Star Maker* emerged, Stapledon noted in the novel's preface, in response to what he perceived as "the plight of our fragmentary and precarious civilization" just as "Europe [wa]s in danger of a catastrophe worse than that of 1914" (*Star Maker* 223). In fact, both *Star Maker* and *The Years* addressed the outbreak of the Spanish Civil War, a conflict in which Stapledon and Woolf were each personally invested. Woolf, of course, would later develop her anti-war treatise, *Three Guineas*, based on text she originally conceived as part of *The Years* and which specifically commented on the war in Spain.

And apparently it was only with the encouragement of his publisher that Stapledon dropped "explicit references to Spain" from his novel (Crossley, *Olaf Stapledon* 241).

Those references that remained would not have been lost to Woolf as she read the novel in the summer of 1937. Particularly that year, Woolf's literary work and private life were preoccupied with the Spanish Civil War. In June after a shopping jaunt to Selfridges, Woolf observed, upon returning to her home at Tavistock Square, "a long trail of fugitives – *like a caravan in a desert* – [who] came through the square: Spaniards flying from Bilbao..." (*D5*: 97; italics mine).[48] Her description of that "shuffling trudging procession" of women, children, and young men, "absorbed – like people on a trek," further demonstrates the interconnections between Woolf's concerns regarding international war, human extinction, and Jeans's descriptions of the new astronomical vistas.

But the casualties of the war in Spain were to strike closer to home. Woolf's nephew Julian Bell, an ambulance driver supporting the Republican effort in Spain, had been killed in July 1937, four months after the publication of *The Years*. She noted in her diary: "If Julian had not died – still an incredible sentence to write – our happiness might have been profound... but his death – that *extraordinary extinction* – drains it of substance" (*D5*: 111; italics mine). Julian's loss seemed to substantiate Woolf's concerns about the very real possibility of human extinction. "Thats one of the specific qualities of this death – how it brings close the immense vacancy, & our short little run into inanity. Now this is what I intend to combat. How? How make good what I protest, that I will not yield an inch or a fraction of an inch to nothingness, so long as something remains?" (*D5*: 105). The "immense vacancy" Woolf hoped to resist is nothing other than future eons of time, and the great abyss of interstellar space, devoid of human existence. Her anxiety about humans' "short little run into inanity," and of "nothingness," was in part indebted to her reading of Darwin, Eddington, and Jeans and their concerns regarding the fact that humans would someday become extinct, never to be repeated in future eons of the universe.[49] It was a topic she had discussed in September 1923 with Maynard Keynes who "talked about palaeolithic man & an interesting theory about the age of man – how the beginning of history about 5,000 B.C. is only the beginning of another lap in the race; others, many others, having been run previously & obliterated by ice ages" (*D2*: 267).

A second world war meant more than the annihilation of literary or aesthetic culture – though Woolf certainly perceived those elements also at risk of being forever lost. "I looked in at the Nat[ional] Gall[ery]," she wrote in September 1938, "being warned by a sober loud speaker to get my gas mask as I walked down Pall Mall. A man repeats this warning through a megaphone as he drives" (*D5*: 174). Global war meant the greater possibility of annihilation of all human civilizations. Often characterized as a highbrow whose definition of "civilization," a major preoccupation for the Bloomsbury group, had to do solely with artistic or intellectual culture, Woolf understood how readily the threat of human extinction eliminates differences of class, ethnicity, and gender. Her vision extended beyond what she saw as T.S. Eliot and Clive Bell's declarations that intellectual culture was inevitably destined for disintegration. Upon hearing in August 1938 a BBC talk by Harold Nicolson on the possibility of another world war, she too lamented: "That is the complete ruin not only of civilisation, in Europe, but of our last lap" (*D5*: 162). She meant that war could foreclose on humanity's race to survive.

Perhaps the most significant interconnection between Woolf and Stapledon and the novels they published in 1937 is their mutual vision for literature as a vehicle for social and political change. It is likely that Woolf valued *Star Maker* for its suggestion of the possibility of peaceful human co-existence, and its potential for reformulating political and social futures. "I don't suppose that I have understood more than a small part," she wrote to Stapledon in July 1937, "– all the same I have understood enough to be greatly interested, & excited too, since sometimes it seems to me that you are grasping ideas that I have tried to express, much more fumblingly, in fiction. But you have gone much further, & I can't help envying you – as one does those who reach what one has aimed at" (quoted in Crossley, *Olaf Stapledon* 248–9, 433 n. 61). Stapledon, likewise, wrote to say he felt that "some of the ideas in [his novel] fall in line with [Woolf's] own thought" (*D5*: 99, n. 21).

In *The Years*, Woolf dreamed the positive possibilities for the future of humanity. This seems clear by her idea to extend nearly 100 years into the future her "detailed account of a family called Pargiter, from the year 1800 to the year 2032."[50] Hermione Lee indicates that Woolf's plan was to develop the novel from the year 1880 to 2012 (*Virginia Woolf* 637). Yet Woolf's vision for the novel pushed beyond simply recording nearly contemporary human experience. As Radin has argued, "Eleanor's vision is of the future and what it will hold for mankind" (*Virginia Woolf's The Years* 109). Radin cites James Hafley's observation that Eleanor comes to learn not only that "she will not disappear into 'the endless night; the endless dark,'" but also "that life is improvable as well as everlasting…" (quoted in *Virginia Woolf's The Years* 109). Despite the devastation of World War I, and the ravages of the Spanish Civil War, Woolf's vision for the future of humanity remained one of hope and positive possibility. In the final scenes at Delia's party, Nicholas again attempts to give a speech, and as earlier is interrupted. When Kitty Lasswade later asks him what he intended to say, Nicholas replies, "I was going to drink to the human race. The human race... which is now in its infancy, may it grow to maturity!" (*TY* 372).

In response to the new findings in astronomy, Woolf and Stapledon endeavored in their fiction and polemical writing to offer radical alternatives to those narratives for human civilization that Darwinian evolution and military history had told time and again – aggression, annihilation, and extinction. Early on in her writing Woolf began working out her own misgivings about the future of human civilization. In the novel *Night and Day* (1919), Katharine Hilbery contemplates humans as mere primitives who eventually die out in a cold and inhospitable universe:

And yet, after gazing for another second, the stars did their usual work upon the mind, froze to cinders the whole of our short human history, and reduced the human body to an ape-like, furry form, crouching amid the brushwood of a barbarous clod of mud. This stage was soon succeeded by another, in which there was nothing in the universe save stars and the light of stars... (*ND* 205)

In comparison to the eons of the stars, Katharine envisions the brief span of human existence from humanity's primitive, animal state to the point of extinction. She also imagines the future in which there is no life in the universe, only the cold light of dying stars.

Woolf's sense of humanity's primitivism and fragility pervades her fiction. These themes reappear in her final novel, *Between the Acts*, which unfolds as a drama of the history of British civilization, even as World War II rumbles in the distance. Framing the narrative is Lucy Swithin's reflections on the relatively recent beginnings of human civilization compared to the long millennia of the dinosaurs and how in the not too distant past dinosaurs grazed in Piccadilly Circus. Her "favorite reading" appears to be H.G. Wells's *The Outline of History* (*BTA* 4), a text that the Woolfs' kept in their own library.[51] Mrs. Swithin, possibly named after the astronomer Swithin St. Cleve in Hardy's *Two on a Tower* (1882) who is awed by the vast expanses of space, is captivated by her primeval visions of "rhododendron forests in Piccadilly" (*BTA* 4). She imagines a time "when the entire continent... was all one; populated, she understood, by elephant-bodied, seal-necked, heaving, surging, slowly writhing, and, she supposed, barking monsters; the iguanodon, the mammoth, and the mastodon; from whom presumably, she thought,... we descend" (*BTA* 4).[52]

By the final pages of the novel, Woolf places the primeval world of the dinosaurs that Lucy envisions in juxtaposition to the rumblings of global war. And again we see Mrs. Swithin engrossed in her Outline of History: " 'England,' she was reading, 'was then a swamp. Thick forests covered the land' " (*BTA* 135). *Between the Acts* closes with Isa and Giles's night of quarreling, and a scene set on a "night that dwellers in caves had watched from some high place among the rocks" (*BA* 135).[53] Yet, *Between the Acts* leaves open the possibility of alternative narratives for human survival in the universe. Either human societies will agree to co-exist in peace or, the novel suggests, humans will continually revert to violence and destroy the last vestiges of culture and civilization. Contemplating her love-hate relationship with her husband Giles, Isa mutters lines from her privately sketched poems or songs her uncle taught her: "To what dark antre of the unvisited earth, or wind-brushed forest, shall we go now? Or spin from star to star and dance in the maze of the moon? Or..." (*BTA* 31).

Isa's question regarding whether humans will "dance in the maze of the moon" or huddle in their caves was the question raised by H.G. Wells at the close of the film *Things to Come* (1936). Initially titled *Whither Mankind?*, the film's conclusion is set in 2036 in the futuristic city Everytown; the world has been restored finally to civility after generations of devastation resulting from fascism and world war. A space gun is readied to launch a capsule, as a young couple have volunteered for a mission to orbit the moon. The local townspeople, opposing what is perceived as unnecessarily dangerous scientific exploration, storm the apparatus just as the gun is fired. They appear, as Wells planned, as a swarm of ants climbing the space gun's girders. Oswald Cabal, Everytown's progressive leader, tracks the launched capsule on a huge telescope mirror which displays multitudes of stars and nebulae in the depths of space. With the massive telescope in the backdrop, Cabal asks: "All the universe or nothingness. Which shall it be?" (quoted in Leon Stover, *The Prophetic Soul* 297). The question is whether humans will continue to eke out an existence as "no more than animals" or seek new adventures on other worlds, as Cabal suggests, "out across immensity [among] the stars" (quoted in *The Prophetic Soul* 297, 296). Isa Oliver's similar question indicates that Woolf, like Wells and Stapledon, believed humans could dream alternative narratives to self-annihilation or extinction. Certainly this was Wells's point in *Things to Come*. Christopher Frayling comments that as Wells worked on the film's production, he insisted a space gun be incorporated though he knew a rocket boosted spacecraft was more scientifically accurate; he deliberately deployed the space gun to depict scientific exploration subverting human aggression (*Things to Come* 66). It is additionally no accident that the astronomer, in the film, from the space gun's astronomical department is William Jeans, presumably a twenty-first century descendent of none other than James Jeans.

Woolf and Stapledon, along with Wells, insisted on the necessity of imagining and writing alternative narratives for our human future. They believed, as J.B.S. Haldane argued in his essay "The Last Judgment," that humans have only limited vision regarding their place in the universe. "Our private, national and even international aims," Haldane asserted, "are restricted to a time measured in human life-spans. 'And yonder all before us lie/ Deserts of vast eternity'" (*Possible Worlds* 311). Evoking Andrew Marvell's poem "To His Coy Mistress," Haldane pointed up the necessity of a global political vision that recognizes our human ephemerality. "Man's little world will end," warned Haldane, unless humans realize "the tiny scale, both temporal and spatial" on which human life is played out in comparison to "the unimaginable vastness of the possibilities of time and space" (*Possible Worlds* 312, 310). Stapledon's first novel, *Last and First Men* (1930) was greatly influenced by this single essay by Haldane (Crossley, *Olaf Stapledon* 190). Yet in 1912, nearly a decade prior to Haldane's essay, Stapledon already had formulated what became the core of Haldane's argument. "I think perhaps the greatest change that has come to the human mind since the middle ages," wrote Stapledon, "is the conception of the infinite heavens, wherein the earth is a point, not the all important centre. [T]his change of conception is very important to the growth of humanity" (quoted in *Olaf Stapledon: Speaking for the Future* 229).

CODA: COSMOLOGY AND THE LEAGUE OF NATIONS

Apollo 15 astronaut Dave Scott has observed: "The significance of Apollo was not so much that man set foot on the moon, but that he set his eye on the Earth."[54] The vistas of earth from space, imagined by turn of the century artists, as well as writers like Woolf and Stapledon, and later glimpsed by astronauts and cosmonauts in the late twentieth century, radically reconfigured the human understanding of earth's position in the universe and the need for peaceful coexistence. "Something significant happened to the astronauts who went to the moon and to the nation that sent them there," writes Frank White, "To some extent, neither the astronauts nor the nation has been quite the same since. . . . [The lunar] missions were shaped by the politics of Earth at the time and produced unpredictable results that will profoundly affect the politics of the future" (*The Overview Effect* 39).

Yet more than twenty years before the earth could be imaged by cameras mounted on the first rockets launched into space, Virginia Woolf, Olaf Stapledon, Karel Čapek, J.B.S. Haldane, H.G. Wells and other modernist writers had already foreseen a very real connection between advances in astronomy and international efforts towards world peace. In The Human Value of the New Astronomy," science writer F.S. Marvin noted in 1929 the "work by which in the strictest sense man is creating his own universe."[55] That work, carried out by the League of Nations and in the field of cosmology, Marvin asserted, promised new hope for human collaboration and world peace: "[T]hroughout the tumult and the disillusionment, two supreme pieces of human organisation have gone on, which in different spheres carry humanity to heights untouched and hardly dreamt of before. The League of Nations and its allied associations is one. The new cosmogony is the other."[56] Marvin claimed that "two Englishman" stood "in the forefront of this new construction," and were responsible for heading these international initiatives for building cooperative human communities. Marvin's comment apparently referred to Leonard Woolf and James Jeans.

While Marvin names neither of the men explicitly, Jeans's work is cited at length in the article, and Leonard Woolf, by his own admission, was a recognized authority on the League. "By 1916 I had a profound knowledge of my subject; I was an authority," wrote Leonard; "This is not retrospective vanity; I can give, at the risk of appearing vain and boastful, a little proof of it" (*Beginning Again* 185). Leonard suggested that he originated the idea of a League. He cited his initial proposal for a "league of states" which was published in the *New Statesman* in 1915, and which called for "the creation of 'an international authority to prevent war'" (*Beginning Again* 189).[57] For Marvin, the efforts of the League of Nations, as well as advances in astronomy, promised a hopeful future for humankind.

In his preface to *Star Maker* Stapledon noted, "And perhaps the attempt to see our turbulent world against a background of stars, may, after all, increase, not lessen, the significance of the present human crisis. It may also strengthen our charity toward one another" ("Preface," *Star Maker* 234). He, like Virginia, hoped to imagine new and different narratives for our human futures. At the close of *Star Maker*, readers glimpse yet another view of the "whole planet, the whole rock-grain, with its busy swarms," even as the narrator queries: "How to face such an age?" (*Star Maker* 407). The answer, the novel suggests, lies in understanding humanity's position in the scale of the universe. There are, says the narrator, "[t]wo lights for guidance. The first, our little glowing atom of community, with all that it signifies. The second, the cold light of the stars, symbol of the hypercosmical reality" (*Star Maker* 408). Stapledon looked to the stars as a guide for our human future. "Strange," says the *Star Maker* narrator, "that in this light...the human crisis does not lose but gains significance" (408).

Likewise, in *The Years*, as Eleanor watches the moths "dashing round the ceiling" and listlessly reads Dante's *Purgatorio*, she senses a possible source of guidance for humanity's fragile existence in the future. She struggles nearly as much to read the English translation as the archaic Italian: "For by so many more there are who say 'ours' / So much the more good doth each possess" (*TY* 185). But the words only "[b]rushed lightly by her mind," and she cannot quite grasp the text's meaning (*TY* 185). Had Eleanor considered the context of the lines their significance might have been clear.[58] In these lines from Canto 15, the Dante character is told that the greater number of persons who embrace a spirit of sharing instead of envy, or of those "who speak of 'ours'" as opposed to "mine," the greater that "Charity burns intensely."[59] In other words, charity increases exponentially as the number of people who exhibit charity increases, even as, Dante is told, a ray of light becomes far more luminous when reflected in a mirror. Virgil admonishes the character Dante: "[T]he more souls...who are in love/the more there are worth loving; love grows more,/each soul a mirror mutually mirroring."[60] The lines suggest Woolf's strategy in the final scene of the pageant in *Between the Acts* when the players holding mirrors reflect images of the villagers back at themselves. Set against the backdrop of a second global war, that novel offers a modernist gesture toward Dante's message of charity. For Dante, charity is the force that drives the universe. The closing line of the entire *Commedia*, as the Dante character makes his way toward the blinding radiance of God, describes this force of the universe as the "love that moves the sun and the other stars."[61] Interestingly, it was Dante's closing line which Aldous Huxley quoted in his sympathy note to Grace Hubble upon her husband Edwin's death. Huxley wrote, "There is nothing to say, dearest Grace, except that we are your loving friends, & that love remains—for it is what 'moves the sun and the other stars,' which is something that Edwin knew even better than Dante."[62] The need to extend charity, it seems, is the message that eludes Eleanor's grasp as "[t]he moths were dashing round the ceiling [and] the book slipped on to the floor" (*TY* 186).

In reading *The Years* and *Star Maker* against the cultural milieu out of which they emerged, we begin to realize the literary as well as the pacifist uses to which Woolf and Stapledon put those astronomical images they glimpsed through their own telescopes. Their novels illuminate even further how modernist writers responded to popular culture and actively challenged, through their art, fascist, and nationalist politics. Certainly, Woolf's creative inspiration drew upon the seemingly infinite vistas of space that many, including even her husband Leonard, found to be terrifying. In 1940, on evenings when she turned her face skyward to watch German bombers raiding the countryside near Monks House, Woolf simultaneously looked to the stars. She could not have helped but be captivated by those stars shining in the inky dark of mandatory blackouts. She noted in her diary in October 1940: "Last night a great heavy plunge of bomb under the window. So near we both started. A plane had passed dropping this fruit. We went onto the terrace. Trinkets of stars sprinkled & glittering. All quiet" (*D*5: 326). A month later she again recorded looking up at what was possibly an enemy plane: "A plane overhead (It was bright starlight)" (*D*5: 336). Her notations regarding the stars on such occasions marked more than simple observation. Rather than being depressed by the minute scale on which our human existence is played out, Woolf looked to the stars as other worlds that signaled the possibility of life, and of a hopeful human future.

6

Three Guineas: *Woolf's global vision*

Virginia Woolf celebrated a global aesthetics that afforded new possibilities for viewing and engaging the world from multiple, even alien, perspectives. She embraced multiple points of view for her own modernist art, as is evidenced in *To the Lighthouse* when Lily Briscoe, having "raised a mountain for the ants to climb over," considered what is needed for a modernist aesthetic vision: "One wanted fifty pairs of eyes," or the complex vision of an insect, in order to more accurately take in the world (*TTL* 198). Woolf owned a telescope, enjoyed in July 1931 the purchase of a Zeiss camera (*D4*: 361), and marveled at the world these devices could reveal. Yet she understood two fundamental principles about visualization technologies, especially photographic technologies. First, she knew that photographic and cinematic images are inevitably framed by a set of rhetorical practices and, secondly, that the deployment of technology is never value free.

She intuited the complex interconnections between technology and the sciences and social and political discourses. Woolf recognized that there are, so to speak, no objective camera angles. "It is a lesson available from photographs of how the world looks to the compound eyes of an insect," writes Donna Haraway, "or even from the camera eye of a spy satellite or the digitally transmitted signals of space probe-perceived differences 'near' Jupiter that have been transformed into coffee table colour photographs."[1] As Haraway points out in a discussion of the cultural and political deployments of visualization technologies, "The 'eyes' made available in modern technological sciences shatter any idea of passive vision" and demonstrate that "all eyes, including our own organic ones, are active perceptual systems, building in translations and specific ways of seeing."[2] Woolf demonstrates, in *Three Guineas*, that visualization technologies like photographic images are inevitably deployed within a network of cultural, scientific, and political practices. In her pacifist polemic, Woolf specifically calls into question the seemingly objective uses of war photography, and more broadly examines the networks by which the sciences have become imbricated with nationalism and militarism.

This chapter argues that *Three Guineas* challenged modernist discourses related to visualization technologies, astronomy, and nationalism. One significant modernist debate had to do with whether the camera can lie. As Susan Squier has shown, the "camera lie" debate emerged among those who first theorized the effects of cinema. Squier cites a 1929 essay by Robert Nichols, "The Movies as Medium," in which Nichols asserted that the art of cinema reveals the extent to which "the camera . . . can lie" (quoted in Squier, *Babies in Bottles* 139). Even James Jeans had considered whether cameras can lie, though from the opposite position. In *The Universe Around Us*, Jeans had argued that the camera served as a perfected retina for the astronomer or cosmologist. More than any other technology since the telescope, he commented, the photographic plate had revolutionized the sciences of astronomy and cosmology. According to Jeans, in observational astronomy, whereas the "eye, betrayed by preconceived ideas, impatience or hope, can and does make every conceivable type of error; the camera cannot lie" (*The Universe Around Us* 36–7). However, what gets occluded, Woolf knew, in claims that the camera cannot lie, or that the camera might serve as the scientist's perfected retina, is the fact that photographs are not neutral objects, but are understood by their cultural and rhetorical framing. Indeed, through her own framing of the photos that were reproduced in the British edition of *Three Guineas*, Woolf exposed those strategies by which photographs of the war in Spain could be used to support specific political agendas.[3] Woolf takes up the camera-lie debate on two fronts: firstly, in terms of the rhetorical framing of photojournalist coverage of the Spanish Civil War; and, secondly, in response to a wireless talk by James Jeans in which he alluded to the new photographic vistas of space in support of a national eugenics program.[4]

THREE GUINEAS AND THE "CAMERA LIE"

In the fictional frame story to *Three Guineas*, a barrister has written to the narrator, asking for women's help in the prevention of war. Even "with the sound of the guns in [his] ears," the barrister wishes to know how in women's opinion men might avoid military aggression (*TG* 4). In reply, the *Three Guineas* narrator searches for an "absolute point of view" from which she and the barrister might collaborate on terms for preventing war (*TG* 9). She points to a collection of photos on her table of "ruined houses and dead bodies" (*TG* 21), sent to her, it seems, by Spanish Republicans seeking support in Britain during the Spanish Civil War.[5] "Here then on the table before us are photographs.... They are not pleasant photographs to look upon. They are photographs of dead bodies for the most part" (*TG* 10). There are also those photographs reprinted in the newspapers which, Woolf's narrator assures, comprise "history and biography in the raw" (*TG* 115). Photographs presumably might provide an absolute point of view from which the narrator and the barrister can collaborate on the prevention of war. As the narrator notes, "Photographs, of course, are not arguments addressed to the reason; they are simply statements of fact addressed to the eye" (*TG* 10).

The persistent refrain regarding the "photographs of dead bodies and ruined houses" (*TG* 95) provides the backdrop and a poignant touchstone for the argument of *Three Guineas*, and may have been inspired by George Steer's report on the Nazi saturation bombing of Guernica in 1937. Steer had published his eyewitness account of the devastation in the *London Mercury*. Having interviewed residents of the town, Steer recalled: "Some of the witnesses were quite dumb. They were digging [bodies] out of *ruined houses*, families at a time, dead and blue-black with bruising...."[6] Despite Woolf's repeated references to photos of dead bodies and ruined houses and to scenes like those Steer observed, Woolf chose not to print such images in *Three Guineas*. As John Whittier-Ferguson has noted, "The...photographs Woolf's narrator describes in detail are the ones we never see: the week's record of carnage from the Spanish Civil War" (*Framing Pieces* 99). Her text in fact describes in detail the kinds of photographs that most of the British public would never see.

PHOTOGRAPHY AND SUBVERSION

With the development of the hand-held camera, and improved film technologies in the 1920s including the flash bulb, photographic images became standard fare in print journalism (D.L. LeMahieu, *A Culture for Democracy* 78). The *Illustrated London News*, like other newspapers, began to incorporate entire sections devoted to photojournalism. Logistically, it was cheaper and less labor intensive to publish photos on one page rather than to disperse them over a paper's entire layout; thus "the 'picture page' became a standard feature of the popular press" (LeMahieu 76). In the *Illustrated London News*, such photo essays, touted as the gleanings of an objective lens, appeared under headings such as "The Camera as Recorder: News by Photography" or "A Window of the World: News of the Day in Pictures."[7]

By the mid-1930s the hand-held camera allowed for the possibility of bringing images of war visually before the British public. Caroline Brothers, in a well researched study, discusses the impact of the hand-held camera on print journalists' coverage of the Spanish Civil War:

Smaller portable cameras, like the Ermanox and the Leica, the manufacture of compact lenses of far greater light passing power than ever before and faster films which, in allowing exposures to be made without flashlight, made possible both night pictures and interior shots – all these were a far cry from the panoramic viewfinders and glass negative plates used by World War One photographers. (*War and Photography* 5–6)

Images of the ravages of the war in Spain were published in both pro-Republican and pro-fascist newspapers in London. However, the photos were heavily censored and not highly graphic.

In examining press coverage of the war in British and French newspapers, Brothers argues that the British press in particular was careful to avoid shocking the public with gruesome war images: "That the representation of injury was in both nations a highly euphemistic affair bespeaks a real unease in the British and French sensibility about confronting war's harsher realities, and about offending readers with 'scenes too gruesome for the public palate' " (*War and Photography* 168).[8] Brothers further has shown that the British press printed largely only those war photographs that reinforced notions of camaraderie and bravery in war.

Images, for instance, of a soldier helping another off the battlefield, or of soldiers convalescing under the care of guardian nurses, appeared in both Britain's pro-Republican and pro-fascist newspapers. The rare photographs of death that were published in British newspapers, Brothers points out, often included no visible signs of the violence of war, such as in the photo of a dead street fighter printed in the pro-Republican paper, the *Daily Herald* [London].[9] Captioned "The Harvest of Civil War," the photo shows a young man, who appears to be merely sleeping, lying dead in a street by a bundle of reeds (*War and Photography* 171). The body appears undamaged, the hair unmatted, the handsome face seemingly peaceful with eyes closed. Next to the body are a bundle of reeds that served to romanticize the death. The photo caption, Brothers comments, aestheticized the death as an appropriate harvesting of a young soldier groomed for war heroism. In Britain more so than in France, Brothers reports, press photographs of the war dead in Spain nearly always obscured blood stains or other signs of violence. "In every case injury was represented obliquely, subdued into metonym, or subsumed in representations of pleasure, security, or comradeship, or suffused with pathos so that the injury itself became a secondary theme" (*War and Photography* 168).

Woolf, on the other hand, refused to aestheticize war. The narrator in *Three Guineas* subverts nationalist manipulation of war images by instead describing in vivid detail the ravages of human aggression. Directing the barrister's attention to her collection of photos, the narrator notes:

This morning's collection contains the photograph of what might be a man's body, or a woman's; it is so mutilated that it might, on the other hand, be the body of a pig. But those certainly are dead children, and that undoubtedly is the section of a house. A bomb has torn open the side; there is a bird-cage hanging in what was presumably the sitting room... (*TG* 10–11)

Such horrific literary snapshots undermine any attempts to rally sentiments of heroism or nationalism. The dead body that resembles "the body of a pig" becomes so abject that no nation would wish to reclaim it. As Brothers' research demonstrates, the kinds of graphic photographs Woolf's narrator describes had not been seen by the British public. The refrain that haunts *Three Guineas*, regarding "dead bodies and ruined houses," calls forth those war images that British newspapers had censored or refused to print. Woolf insisted on evoking such images in order to demonstrate the raw brutality of human aggression.

Brothers reports that in only three cases did British papers publish graphic images of death related to the war in Spain (*War and Photography* 175). In one instance, photographs of some seventy Spanish children, who had been mutilated and killed in a Nazi bombing raid, appeared (along with apologies and an editor's justification) in the 12 November 1936 issue of the *Daily Worker*. In those photos, as Brothers has noted, the children's faces and clothes are visibly blood-stained. Unlike the soldier of "The Harvest" photo, their wounds and mouths are gaping, and their dead eyes remain open. "The cardboard labels on the children's chests," Brothers aptly claims, "signify their transformation in death into objects to be catalogued, photographed, and employed as propaganda" (*War and Photography* 176). The images were among "the most horrific to appear in the press" in either France or in Britain (*War and Photography* 175). Woolf's reference in *Three Guineas* to "dead children" may refer to these particular photos. In fact, she wrote to her nephew Julian Bell in November 1936: "This morning I got a packet of photographs from Spain all of dead children, killed by bombs – a cheerful present" (*L6*: 83). Yet, given that Woolf's purpose in evoking images of war dead was to stir anti-war sentiment, why hadn't she simply included in *Three Guineas* several of those graphic photographs? Certainly, such images of unnecessary death and destruction would have been rhetorically powerful for a pacifist argument.

Perhaps Woolf preferred her literary snapshots of war dead as a means of subverting the photographic essay, which had emerged in newsprint as an objective framer of events. As Brothers demonstrates, war photographs were used as propaganda for both sides, and similar images were printed by pro-fascist and pro-Republican newspapers alike. Sensitive to the ways that politics drives what appears in print, the *Three Guineas* narrator complains:

> Therefore if you want to know any fact about politics you must read at least three different papers, compare at least three different versions of the same fact, and come in the end to your own conclusion. Hence the three daily papers on my table... In other words, you have to strip each statement of its money motive, of its power motive, of its advertisement motive, of its publicity motive... before you make up your mind about which fact about politics to believe... (*TG* 95, 96)

Woolf's unsettling word-pictures of "dead bodies and ruined houses" serve as a powerful strategy for subverting the rhetoric of nationalism and heroism. Her resistance to including war photographs in *Three Guineas*, despite the fact that she had access to such images, exposed the ways photojournalist coverage of the Spanish Civil War was manipulated for propagandistic means. She would refuse to do likewise.

Of course, one might argue that since it was convention to censor war images, Woolf simply exercised the same discretionary standards established for print journalism. Yet, the rhetorical framing of the photos she did include in *Three Guineas* indicates Woolf made very deliberate choices about the photos in her text. John Whittier-Ferguson has called attention to the duplicity of the narrator's claim that photographs serve only as mere "statements of fact addressed to the eye" (*TG* 10). The photos Woolf actually published in *Three Guineas* exposed what she saw as Britain's ignoble glamorizing of military aggression in the ornament and parading of military dress. In order to "demonstrat[e] how easily images, set in a polemical context, become part of that polemic," Whittier-Ferguson points to the humorous image that appeared in British editions of *Three Guineas* of the horse's backside photographed next to a line-up of men in full military dress (*Framing Pieces* 99). Other photos poked fun at the extravagance of professional garb and military uniforms on which "metal objects cut in star shapes or in circles glitter and twinkle" (*TG* 19). Military fanfare and the attire of men in the professions, the narrator claims, "make us gape with astonishment" (*TG* 19). Those "pieces of metal, or ribbon, coloured hoods and gowns" are characterized as "a barbarity" which serve only to romanticize military rank and "induce young men to become soldiers" (*TG* 20, 21). The narrator of *Three Guineas* ridicules the inanity of such baubles:

"A woman who advertised her motherhood by a tuft of horsehair on the left shoulder would scarcely, you will agree, be a venerable object" (*TG* 20–1). It is among the educated, and their love of costume, that Woolf finds the psychological seeds that produce public acceptance of war:

We can say that for educated men to emphasize their superiority over other people, either in birth or intellect, by dressing differently, or by adding titles before, or letters after names are acts that rouse competition and jealousy – emotions which, as we need scarcely draw upon biography to prove, nor ask psychology to show, have their share in encouraging a disposition towards war. (*TG* 21)

Beyond her critique of militarism, Woolf develops in *Three Guineas* a direct repudiation of professions in the sciences that have been implicated in acts of aggression against women and others.

ASTRONOMY, EUGENICS, AND NATIONALIST POLITICS

The extent to which discourses in the sciences are central to the argument of *Three Guineas* has not been fully explored. In particular, the text's interconnections with the work of James Jeans has not been traced. The link between Jeans and *Three Guineas* most likely dates to a sensational and highly controversial wireless talk given by Jeans in 1930. In the spring of that year, the BBC had scheduled a series of radio lectures titled "Points of View." Designed to present the opinions of several widely recognized scholars and public figures, the "Points of View" series included, in addition to Jeans, writers George Bernard Shaw, G. Lowes Dickinson, H.G. Wells, Hilaire Belloc, as well as Oliver Lodge and J.B.S. Haldane. Composer and author Ethel Smyth also participated in the talks.

From the perspective of their professions, presenters were commissioned to speak on a national or international issue. Jeans selected eugenics as it related to the field of astronomy as the topic for his talk.[10] The great vistas of intergalactic space, Jeans claimed, had taught the importance of Britain's national eugenics movement. While there is no clear evidence that Woolf listened in on Jeans's controversial broadcast, it is probable that given her own interest in cosmology and the future of human civilization, Woolf either heard about this talk or read the published lecture in the BBC's magazine, the *Listener*.[11] In addition, in the spring of 1930, when Jeans delivered his talk, some of Woolf's closest associates, including Vita Sackville-West, Harold Nicolson, George Rylands, T.S. Eliot, and Desmond MacCarthy were also doing BBC presentations. I want to suggest that in *Three Guineas* Woolf responded to Jeans's broadcast by challenging the ways the rhetoric of eugenics could easily be deployed in the service of nationalism. Ultimately, the Society of Outsiders Woolf posits in *Three Guineas*, an experiment in feminist pacifism, positions itself in direct opposition to the nationalist underpinnings of Britain's eugenics movement.

While the connection between astronomy and eugenics may seem at best tenuous, Jeans had clearly found a link between the two disciplines. "[B]ecause I am an astronomer," he stated in that BBC broadcast, "I am apt to see the problems of to-day set against a background of time in which the whole of human history shrinks to the twinkling of an eye, and to think of these problems specially in relation to man's past history on earth" (*More Points of View* 55). Jeans considered the project of eugenics as a means of ensuring the future of humans' long-term survival on the planet.

Gigantic reptiles, dinosaurs, ruled the earth for millions of years, but failed to retain their supremacy. Then huge animals, terrible in their weight and strength, but almost brainless, governed for many million years more. Man has ruled only for a fraction of one million years. Why should he suppose that he has come to stay? (*More Points of View* 56)

New telescopic and photographic technologies had pushed back the great age of the universe which, astronomers and geologists had shown, dated to billions of years. If humans planned to survive for even a fraction of that time, Jeans argued elsewhere, they must "learn how to harness the forces of nature, and to make a world worthy for mankind to live in" (*The Universe Around Us* 331). He concluded his widely-read volume *The Universe Around Us* (1929) with this admonition: "[W]e seem to discern that the main message of astronomy is one of hope to the race and of responsibility to the individual – of responsibility because we are drawing plans and laying foundations for a longer future than we can well imagine" (331).

In his BBC talk, Jeans suggested that a national eugenics program could provide a new technology or weapon by which humankind might protect itself against extinction, which the dinosaurs only too well had demonstrated every species must face. "It is our use of this weapon that will mould the future of our race for good or for ill," admonished Jeans in his steady and matter-of-fact voice: "If we are to make the earth a paradise again, it seems to me that our first task, our first duty, is, at all costs, to prevent the moral, mental, and physical wreckage of to-day from reproducing itself and starting a new sequence of unhappy lives trailing down through endless generations" (*More Points of View* 57, 59). Through a national eugenics program, he argued, humans could delay and perhaps even avoid the "decay, defeat and extinction" by which the dinosaurs met their end (*More Points of View* 57).

Having attended Cambridge just at the turn of the century, Jeans was connected to its intellectual community. In the early decades of the twentieth century, Susan Squier has noted, "Britain was in a eugenic fervor, fueled both by anxiety over perceived racial degeneration and by hopes of using prenatal culture to produce racial perfection" (*Babies in Bottles* 175).[12] Francis Galton, the recognized father of eugenics, had established by 1909 the Eugenics Education Society in Cambridge (*Babies in Bottles* 175). By the early 1910s, "Eugenics Society meetings were crowded with hundreds of students, dons and townspeople" (*Babies in Bottles* 175). Driven by a concern for the long-term survival of humans, Jeans criticized Britain for its failure to allow "the weaker and less successful to go to the wall": "There is no weeding out of the unfit, we save nearly all our babies indiscriminately – good and bad, strong and weak, healthy and diseased" (*More Points of View* 60). England in the future, he argued, "will consist far too largely of hospitals, prisons and lunatic asylums. Its population will contain too many unemployed, and too many unemployables" (*More Points of View* 61). Echoing a line from Blake's "Milton," Jeans suggested the nationalist underpinnings of his eugenics proposal: "If we are to 'build Jerusalem in England's green and pleasant land,' we must, I think, reverse our present policy" (*More Points of View* 62).[13]

The broadcast received a sensational response. Letters from BBC listeners so overwhelmed Jeans that he requested assistance from staff members in making replies.[14] The public reaction to this single radio talk revealed, too, the deep and conflicted concerns of the British public with regard to eugenics. Of the letters that have been preserved, the majority which expressed appreciation for Jeans's talk represented educated and skilled artisans, as for instance, nineteen-year-old watch and clock maker E.C. Cull, who humbly observed:

My views on politics are not formed sufficiently for me to venture any opinion so I will say nothing on that score. I am in entire agreeance [sic] with your views on the undesirability of the mentally and physically unfit reproducing their kind. The trouble to me seems, however, where one could start. So many people to-day are really unfit and one can't stop them all from marrying.[15]

More striking was the number of working-class listeners who applauded Jeans's views.

In one of the most poignant responses, a self-described "working man" William Brown, who characterized his neighborhood as "a rather thickly populated district" in which "the splendour of the Heavens is always partly obscured by a veil of smoke," apologized for "taking this liberty, and intruding, on your [Jeans's] valuable time."[16] Brown, who had read Jeans's technical and popular astronomy texts, including *The Universe Around Us*, simply wanted to "congratulate and thank" Jeans for his talk over the "Ether." Even respondents who might be categorized by Galton as "unfit" acclaimed Jeans's position on eugenics. For instance, A. H. Pretty, a disabled soldier turned barrister, wrote to Jeans immediately upon hearing the broadcast:

> As an ordinary man, I beg to thank you most heartily for your 'Point of View', to which I have just listened on the wireless.... [M]y wife, my daughter & myself, all agree that your 'Point of View' was the best that we have heard, & we agree with every word you said, though we are none of us scientists...[17]

There were, of course, those working-class members of the wireless audience, like Charles Barton, a self-proclaimed "factory rat," who promptly reminded Jeans of his responsibility as a scientist to devise "identical test conditions [for] each class before deciding our unworthiness to reproduce our stock."[18]

In all fairness, it must be noted that Jeans's eugenic vision was rooted in the widely held notion that "professional and other successful classes" including "skilled artisans" were declining in number while birthrates among "the unfit" continued to rise (*More Points of View* 60, 61).[19] Jeans had argued that the success of a national eugenics program would depend upon "good raw material in the form of children born from the best possible stock," unequivocally equated in his mind with the "professional and other successful classes" (*More Points of View* 60). His views were closely aligned with those of his good friend, Dr. Marie Stopes, a feminist sexologist who established the first birth control clinics in London. The Jeans family for some time lived near the Stopes family, and the two frequently got together for dinner and tennis.[20] Correspondence between Jeans and Marie Stopes reveals the extent of their great admiration for one another. In 1935, for instance, Jeans sent Marie a volume titled *"Driftweed" and Later Poems*, by his first wife Charlotte (Charly), which he had published shortly after her death. Several of the poems had been written for Jeans. Upon reading the volume, Marie immediately drafted a sympathetic letter: "I almost never dream of people," wrote Marie, "but I dreamt of you last night, & I hope that the friendship & sympathy the dream expressed may really reach you."[21] Stopes's dedication to making birth control available in London was grounded in her own eugenics agenda. Perhaps as a result of her training as a paleobotanist Stopes, like Jeans, had thought about human existence in the long term.[22] June Rose contends, "Marie was an elitist, an idealist, interested in creating a society in which only the best and the beautiful survive."[23] Stopes, apparently, advocated involuntary sterilization, not a widely-respected position, in "cases of inherent disease, drunkenness or bad character."[24] Christina Hauck has shown that Woolf, too, expressed anxiety over what was perceived as a higher birthrate in the lower classes.[25] Yet, despite her own conflicted concerns regarding disparity of birthrates between the lower and upper classes, Woolf nevertheless was skeptical of the rhetoric of eugenics.[26]

Francis Galton had complimented the Stephen family by listing them in *Hereditary Genius* (1869).[27] The first chapter of this volume, ti- tled "Classification of Men According to Their Reputation," announces Galton's intention to demonstrate "how large is the number of instances in which men who are more or less illustrious have eminent kinsfolk" (*Hereditary Genius* 5).[28] Woolf nevertheless appears to have had little re- spect for Galton's eugenic objectives. Her novel *Night and Day* (1919) mocks the text that launched the pseudo-science of eugenics. Upon noting that Rodney Denham had "accused Katharine Hilbery of belonging to one of the most distinguished families in England," the narrator of *Night and Day* mentions Galton's book and comments that the Alardyces, the Hilberys, the Millingtons, and the Otways seem to prove Galton's notion that moral character is a product of good genes. However, the narrator comments wryly: "It is true that there were several lamentable exceptions to this rule in the Alardyce group, which seems to indicate that the cadets of such houses go more rapidly to the bad than children of ordinary fathers and mothers ..." (*ND* 31). In addition, Woolf apparently disliked Vita Sackville- West's eugenicist novels *Heritage* and *The Dragon in Shallow Waters*, both of which depicted England's poor as a distinctly separate race from the middle and upper classes.[29] Despite her obvious fascination with Jeans, Woolf remained skeptical of proposals for a national eugenics plan, if for no other reason than their inherent nostalgia for British nationalism and imperialism.

In *Three Guineas*, the Society of Outsiders calls for a more global vi- sion in ardent resistance to nationalist rhetoric. The narrator claims, "As a woman I want no country. As a woman my country is the whole world" (*TG* 109). The Outsiders "bind [themselves] to take no share in patriotic demonstrations; to assent to no form of national self-praise" and refuse to attend "all such ceremonies as encourage the desire to impose 'our' civiliza- tion or 'our' dominion upon other people" (*TG* 109). Furthermore, Woolf rejected eugenics on the grounds that it inevitably perpetuated the class system. As Jill Graham has demonstrated, in *Three Guineas*, Woolf actually proposed a means for disintegrating class barriers. Indeed, the third and final guinea, to be contributed by the anonymous and secret Society of Outsiders in an effort to prevent war, would be given on the condition that "a wage... be paid by the State to those whose profession is marriage and motherhood" (*TG* 110–11). It is true that the narrator of *Three Guineas* argues a wage should be paid to "mothers of educated men," and additionally applauds the effects this would have on the falling birthrate "in the very class where births are desirable – the educated class" (*TG* 110, 111). However, the proposal calls for the State to pay a wage to *all* mothers (*TG* 111). Such a proposal, as Graham contends, would effect a disruption of the class system:

Without wishing to cover the scent of eugenics with a deodorant spray, I still feel that there's something of a Swiftian 'modest proposal' in the way V[irginia] W[oolf] presents her ideas here. In order to sell the idea of paying 'the child-bearing force,' she has to point out to the educated class the particular benefits the proposed idea has for them. The benefits to working class people, by contrast, are fairly obvious. If bearing and raising children were paid work (for I don't recall her saying anywhere that working-class women should NOT be paid to bear and raise their children), there would ensue some erosion of the class system itself.[30]

Woolf's proposal calls for "a wage to be paid by the State to those whose profession is marriage or motherhood," and motherhood is not, finally, a profession respective of class.

HOW WOMEN CAN HELP PREVENT WAR

How can women help to prevent war? The central question which haunts *Three Guineas* happened to be the culminating concern for another of the "Points of View" talks given by Woolf's then new acquaintance and fast friend Ethel Smyth.[31] Woolf apparently had not heard Smyth's wireless talk as evidenced by her letter to Ethel written in March 1930: "[A]nd then about your Broadcast. The gardener's wife stopped me in the road and gave me an account of it, and my sales [sic] jumped up" (*L4*: 149).[32] The talk it seems provoked the argument of *Three Guineas*, which shares significant similarities with the themes and content of Smyth's presentation, or was inflected by Woolf's conversations with her.

At the conclusion of her rambling broadcast, Smyth commented: "I must now pass on to my most important part of my Point of View. I had often asked myself, 'How can women help to prevent another war?'" (*More Points of View* 89). "Still, nowadays a war cannot be fought without women's help and we ought to face the issue now," asserted Smyth. "[T]he thought of another war – a war of poisonous germs, of gas, of hideous mechanical ingenuity, a war which will end civilisation – is to me, as to most people, the worst of nightmares..." (*More Points of View* 89). Smyth argued that the answer to the question of preventing war would involve eradicating nationalist sentiment. We must, she declared, teach children to attain a more global vision: "Well, it seems...that the old exclusively English view of geography, history, politics, etc. should be extirpated in children, and a mentality substituted that is ready to take the views and aspirations of other countries into account" (*More Points of View* 90). Like Woolf who disapproved of military fanfare, Smyth contended, "The difficulty about peace is that it is so much less romantic than war" (*More Points of View* 90). Britain's youth must not be given "the impression that peace is a dull, drab, negative kind of thing fit only for the timid and the selfish" (*More Points of View* 90, 91).

Three Guineas, likewise, builds on the themes of rethinking educational curriculum to promote global perspectives, as well as the importance of women's work in subverting militarism and nationalism. Woolf's narrator calls for the establishment of a new "experimental" college for women, the aim of which would be to "cooperate; discover what new combinations make good wholes in human life" (*TG* 34). Even as Smyth had suggested, *Three Guineas* in answer to the question regarding how to prevent war asserts the necessity of securing *the world*, and not simply England, as a more livable place for all peoples. And such a world, Woolf reasoned, would require a radical resistance to nationalism. It is not simply that Woolf lifted arguments from Smyth's radio broadcast or Smyth from Woolf, but that similar rhetoric regarding a need for rethinking human aggression well preceded the publication of *Three Guineas*.[33] Woolf's contribution was to demonstrate how discourses of science, such as in geology, paleontology, and astronomy, had been deployed to reify and endorse a national eugenics program. Though greatly enamored of advances in the sciences, and of technologies like the camera and the telescope, Woolf imbedded in the text of *Three Guineas* a commentary on the imbrication of the sciences with social and political rhetorics regarding nationalism and militarism.

EXPOSING THE IMBRICATIONS OF POLITICS
AND THE SCIENCES

Three Guineas is, finally, a book about science, about experiments and scientific practices. It is in a sense a lab report of the Society of Outsiders and

women's own "effective experiment[s] in the prevention of war" (*TG* 116).
Even the structure of the text, with its amalgamation of news reportage,
epistolary framing, essay, and biography, allows Woolf to experiment with
a hybrid genre that cannot be dismissed as simply fiction or empty polemic.
The members of the Society of Outsiders, as their title suggests, position
themselves at the periphery of the science academy and its political structure. In order to disrupt cultural and scientific discourses, the Outsiders
adopt what Donna Haraway calls the "capacity to see from the periph-
eries."[34] They operate "[b]y making their absence felt" (*TG* 119). Indeed,
the Society, we learn, has already successfully conducted three "effective
experiment[s] in the prevention of war" including refusing to " 'darn a sock
to help in a war,' " as well as the "very original experiment" of declining sports
awards, and "an experiment in passivity" which involved desisting from attending church (*TG* 116, 117). And these experiments, the narrator insists,
were actual, not hypothetical; evidence of their effectiveness can be found
in the articles she cites from *The Times* [London] and the *Daily Herald*.
As part of the Outsiders' experiments in resisting aggression, women had
refused to accept for their achievements baubles and trinkets, medals and
awards, such as those "decorated ink-pots" awarded by "President Hindenburg for scientists and other distinguished civilians" (*TG* 114; 179, n. 19).[35]
Such baubles point up the sciences' complicity with social and political
aggrandizement. The Outsiders, instead, "practise their profession exper-
imentally, in the interests of research and for the love of the work itself"
(*TG* 112), and in opposition to scientific practices that exclude women and
others.

One example of the sciences excluding women appears in a news report of
women petitioning in 1869 to matriculate at the Royal College of Surgeons
in Edinburgh:

'A disturbance of a very unbecoming nature took place yesterday afternoon in front
of the Royal College of Surgeons.... Shortly before four o'clock... nearly 200
students assembled in front of the gate leading to the building....' The medical
students howled and sang songs. 'The gate was closed in their [the women's]
faces....' (*TG* 65)

This account of insensitivity to women who wish to study medicine is
immediately followed by a brief but dramatic glimpse of what goes on
inside the Royal College of Surgeons: " 'Dr. Handyside found it utterly
impossible to begin his demonstration... a pet sheep was introduced into
the room' " (*TG* 65). Handyside's demonstration, disrupted by the male
students' show of force against the prospect of women students, will be

the vivisection of a domesticated sheep. In that cinematic break to the vivisection scene, at the instant of the gate being closed to the women, the text juxtaposes a scientific indifference to the suffering of a demonstration animal with an institutional indifference to women. And such institutional indifference, *Three Guineas* argues, ultimately manifests itself in the kind of outright violence associated with war.

In another instance of the sciences excluding women, Newnham and Girton students had petitioned for the right to place the title BA after their names which incited Cambridge's male undergraduates to vandalize the Newnham school gate. Woolf cites, not accidentally, the revered physicist Sir J.J. Thomson, OM, FRS, who reported on the "determined opposition" exhibited by those Cambridge undergraduates who staunchly rejected the women's petition (*TG* 29).[36] Largely known for his work in atomic physics, Joseph John Thomson followed Lord Rutherford as Cavendish Professor at Cambridge, and became Master of Trinity College in 1919 (*Recollections and Reflections* 241). Thomson was knighted for his work in the discovery of the electron and for having identified it as the carrier of a negative charge of electricity. Whereas Thomson celebrated his distinctions by proudly listing his titles after his name, as on the title page to his memoir *Recollections and Reflections*, Woolf abjured them. When in February 1932, Thomson extended to Woolf an invitation to give the Clark Lectures the following year, Woolf delighted in the opportunity to conduct her own Outsiders' experiment. To accept would have meant for her a particular honor. Her father Leslie Stephen had been a Clark lecturer in 1883, and her colleague T.S. Eliot had given the Clark Lectures in 1926 (*D4*: 79, n. 33). She noted in her diary: "And this morning I opened a letter; & it was from 'yours very sincerely J.J. Thompson [sic]" – Master of Trinity; & it was to say that the council have decided to ask me to deliver the <Ford> Clark Lectures next year" (*D4*: 79). She was pleased to refuse the lectureship particularly as this was, she "suppose[d,] . . . the first time a woman has been asked" (*D4*: 79).

It was not science in general, but science rallied in support of aggression, that Woolf wished to expose and resist. At her most caustic, she associated the sciences with fascism. "Science, it would seem, is not sexless; she is a man, a father, and infected too" with the infantile fixation Woolf identifies at the heart of fascism (*TG* 139). In fact, in the mid-1930s as David Bradshaw points out, the Woolfs helped establish two organizations of artists and scientists who collaborated in the promotion of world peace. Both Leonard and Virginia were involved in helping establish the British Section of an organization titled the International Association of Writers for the Defense of Culture (IAWDC), as well as another organization titled For Intellectual Liberty (FIL).[37] The organizations comprised largely literary writers as well as several scientists and science writers. The British Section of the IAWDC included among others Sylvia Townsend Warner, Naomi Mitchison, Edward Sackville-West, and Olaf Stapledon; among those who attended meetings or supported For Intellectual Liberty were Leonard and Virginia, Vanessa Bell, E.M. Forster, Gerald Heard, J.D. Bernal, C.P. Snow, Aldous Huxley, and Arthur Eddington.[38]

Thus when the narrator of *Three Guineas* refuses to sign a manifesto "to protect culture and intellectual liberty," the text is commenting on peace organizations that the Woolfs helped found (*TG* 85). The minute book, for instance, to the inaugural FIL meeting records Leonard's explanation of that organization's purpose: "to discuss the possibilities of international co-operation for the defence of culture, liberty and peace."[39] Virginia had also served on an organising committee of a British delegation to the International Congress of Writers, out of which the IAWDC was formed, to be held in Paris in 1935.[40] Along with Aldous Huxley and E.M. Forster, she was to travel to Paris to represent Britain at the Congress; however, in June 1935, Virginia decided not to make the trip, reports Bradshaw, "although Forster and Huxley attended."[41] To serve as a delegate to the Paris Congress meant that Virginia would have specifically represented British writers. Yet, nationalism was the very thing that Woolf's Society of Outsiders rejected. They adopted instead a more global vision that refused to recognize nations as so many "chalk marks," scored upon the surface of the earth, "within whose mystic boundaries human beings are penned, rigidly, separately, artificially" (*TG* 105). Like the Society of Outsiders who question whether they should sign a "manifesto pledging [them]selves 'to protect culture and intellectual liberty,'" the very concerns of FIL and IAWDC, Woolf was guarded about the effectiveness of such organizations (*TG* 85). Moving beyond nationalism required a more global vision.

In 1938, Olaf Stapledon called for greater collaboration between artists and scientists in resistance to fascist regimes. Stapledon asserted that artists alone were "in too weak a position" to effect social or political change.[42] Woolf, however, refused to believe that the work of artists was ineffectual in promoting world peace. Repudiating complaints that Bloomsbury intellectuals were out of touch with the realities of war, she defended Bloomsbury and the use of art, whether painting or literature, in resisting human aggression. What Woolf hoped for in writing and publishing, as Pamela Caughie has argued, was not that her work should "reveal truth" but rather that it might "change behavior" (*Virginia Woolf & Postmodernism* 32). She found in literature, and the work of her colleagues like Roger Fry, a viable means for "checking Nazism" (*L6*: 414).

From those tiny worlds she glimpsed at the end of her telescope and in the pages of James Jeans's popular astronomy texts, Woolf forged a global aesthetic vision. It was a vision grounded in what she called the "liberating & freshening" vistas of the stars, both as she observed them from the verandah at Monks House and during air raid blackouts. Images of earth's globe etched against the black abyss of space that she may have seen in Flammarion's *Astronomie Populaire* depicted earth as an oasis of life in a cold and alien universe. In "A Walk by Night" (1905), Woolf recalled a walk homeward after dark, and her sense of "the trackless ocean of the night" (*E1*: 81). In that essay, she depicts the earth as a lonely mooring in the trackless expanse of space: "A ship at sea is a lonely thing, but far lonelier it seemed was this little village anchored to the desolate earth and exposed every night, alone, to the unfathomed waters of darkness" (*E1*: 82). Those unfathomed waters of darkness refer to the expanses of intergalactic space. Her sense of earth as an oasis of life in the empty wastes of space is perhaps best reflected in that much cherished image of the porpoise "fin rising on a wide blank sea" which she evoked so frequently in *The Waves* and elsewhere (*D3*: 153).[43] Bernard notes, "Leaning over this parapet I see far out a waste of water. A fin turns. This bare visual impression is unattached to any line of reason, it springs up as one might see the fin of a porpoise on the horizon…I noted under F., therefore 'Fin in the waste of waters'" (*TW* 189). Later, when Bernard gets a hint of his own death, he remarks, "Now there is nothing. No fin breaks the waste of this immeasurable sea…. The scene is like the eclipse when the sun went out and left the earth, flourishing in full summer foliage, withered, brittle, false" (*TW* 284). That image of the undisturbed wastes of the immeasurable sea evoked for Woolf the moment when the earth shriveled under a sky darkened by a solar eclipse. She once noted that she "saw human beings at the beginning of a vast enterprise" presumably to survive long ages into the future (*D3*: 155). In "The Sun and the Fish," the sublime opposition of the Zoological Gardens' aquariums to her memory of the 1927 eclipse was intended to "sho[w] us a dead world and an immortal fish" (*CE4*: 138). Gazing at the moon and stars reminded Woolf not only of the possibility of life on other worlds even as a porpoise fin breaking the ocean surface indicates life in what is otherwise a seemingly limitless abyss, but also of the fragility of life on our planet.

"A common interest unites us; it is one world, one life," the narrator declares at the close of *Three Guineas*. Woolf's feminist outsiders' politics, her rejection of any affiliation with country or nation, reflect her desire to embrace all peoples in one global community. How might a writer re-imagine her world? The narrator of *Three Guineas* answers: "'And do not [only]... dream dreams about ideal worlds behind the stars; consider actual facts in the actual world'" (*TG* 97). What appears to be a throw-away line about "ideal worlds behind the stars" may have been a comment directed toward H.G. Wells or James Jeans. Instead of simply dreaming of "ideal worlds" beyond our solar system, or of some eugenically perfected civilization here on earth, Woolf suggested that we might dream instead of a "unity that rubs out divisions as if they were chalk marks only" on our own small globe (*TG* 143). Virginia Woolf produced some of her best novels in the interwar years, in the wake of the Great War, and in the shadow of World War II. Yet Woolf maintained a hopeful vision for the future of humanity. It was a vision that called for breaking down barriers of nationality and difference and for finding alternatives to global war on this fragment of a grain of sand we call Earth.

Notes

INTRODUCTION: FORMULATING
A GLOBAL AESTHETIC

1. Joanne Trautmann Banks, "Some New Woolf Letters." *Modern Fiction Studies* 30.2 Summer 1984: 198. Elizabeth Nielsen's doctoral dissertation on Woolf apparently "was rejected as too modern" (*D5*: 145, n. 13). However, Nielsen earned a PhD at Northwestern University in 1943; the title of her dissertation was "Attitudes of English Writers (1690–1750) Toward the English Poor." She went by the name of E.E. Nielsen, and later "became a professor of literature, first at Santa Barbara College," and then from 1950 to 1977 at what was then California State College, Long Beach (Banks, "Some New Woolf Letters" 200, n. 110).

2. Judith Killen's dissertation, "Virginia Woolf in the Light of Modern Physics" (University of Louisville 1984), remains one of the most comprehensive book-length studies on Woolf and the new physics. She offers close readings of *The Waves, The Years, Between the Acts* and discusses how the novels' plot, themes and language are shaped by Woolf's understanding of the new physics. Killen also was among the first to comment on Woolf's interest in astronomy. More recently, Ann Banfield, in *The Phantom Table* (2000), has published a carefully researched study of the extent to which Woolf's fiction and essays engage with Bertrand Russell and the Cambridge debates regarding the nature of material phenomena, and other discourses in the philosophy of science. Gillian Beer's volume, *Virginia Woolf: The Common Ground* (1996), uncovers fascinating connections between Woolf's work and advances in physics. Jane Goldman, in *The Feminist Aesthetics of Virginia Woolf* (1998), offers an in-depth exploration of how Woolf's account of the 1927 solar eclipse elaborates Woolf's literary use of color and myth, as well as how color is linked to Woolf's feminist politics.

3. See James Jeans, *Astronomy and Cosmogony* 421; also Jeans, *The Mysterious Universe* 3.

4. "How mysterious is the Universe!" Cartoon by Will Dyson. *Everyman* 18 Jan. 1931. Taken from James Jeans's private notebooks of news clippings which do not include page numbers.

5. Peter Hingley, librarian at the Royal Astronomical Society in London, graciously directed me to Holst's work.
6. This study examines the popular and largely secular response to the new vistas of space, and does not address astrology or mysticism in relation to the popular interest in astronomy.
7. Woolf knew of Humbert Wolfe by at least 1940 when she noted in her diary how Wolfe's poetry had been "striking odd little sparks from Tom [Eliot]'s 'genius' vanity" (*D5*: 268).
8. Letter from Nigel Nicolson to Holly Henry, dated 1 March 1998.
9. Letter from Nigel Nicolson to Holly Henry, dated 1 March 1998.
10. Leonard and Sydney-Turner shared rooms during their undergraduate days at Cambridge. Sydney-Turner was a classics scholar whom Mark Hussey claims was perhaps the "inaugural member of the Bloomsbury Group" (*Virginia Woolf A to Z* 281).
11. I. Grattan-Guinness, "Russell and G.H. Hardy: A Study of Their Relationship." *Russell: A Journal of Bertrand Russell Archives* 2.2 (Winter 1991): 166.
12. I. Grattan-Guinness, "Russell and G.H. Hardy: A Study of Their Relationship" 167.
13. Letter from R.K. Gaye to James Jeans, dated 1 Feb. 1903, The James Jeans Papers, The Royal Society of London.
14. Letter from R.K. Gaye to James Jeans, dated 1 Feb. 1903, The James Jeans Papers, The Royal Society of London.
15. See Joseph Rouse, "What are the Cultural Studies of Scientific Literature?" *Configurations* 1.1 (Winter 1993): 57–94. See also Donna Haraway, *Simians, Cyborgs, and Women: The Reinvention of Nature*. New York: Routledge, 1991.
16. *The Letters of Vita Sackville-West to Virginia Woolf*. Ed. Louise De Salvo and Mitchell, A. Leaska. New York: William Morrow, 1985: 92.
17. *The Letters of Vita Sackville-West to Virginia Woolf* 181. Actually, Ceres was the first asteroid ever discovered, by Italian astronomer Giuseppe Piazzi in Palermo, Sicily. It is also the largest asteroid in our solar system measuring about 600 miles in diameter.
18. *The Letters of Vita Sackville-West to Virginia Woolf* 191.
19. *The Letters of Vita Sackville-West to Virginia Woolf* 365, 366.
20. *The Letters of Vita Sackville-West to Virginia Woolf* 331. See also *Virginia Woolf in the Age of Mechanical Reproduction* (2000), edited by Pamela Caughie, for a collection of essays on Woolf and technology.
21. "The Clothbound Universe: Popular Physics Books, 1919–39." *Publishing History* 40 (1996): 54.
22. I am very grateful to Susan Squier for pointing out to me Felski's work on the popular sublime.
23. "Books in General." *The Listener* 19, Nov. 1930: 844.
24. S.C. Roberts, who first encouraged Jeans to publish popular astronomy texts through Cambridge University Press, recalls how, while in the Alps, Susi and Jeans met and then spent the evening on a hotel terrace talking about the stars and about music. "It was a brilliant starlit night and Susi asked many questions

about the stars, which Jeans was only too ready to answer. There was also much talk about music" (Roberts, "A Memoir," *Sir James Jeans: A Biography* xiv).

1 STARS AND NEBULAE IN POPULAR CULTURE

1. Sharon Begley, "When Galaxies Collide." *Newsweek* 3 Nov. 1997: 30-7.
2. John Nobel Wilford, "Fireworks in Deep Space as Two Galaxies Collide." *New York Times* 22 Oct. 1997: A24.
3. Andromeda actually lies roughly 2.2 to 2.3 million light-years from the Milky Way.
4. Richard Berendzen, Richard Hart and Daniel Seeley, *Man Discovers the Galaxies* 11.
5. Robert Smith's *The Expanding Universe: Astronomy's Great Debate 1900–1931* offers a well researched account of the developments leading up to Hubble's determination that entire galaxies existed beyond the Milky Way. Another valuable text in this regard is Berendzen, Hart, and Seeley's *Man Discovers the Galaxies*.
6. Quoted in Alexander Sharov and Igor Novikov, *Edwin Hubble: The Discoverer of the Big Bang Universe* 34.
7. Joel Stebbins, quoted in Berendzen, Hart and Seeley, *Man Discovers the Galaxies* 137. Stebbins was then secretary of the Council of the American Astronomical Society (Gale Christianson, *Edwin Hubble: Mariner of the Nebulae* 160).
8. Hubble's velocity/distance calculations for the recession of extra-galactic nebulae were too large by approximately a factor of 10.
9. "Eddington and the Idiom of Modernism," *Science, Reason, and Rhetoric* 303.
10. In January 1930, the planet Pluto had been discovered by Tombaugh, then an astronomer's assistant working at the Lowell Observatory in Arizona (James Stokley, *Stars and Telescopes* 211).
11. Judith Killen was among the first to discuss Woolf's access to scientists through Ottoline Morrell ("Virginia Woolf in the Light of Modern Physics," Diss. University of Louisville, Nov. 1984: 36–7, 195). Michael Whitworth also makes this point in "Virginia Woolf and Modernism," *The Cambridge Companion to Virginia Woolf* 149.
12. Gillian Beer, " 'Wireless': Popular Physics, Radio and Modernism," *Cultural Babbage* 150.
13. Killen lists a sizeable sampling of the plethora of newspaper and journal articles published between 1910 and 1939 on cosmology, the new physics, relativity, and related topics.
14. Dickie Spurgeon, "The Athenaeum," *British Literary Magazines* Vol. 2: 21.
15. "The Nation and Athenaeum," *British Literary Magazines* Vol. 4: 270.
16. "Solid Objects" and "Kew Gardens," appeared in the *Athenaeum* in 1920 while "Mr. Bennett and Mrs. Brown" was published in a December 1923 issue of the *Nation & Athenaeum*.

17. "Virginia Woolf and Modernism," *The Cambridge Companion to Virginia Woolf* 149.

18. "Virginia Woolf and Modernism," *The Cambridge Companion to Virginia Woolf* 149.

19. Dickie Spurgeon, "The Athenaeum," *British Literary Magazines* Vol. 2: 22.

20. See "Daedalus and Icarus." *Nation & Athenaeum* 34.25 (22 Mar. 1924): 890, and "Ad Astra?" *Nation & Athenaeum* 45.26 (28 Sept. 1929): 829.

21. See F.W.N. Sullivan's "Einstein's Problem" and Clive Bell's, "Matisse and Picasso," in *Athenaeum* 4698 (14 May 1920): 641–4. Numbers listed after the title of this journal are issue and not volume numbers.

22. *Athenaeum* 4649 (6 June 1919): 433, 434.

23. J.W.N. Sullivan, "Stellar Universes." *Athenaeum* 4671 (7 Nov. 1919): 1156.

24. Michael Whitworth, "The Clothbound Universe." *Publishing History* (1996): 74.

25. Miranda Seymour, *Ottoline Morrell* 294. David Bradshaw notes that Woolf wrote of Sullivan in her diary though not entirely in flattering terms. According to Bradshaw, "Sullivan was also a close friend of Aldous Huxley between the war years, especially in the early 1920s, and a major influence on the development of his thought" ("The Best of Companions: J.W.N. Sullivan, Aldous Huxley, and the New Physics, (Part I)," *Review of English Studies* [1996]: 188–9).

26. "Science and Literature." *Athenaeum* 4650 (13 June 1919): 464.

27. "Science and Literature." *Athenaeum* 4650 (13 June 1919): 464.

28. The information on the total solar eclipse of 1927 was previously published in "Eclipse Madness, 1927." *Astronomy & Geophysics: The Journal of the Royal Astronomical Society* 40.4 (August 1999): 17–19.

29. Virginia and Leonard, along with Vita's family and cousin Eddy Sackville-West, Virginia's nephew Quentin Bell, Saxon Sydney-Turner, and Rachel Strachey traveled together by overnight train to see the eclipse.

30. "Eclipse Madness." *Nation & Athenaeum* (9 July 1927): 477–8.

31. "Corrected Path of Eclipse." *The Times* 21 May 1927: 9.

32. "Plans of London Public." *The Times* 29 June 1927: 16.

33. "In the Totality Belt." *The Times* 27 June 1927: 14.

34. "In the Totality Belt." *The Times* 27 June 1927: 16.

35. A respected and widely-read periodical, *Punch* published editorial cartoons spoofing national and international politics, cultural and social events, and the arts.

36. Woolf was right about the solar eclipse of 11 August 1999, which was the last total solar eclipse visible in England before the year 2000. During that event, totality was visible along Cornwall's southern coast.

37. "On the North-East Coast." *The Times* 30 June 1927: 18.

38. "Eclipse Madness." *Nation & Athenaeum* 41.14 (9 July 1927): 477.

39. In her detailed study of Woolf's accounts of the solar eclipse of 1927, Jane Goldman asserts that Woolf's use of color and light reflected her appreciation for suffrage art and English Post-Impressionism.

40. Though named after the British astronomer Edmund Halley (1656–1742), appearances of Halley's comet have been recorded for centuries. The Bayeux tapestry, for instance, dating from about 1100 AD, includes an image of Halley's comet. In actuality, there are hundreds of comets and asteroids whose orbits intersect with the earth's orbit. Halley's comet happens to be more widely known.

41. Gary Kronk, "Comet Hysteria" 2 of 3. <http://www.maa.mhn.de/Comet/Hale-Bopp/hbhysteria.html>. Accessed on 12 Dec. 2001. Gary Kronk is an amateur astronomer and an expert on comets.

42. S.A. Mitchell, "The Return of Halley's Comet." *American Review of Reviews* 41.4 (April 1910): 443.

43. The appearance of the comet Hale-Bopp in March 1997 inspired thirty-nine members of a religious group, who operated a computer web business titled Higher Source, to take their lives. This was reportedly the largest mass suicide in US history. Members of the group, whose private web page was titled "Heaven's Gate," believed that an alien ship, located behind Comet Hale-Bopp, had arrived to take them to another planet.

44. Donald Gropman, *Comet Fever*. Illustrations in this text do not have page numbers.

45. The description in "The Star" of newspaper headlines announcing the close approach of an asteroid became a reality in March 1998 when it was reported that an asteroid might strike earth. One London newspaper, headlined "We're all doomed (or at least we might be) as giant asteroid heads for Earth," reported that "at 17.30 GMT on 26 October 2028" an asteroid will closely approach earth and that "a collision with Earth is easily possible" (*Evening Standard* [London] 12 March, 1998: 1). While the report was quickly discredited, the explosive 130,000 mph-collision of fragments of comet Shoemaker-Levy with Jupiter in 1994 made it very clear that earth has been subject to such disasters. In fact, US congressional hearings were held in the summer of 1998 to investigate the possibility of developing technology that could break up asteroids or comets passing dangerously close to our planet. See the NASA web site on "Congressional Hearings on Near Earth Objects and Planetary Defense" ("NASA's Current Efforts/Future Plans: NEOs" <http://impact.arc.nasa.gov/congress/1998_may/>). More recently, in June 2002, a soccer-field sized asteroid just missed impact with earth by only 75,000 miles ("Asteroid Passes in 'Close Shave,'" *The Press-Enterprise* [Riverside, CA] 21 June 2002: A2). A few weeks later news reports indicated that an asteroid might hit the earth in February 2019 and cause "a global catastrophe" ("Asteroid Comes Collision Risk," *The Press-Enterprise* [Riverside, CA] 25 July 2002: A13). It is interesting to note that Wells's story prefigured, nearly 100 years in advance, the plots of the 1998 Hollywood block buster movies *Armageddon* and *Deep Impact*.

46. Wells's prediction of such catastrophic events closely matches the details of a report given during US congressional hearings in 1998 on the threat of a collision with Near-Earth Objects. Should such an object strike the earth, Clark

R. Chapman reported, "hundreds of thousands of people" could be killed or subject to tsunamis and "other kinds of natural disasters like great floods or magnitude 8 earthquakes" ("Statement on the Threat of Impact by Near-Earth Asteroids," <http://impact.arc.nasa.gov/congress/1998_may/chapman.html>). At the time of his report, Dr. Chapman, an expert on asteroids and studies of impact craters on planetary surfaces, was a research scientist in the Boulder, Colorado, Space Studies Department.

47. Stephen Kern, *The Culture of Time and Space* 184.
48. This was not the first or last of the eclipse expeditions to prove Einstein's theory. Einstein himself sought observational evidence regarding how the gravitational mass of a body might warp the space surrounding it. He recruited the German astronomer Erwin Freundlich to carry out in August 1914 an eclipse expedition to southern Russia, but with the eruption of the World War I, Freundlich and members of his team were arrested, and traded back to the Germans for several Russian officers; the eclipse expedition had to be aborted (Clark, *Einstein: The Life and Times* 175–6). In 1922, when more efficient telescopic equipment became available, Freundlich attempted an expedition to Christmas Island in the Pacific to photograph a solar eclipse, but the research was prohibited by poor weather (Clark 301–2). He tried for a third time in 1926, but was unable to obtain viable results, again due to weather conditions (Klaus Hentschel, *The Einstein Tower* 103). Finally, in 1929, Freundlich traveled to Sumatra to measure the deflection of star light by the sun's mass; this time he was successful, but his results did not corroborate those predicted by Einstein's theory (*The Einstein Tower* 116). More recent investigations of Einstein's calculation for the deflection of light by the sun have confirmed his figures. It is interesting to note that photographs taken by the Hubble Space Telescope of an effect astronomers today call gravitational lensing provide visual confirmation of Einstein's notion of curved space.
49. Qtd. in Ronald Clark, *Einstein: The Life and Times* 233.
50. David Bradshaw, "The Best of Companions: J.W.N. Sullivan, Aldous Huxley, and the New Physics (Part I)." *Review of English Studies* 194.
51. Judith Killen, "Virginia Woolf in the Light of Modern Physics" 43.
52. Judith Killen cites these examples as well.
53. Abraham Pais, *Einstein Lived Here* 179; also 267 n. 189.
54. Moszkowski's book, *Einstein, the Searcher*, comprises a collection of his interviews with Einstein. The text was criticized as much of the work represents Moszkowski's paraphrasing of Einstein's conversations.
55. "An Abstruse Theory." *Athenaeum* 4723 (5 Nov. 1920): 621.
56. "An Abstruse Theory." *Athenaeum* 4723 (5 Nov. 1920): 621. A physics professor at University College London until 1900, Lodge had published throughout the 1920s texts on physics, electricity, the ether, and relativity.
57. Woolf presented a paper that would become "Character in Fiction" to the Cambridge Heretics, a group of leftist intellectuals including scientists, on 18 May 1924. The evening she presented her essay she dined with physiologist J.B.S. Haldane and then proceeded to the reading.

58. See Mark Hussey, "*To the Lighthouse* and Physics: The Cosmology of David Bohm and Virginia Woolf." *New Essays on Virginia Woolf*. Ed. Helen Wussow. Dallas: Contemporary Research Press, 1995: 79. The passage from "Character in Fiction" often associated with developments in the new physics reads: "In the course of your daily life this past week you have had far stranger and more interesting experiences than the one I have tried to describe. You have overheard scraps of talk that filled you with amazement. You have gone to bed at night bewildered by the complexity of your feelings. In one day thousands of ideas have coursed through your brains; thousands of emotions have met, collided, and disappeared in astonishing disorder" (*E*3: 436).

59. "A Mathematical Universe." *Hibbert Journal* 29 (1930): 401.

60. Jeans invariably referred to humankind as "man," as did Woolf and nearly all of her contemporaries. Throughout this study I have cited the quotations as they appeared in the original without further comment.

61. Edward Shanks, "Do We Matter?" *Evening Standard* [London] 5 Nov. 1930: 7.

62. S.C. Roberts, *The Evolution of Cambridge Publishing* 63.

63. Jeans's *The Mysterious Universe* (1930) included chapters on modern physics and relativity as well as on astronomy and cosmology.

64. S.C. Roberts, *The Evolution of Cambridge Publishing* 63.

65. Michael Whitworth, "The Clothbound Universe." *Publishing History* 65.

66. "Science and Sentiment Are Best Sellers!" *Sunday Express* [London] 29 March 1931: 8.

67. Michael Whitworth, "The Clothbound Universe." *Publishing History* 71.

68. For more information on women and science popularization in the nineteenth century see *Natural Eloquence: Women Reinscribe Science*. Eds. Barbara Gates and Ann Shteir, 1997. Gerald Dennis Meyer's *The Scientific Lady in England 1650–1760* (1955) examines women's earlier work and interest in the natural sciences.

69. "Constructing Victorian Heavens: Agnes Clerke and the 'New Astronomy,'" *Natural Eloquence* 70.

70. See the correspondence between Hale and Clerke archived at the Beckman Institute at the California Institute of Technology, in Pasadena, CA. I am grateful to the Beckman Institute for allowing me to research their holdings of the George Ellery Hale Papers.

71. Berendzen, Hart, and Seeley, *Man Discovers the Galaxies* 22.

72. UCL's records indicate Williamson was a volunteer assistant from at least 1929 to 1931. She was appointed Honorary Assistant in Astronomy at UCL's Department of Applied Mathematics and Mechanics in February 1927, and she held this post until the 1932–33 session. She was then appointed Assistant in Astronomy from 1933–34, and remained in this position until the 1945–46 academic year. According to Royal Astronomical Society Librarian Peter Hingley, Williamson was a member of the Royal Astronomical Society from 1924 through 1977. The 13 June 1924 issue of the Society's professional journal, *Monthly Notices*, lists Williamson's nomination for election to the Fellows of the Society. Williamson died in 1980.

73. I am grateful to Derek McNally of the University of London Observatory for this information.

74. Patricia Phillips has argued that this may have resulted from changes in women's educational curricula, which at the end of the nineteenth century became focused on the classics instead of the sciences (*The Scientific Lady* 249). Phillips contends that as scientific research was becoming "highly specialized and politically and strategically important – in other words, just as science was poised to become a respectable profession – women were finally excluded" (*The Scientific Lady* 257).

75. The 42-inch reflector at Lowell Observatory in Arizona became operable in 1909.

76. Letter to Jeans dated 25 May 1920. George Ellery Hale Papers, Box 23. The Beckman Institute, California Institute of Technology, Pasadena, CA.

77. Grace Hubble memoirs titled "Some People," The Edwin Hubble Papers, HUB 82(17), Box 8, The Huntington Library, San Marino, CA.

78. Hubble preferred the term extra-galactic nebulae to the term galaxy, though the terms are used interchangeably in this study.

79. Letter from Jeans to Hubble dated 22 Feb. 1938. The Edwin Hubble Papers, HUB 718, Box 16.

80. In December 1929, multiple papers in the US listed Jeans's *The Universe Around Us* on their best seller lists. As one example see "Christmas Suggestions," *Call* [Paterson, NJ]] 7, Dec. 1929. This citation is taken from James Jeans's private notebooks of news clippings, which do not include page numbers. I am grateful to Jeans's son, Christopher Jeans, for inviting me to read through his father's papers and notebooks archived at his home in Cambridge.

81. "Hoover Gets First 12 Books for White House Library." *New York American* 26 April 1930, midnight ed.: 2.

82. See Grace Hubble's diary titled "Travels 1934," The Edwin Hubble Papers, HUB 74, Box 4.

83. Grace Hubble's diary titled "September 1936 Travel Diary," The Edwin Hubble Papers, HUB 75, Box 5.

84. Letter from Sir Carleton K. Allen dated 29 Dec. 1936. The Edwin Hubble Papers, HUB 102, Box 9.

85. Letter from Hugh Walpole to Edwin Hubble dated 11 Sept 1934. The Edwin Hubble Papers, HUB 987, Box 20.

86. Grace Hubble's memoirs titled "Some People." The Edwin Hubble Papers, HUB 82 (17), Box 8.

87. Walpole's book is listed in Elizabeth Steele's "Addendum" to the Holleyman and Treacher *Catalogue of Books* owned by the Woolfs, published in *Virginia Woolf's Literary Sources and Allusions* 337. Hugh Walpole corresponded frequently with Grace Hubble both while he lived in California and from England. He also befriended, and corresponded with, Virginia Woolf.

88. In 1910, Edwin earned a Rhodes Scholarship to attend Oxford for three years, and while there served on the crew team with Trevenan Huxley. A brother to Aldous, Trevenan killed himself in his early twenties.

89. From a memoir titled "The Astronomer" by Grace Hubble. The Edwin Hubble Papers, HUB 82 (7), Box 7. A globular cluster is a roughly spherically symmetrical group of stars. The 200-inch telescope then under construction at Mount Palomar became operational by 1948.

90. Letter to Grace Hubble from Maria Huxley dated 9 August 1943. The Edwin Hubble Papers, HUB 692, Box 16. The section in brackets appears in the letter as scratched out.

91. Letter to Grace Hubble from Maria Huxley dated 9 Jan. 1944. The Edwin Hubble Papers, HUB 1083, Box 16. The novel by Huxley that Grace may have edited was perhaps *Time Must Have a Stop* (1944).

92. I am grateful to the Royal Society in London for allowing me to research their holdings of the James Jeans Papers.

93. Robert Smith, *The Expanding Universe: Astronomy's 'Great Debate' 1900–1931* 4.

94. Edward Shanks, "Do We Matter?" *Evening Standard* 5 Nov. 1930: 7.

95. "Mankind Just An Accident: Ice Age of Universal Death Must End the World." *Daily Herald* 5 Nov. 1930: 1.

96. H. Gordon Garbedian, "The Star Stuff That is Man." *New York Times Magazine* 11 Aug. 1929: 5:1 (italics mine).

97. H. Gordon Garbedian, "The Star Stuff that is Man" *New York Times Magazine* 11 Aug. 1929: 5:1.

98. Over the course of his publishing career, Jeans would rethink his position on the rarity of life in the universe. The sheer millions of galaxies glimpsed through the 100-inch telescope ultimately suggested that solar systems must be plentiful and that many may be similar to our own. The 1944 edition of *The Universe Around Us* was revised to report that "the number of planetary systems in the whole of space must be almost unthinkably great. Millions of millions of these must be almost exact replicas of our solar system, and the millions of their planets must be almost exact replicas of our earth" (Jeans, *The Universe Around Us*. 4th ed. Cambridge University Press, 252–3). All other references for *The Universe Around Us* indicate the 1929 edition.

99. "What Are the Stars?" *The Universe of Stars* 5.

100. Quoted. in Gordon Garbedian, "The Star Stuff That is Man." *New York Times Magazine* 11 Aug. 1929, 5:2.

101. I am grateful to my colleague Harvey Quamen for pointing out to me the theory of nucleosynthesis.

102. "Centre of Universe Located by Shapley." *New York Times* 20 Nov. 1928: A1.

103. "The Progress of Science. New Views on the Universe." *The Times* 5 Jan. 1925: 18.

104. H. Gordon Garbedian, *New York Times Magazine* 24 Feb. 1929: 5:1.

105. H. Gordon Garbedian, "Our Universe Bares its Heart." *New York Times Magazine* 24 Feb. 1929: 5:1.

106. H. Gordon Garbedian, "Our Universe Bares its Heart." *New York Times Magazine* 24 Feb. 1929: 5:1. Here again, the center of the Milky Way galaxy is referred to as the center of the universe.

107. H. Gordon Garbedian, "The Star Stuff That is Man" *New York Times Magazine* 11 Aug. 1929: 5:1.
108. For example, see "Stars Seen Now as They Were 'Inconceivable Ages Before Man.'" *Illustrated London News* 15 Nov. 1930: 873. Also see "Photography Records a Stellar Explosion." *Illustrated London News*, 18 June 1938: 1097.
109. See "Mystical Mathematics of the City of Heaven." *Illustrated London News* 22 Nov. 1930: 922–3. Lucien Rudaux produced imaginary but scientifically sound and quite dramatic paintings of landscapes from other planets in our solar system for popular audiences. Many of these were featured in the *Illustrated London News* from at least 1930 on. His illustrations of Jupiter and of Mars as seen from a satellite moon were used by the newspaper to illustrate announcements of book publications by Sir James Jeans. "But his masterwork was a 'coffee-table' volume titled *Sur les Autres Mondes* (*On Other Worlds*) (1937). More than 400 illustrations, including 20 full-page color paintings, gave readers the most accurate and spectacular look at the solar system of that era" (Ron Miller, "The Astronomical Visions of Lucien Rudaux." *Sky & Telescope* [Oct. 1984]: 293–295).
110. "The Universe. Sir James Jeans on Astronomy." *The Times* 13 Sept. 1929. Cited from James Jeans's notebooks, which do not include the page numbers for articles and reviews. At least eighteen news articles preserved by Jeans reprinted this table, which suggests that the table spoke to some sort of popular anxiety about the human place in the universe.
111. "The Universe. Sir James Jeans on Astronomy." *The Times* 13 Sept. 1929.
112. *Daily Record & Daily Mail* [London] 10 Sept. 1929: 23. Other examples include the *Evening News* [Carmelite House] which ran a story headlined "A Great Astronomer Looks at Man a Million Million Years Hence . . . Frozen Seas, Vanished Mountains and the Human Race Racing Certain Extinction" (10 Sept. 1929). The *Sunday Worker* [London] likewise published an article titled "The End of the World is Still a Long Way Off – But it Will be Very Cold a Million Million Years Hence" (20 Oct. 1929). These articles are cited from Jeans's notebooks of news clippings, which do not include page numbers.
113. "The Human Value of the New Astronomy." *Hibbert Journal* 27, January 1929: 249.
114. "The Scientific Contribution." *Athenaeum* 4696 (30 April 1920): 577.
115. "Ad Astra?" *Nation & Athenaeum* 45.26 (28 Sept. 1929): 829.
116. Notice the link Jeans makes between Alpine climbing, suggested by the reference to Mont Blanc, and the long vistas of time presented by astronomy. See the Introduction for a discussion of the connection between the desire for the sublime associated with astronomy and with mountain climbing.
117. David Bradshaw comments that a concern regarding the topic of civilization "permeates Woolf's whole literary output as a novelist" ("The socio-political vision of the novels," *The Cambridge Companion to Virginia Woolf* 199).

118. Letter from Clive Bell to Saxon Sydney-Turner dated April 1908. The Leonard Sydney Woolf Collection, the Huntington Library, HM 57624.

2 FROM HUBBLE'S TELESCOPE TO "THE SEARCHLIGHT"

An earlier version of this chapter appeared in *Virginia Woolf in the Age of Mechanical Reproduction*. Ed. Pamela Caughie. New York: Garland (2000): 135–58.

1. J.W. Graham, "The Drafts of Virginia Woolf's 'The Searchlight' " *Twentieth Century Literature* 22.4 (December 1976): 380, 381.
2. Taylor's telescope story made such an impression on Woolf that she mentioned the story in a short review of *Guests and Memories: Annals of a Seaside Villa* (1924) by Una Taylor, Henry Taylor's daughter (*E4*: 10–11).
3. Ellipses that appear in brackets indicate my deletion of text. Woolf used ellipses throughout this story as a device for deploying her narrative scoping strategies. All ellipses not in brackets in "The Searchlight" citations are Woolf's.
4. Stephen Spender, *Recollections of Virginia Woolf by her Contemporaries* 219. Spender, a literary critic and essayist, was a close friend to Leonard and Virginia Woolf.
5. I am very grateful to Susan Squier for her insights on this point.
6. J.W. Graham, "The Drafts of Virginia Woolf's 'The Searchlight' " 381. In more recent work on the drafts of "The Searchlight," Jane de Gay has argued that the story of "A Scene from the Past," which is set at Freshwater and in which Sir Henry Taylor discusses love with a young woman, was first drafted in 1941. Jane de Gay convincingly claims that "the Freshwater story of 1941 had its own momentum, and that with its different framing narrative and title, it was developing away from the Ivimey version and the searchlight motif" ("An Unfinished Story: The Freshwater Drafts of 'The Searchlight,' " *Virginia Woolf Turning the Centuries* 209).
7. Letter from E.M.Forster to Virginia Woolf dated 7 November 1931, held at The Archive Centre at King's College Cambridge. See file titled EMF xviii/ Woolf, V. I am grateful to The Society of Authors, who serve as agent for the Provost and Scholars of King's College, Cambridge, for permission to cite from Forster's letter. A book review titled "The Biological Telescope," published in the *New Statesman and Nation*, suggests the public largely understood the telescope as a device for looking back in time. In a review of books on evolution and botany, the anonymous writer notes, "Yet biology, too, has a telescope, a colossal metaphorical instrument, pointing back into remote time rather than out into remote space. It is, of course, the evolution theory..." ("The Biological Telescope." *New Statesman and Nation* 2.24 [8 Aug. 1931]: 171).
8. Astronomers today claim that the Hubble Space Telescope's deep field images afford nearly 90 per cent look-back time to the Big Bang. This, however, is not due to the curvature of space, but to the vast distances of intergalactic space

and the nearly 14 billion years light emitting from the most distant and ancient galaxies has traveled before reaching earth.

9. Gillian Beer, *Virginia Woolf: The Common Ground* 41. This collection of essays traces many important connections between Woolf's interest in Eddington, Jeans, and the new physics.

10. Qtd. in Jocelyn Bartkevicius, "A Form of One's Own: Virginia Woolf's Art of the Portrait Essay." *Iowa Review* 22.1 (Winter 1992): 128.

11. Quoted in Bartkevicius, "A Form of One's Own: Virginia Woolf's Art of the Portrait Essay" 128.

12. Quoted in J.W. Graham, "The Drafts of Virginia Woolf's 'The Searchlight' " 384.

13. Letter to Virginia Woolf, 23 February 1929, *The Letters of Vita Sackville-West to Virginia Woolf* 328.

14. Woolf notes in her diary that they purchased the telescope from Williamson (*D5*: 58); however, Nicolson and Trautmann claim that Williamson gave the telescope to Woolf (*L6*: 158, n. 3).

15. Michael Crowe, *The Extraterrestrial Life Debate 1750–1900: The Idea of a Plurality of Worlds from Kant to Lowell* 48.

16. Judith Killen was among the first to point out that Woolf incorporated elements of Jeans's texts into her novels, and further noted that Isa Oliver in *Between the Acts* considers reading Eddington or Jeans ("Virginia Woolf in the Light of Modern Physics" 93, 161).

17. "Eddington and the Idiom of Modernism," *Science, Reason and Rhetoric* 304.

18. Also, in *The Years*, Rose as a young girl imagines herself as a military messenger on horseback delivering a secret message to an awaiting general, whom she envisions standing at the watch "with his telescope to his eye"; likewise, there is the altercation between Rose and the boy named Erridge who "broke the microscope," another scoping device (22, 136). In *Orlando*, a telescope appears along with "globes, maps . . . and mathematical instruments" on a heap of "ill-assorted objects, piled higgledly-piggledly in a vast mound" which Orlando envisions while motoring near St. James Park (149). Woolf's short story "Scenes from the Life of a British Naval Officer" also includes a scene in which the officer looks through a telescope, and somehow the officer's militarism is linked to the restricted view of his scope. The story appears in the second edition of *The Complete Shorter Fiction of* Virginia Woolf edited by Susan Dick.

19. "Half of Thomas Hardy," *Nation & Athenaeum* 44 (24 November 1928): 290. The telescope evoked in Woolf's review was no mere trope. The review opens with an anecdote about Hardy's father who "would stroll on to the heath alone with [a] telescope that had belonged to some sea-faring Hardy and 'stay peering out into the distance by the half-hour' " ("Half of Thomas Hardy" 289). Woolf further recounted how Thomas Hardy himself "had once stood on the heath and put that same brass telescope to his eye" and by chance had seen a man die on the gallows ("Half of Thomas Hardy" 289).

20. "Half of Thomas Hardy" 290.

21. "The Fatal Accident on the Matterhorn," *Peaks, Passes and Glaciers* 51. Whymper's published account of the accident appeared in *The Times* [London] in August of 1865 (*Peaks, Passes and Glaciers* 52). In March 1940, Woolf recorded in her diary that she was reading Whymper, which Anne Oliver Bell and Andrew McNeillie note may have been the biography of Edward Whymper by Francis Sydney Smythe, published that year. See F.S. Smythe, *Edward Whymper*. London: Hodder and Stoughton, 1940.

22. H. Gordon Garbedian, "The Star Stuff That is Man" *New York Times Magazine*, 11 August 1929: 5:2.

23. H. Gordon Garbedian, "The Star Stuff That is Man," *New York Times Magazine* (11 August 1929): 5:2.

24. Russell, "A Free Man's Worship," *Mysticism and Logic* 46; Banfield, *The Phantom Table* 344.

25. Quoted in Bertrand Russell, "A Free Man's Worship," *Mysticism and Logic* 47.

26. "A Free Man's Worship," *Mysticism and Logic* 47.

27. See Chapter One for a discussion of Wells's story "The Star," in which an asteroid has slammed into Neptune and has accumulated into a huge flaming mass which narrowly misses earth. The story concludes with a scene in which a group of Martian astronomers comment on their telescopic observations of the effects of the asteriod's near miss of earth: " 'Considering the mass and temperature of the missile that was flung through our solar system into the sun,' one wrote, 'it is astonishing what a little damage the earth . . . has sustained" (Wells, "The Star" 691). The Martian account of the asteroid's near-collision with earth, Wells's narrator claims, "only shows how small the vastest of human catastrophes may seem, at a distance of a few million miles" ("The Star" 691). Woolf too played out in miniature the history of England in the pageant in *Between the Acts*, a novel that spans the ages, from prehistory to World War II.

28. Hardy wrote of the dying universe in *Two on a Tower*. See the discussion of Hardy's *Two on a Tower* in the Introduction. In Tennyson's poem "The Dawn" (1892), the speaker of the poem speculates whether "twenty million of summers are stored in the sunlight still" (*The Poems of Tennyson*. ed. Christopher Ricks, 2nd. ed., vol. III: 247). In Flammarion's novel *Omega*, the narrator comments: "The heat of the sun and of all the stars seems to be due to the transformation of their initial energy of motion, to molecular impacts [fission]; the heat thus generated is being constantly radiated into space, and this radiation will go on until every sun is cooled down to the temperature of space itself" (287).

29. J.W. Graham, "The Drafts of Virginia Woolf's 'The Searchlight' " 388. Anne Olivier Bell and Andrew McNeillie note, "From 7 September until 3 November [1940] an average of 200 German bombers attacked London every night; from 10 September, instead of relying upon interception and directed anti-aircraft fire, the defensive tactic was transformed into a continuous barrage of anti-aircraft fire accompanied by a blaze of weaving searchlight beams – a measure immensely heartening to Londoners" (*D5*: 318, n. 5).

30. While it is debated whether telescopes date back to ancient Egypt and China, traditionally the telescope is believed to have first emerged in Europe.

31. It was not, apparently, until sometime in the autumn of 1609 that Galileo recorded his earliest telescopic astronomical observations (Annibale Fantoli, *Galileo: For Copernicanism and for the Church* 104).

32. Galileo had, in fact, in a letter to the Doge Leonardo Donato dated August 1609, described the telescope's military potential:

    I have made a telescope, a thing for every maritime and terrestrial affair and an under-taking of inestimable worth. One is able to discover enemy sails and fleets at a greater distance than customary, so that we can discover him [the enemy] two hours or more before he discovers us, and by distinguishing the number and quality of the vessels judge of his force whether to set out to chase him, or to fight, or to run away. (Quoted in Bernal, *The Social Function of Science* 187, n. 2.)

    Bernal describes Galileo as a professor of military science (*The Social Function of Science* 168). I have been unable to corroborate that title through any other source; however, one of Galileo's projects while he was at the University of Padua focused on ordnance trajectories and the velocity of artillery shells (James Reston, *Galileo: A Life* 84). Timothy Ferris and Annibale Fantoli independently note that Galileo's initial interest in the telescope was based on its marketability for military use (*Coming of Age in The Milky Way* 86–7; *Galileo: For Copernicanism and For the Church* 103).

33. "Virginia Woolf's Keen Sensitivity to War: Its Roots and Its Impact on Her Novels," *Virginia Woolf and War: Fiction, Reality, and Myth* 15.

34. Bazin and Lauter, "Virginia Woolf's Keen Sensitivity to War: Its Roots and Its Impact on Her Novels" 15.

35. The holograph version of this text is dated 29–30 November 1928, and is located in the Berg Collection. I am grateful to Stuart N. Clarke for this information.

36. Ann Banfield notes that images of flight in Woolf's essay "The Moment: Summer's Night" evoke for Woolf the possibility "to imagine other worlds" (*The Phantom Table* 186). Woolf comments in that essay that flight affords new perspectives of earth without "boundaries, these pryings over hedge into hidden compartments of different colours," and allows the human imagination to soar to the mountaintops to "visit in splendour, augustly, peaks; and there lie exposed, bare, on the spine [of the mountain], high up, to the cold light of the moon rising, and when the moon rises, single, solitary, behold her..." (*CE*2: 294–5).

37. In July 1931, Virginia wrote to Ethyl Smyth about the quality of a Zeiss camera that she and Leonard purchased: "[W]e rushed with impetuosity into a camera shop... and bought a superb Zeiss camera, costing £20, and said to be unrivalled in the portrayal of the human – if mine can be said to be human – face" (*L*4: 361). Likewise, the planetarium that Vita Sackville-West visited in Berlin may have been built by the Zeiss company. In 1920 or so, the Carl Zeiss Optical Works had designed and manufactured the modern planetarium. Zeiss also provided optical equipment to Mount Wilson Observatory. Edwin Hubble also owned a pair of Zeiss field-glasses. As Grace Hubble recalls, "He bought these in London, while he was abroad in 1922, and on Christmas Eve, when

he was on Mt. Wilson observing, sent them to me with a note: 'I have taken the liberty of testing and adjusting the lenses and prisms in our optical shop. You should be able to pick up the satellites of Jupiter' " (The Edwin Hubble Papers, the Huntington Library, HUB 7 82[9]).

38. Burstein has theorized that the pre-World War I "English penchant for knowing more about insects" coincided with a mass interest in "things with 'the works on the outside'" like insects and soldiers ("Waspish Segments: Lewis, Prosthesis, Fascism," *MODERNISM/modernity* 156–7). Woolf's question regarding humans' relation to insects appears in a diary entry written within less than one week of her learning that the Eton tutor and his fiancée had fallen into a ravine in Switzerland and had died (*D3*: 315).

39. In May 1940, Woolf recorded in her diary the sound of war planes fighting overhead near Rodmell: "Pop-pop-pop, as we play bowls. Probably a raider over Eastbourne way" (*D5*: 284). In that same entry she noted her formulation of the crucial element to the "Thoughts on Peace" essay: "This idea struck me....Thinking is my fighting" (*D5*: 284). Beer points out that the Woolfs were "living near Gatwick aerodrome in the 1930s – first a place for light aircraft then a military airfield" (*Virginia Woolf: The Common Ground* 4).

40. Killen notes that Woolf read Whitehead's text ("Virginia Woolf in the Light of Modern Physics" 39).

41. Sharov and Novikov, *Edwin Hubble: The Discoverer of the Big Bang Universe* 93–4.

42. "The Scientist at War," *The Nature of Science and Other Lectures* 66.

43. Quoted in Sharov and Novikov, *Edwin Hubble: The Discoverer of the Big Bang Universe* 100.

44. "The War That Must Not Happen." *The Nature of Science and Other Lectures* 75.

45. "The War that Must Not Happen." *The Nature of Science and Other Lectures* 81.

46. "Dreams and Facts." *Athenaeum* 4643 (25 April 1919): 232.

47. Letter to Robert Nichols, 17 February 1930, *The Letters of Aldous Huxley* 330.

48. Letter from Woolf to Vita Sackville-West, 3 December 1939, *The Letters of Vita Sackville-West to Virginia Woolf* 429.

3 MAPS, GLOBES, AND "SOLID OBJECTS"

1. As editor of *Cornhill* magazine, Leslie Stephen often included articles on popular astronomy in issues of the journal. Given the popularity of Flammarion's texts, and that Woolf read in French, it is likely she knew his work.

2. The date of this diary entry is 27 February 1926. Woolf's comment regarding the moon rising over Persia refers to letters Vita Sackville-West had sent to Virginia during her journey to Persia from January to May 1926. In January, Vita wrote to Virginia to say that she would visit at night the Temple of Amen, considered the greatest of the Egyptian temples at Karnak, and noted "It is full moon, and it quite frightens me to think what it will be like" (*The Letters of Vita Sackville-West to Virginia Woolf* 94). In *Passenger to Teheran*, which Leonard

and Virginia published in November 1926, Vita recorded her impressions of the temple in moonlight: "Piled on fantastic ruin, obelisks pricked the sky; the colossal aisle soared...shafts of light struck the columns...The black, enormous temple was shot through and through by those broad beams of light" (45). The light of the moon on the Temple, part of the ruins at Thebes on the Nile, evoked for Vita a sense that "both are old [the moon and the temple], so old that both have become unreal to us; unreal and charged with a significance we are quite at a loss reasonably to interpret..." (*Passenger* 42). Interestingly, Ann Banfield cites Woolf's diary entry about the moon over Persia to illustrate how Woolf's "moments of being," in Banfield's terms, "hold within themselves eternity" (*The Phantom Table* 372).

3. Leslie Stephen, *An Agnostic's Apology* 87; Ann Banfield, *The Phantom Table* 312.

4. Ann Banfield's *The Phantom Table* (2000) is by far the most comprehensive study of Woolf's work in relation to that of Bertrand Russell. See also Jaakko Hintikka, "Virginia Woolf and Our Knowledge of the External World," *The Journal of Aesthetics and Art Criticism* 31.1 (Fall 1979): 5–14 and Joanne Wood, "Lighthouse Bodies: The Neutral Monism of Virginia Woolf and Bertrand Russell," *Journal of the History of Ideas* 55.3 (July 1994): 483–502. Killen in "Virginia Woolf in the Light of Modern Physics" comments on Woolf's conversations with Russell and the scientific debates driven by advances in atomic physics.

5. I borrow this phrase from J.B.S. Haldane's essay "Possible Worlds," which is discussed in the pages that follow. According to Russell, the phrase, which also happened to be a favorite phrase of Edwin Hubble's, was drawn from the work of Gottfried Wilhelm von Leibniz (Russell, *Our Knowledge of the External World* 190).

6. Gertler's work was revered by Vanessa Bell, as well as art critic Roger Fry and artist Duncan Grant (Hussey, *Virginia Woolf A to Z* 101).

7. James Jeans also apparently referred to Russell's blue spectacles to make the point that mathematics provides one means by which cosmologists can create models of the physical universe. See a discussion of this in Chapter Four.

8. Russell contended that mental phenomena, or the various appearances of an object, are just as real as physical phenomena: "It is supposed that the table (for example) causes our sense-data of sight and touch, but must, since these are altered by the point of view and the intervening medium [the blue spectacles] be quite different from the sense-data to which it gives rise...The first thing to realise is that there are no such things as 'illusions of sense.' Objects of sense, even when they occur in dreams, are the most indubitably real objects known to us" (*Our Knowledge of the External World* 92–3). Interestingly, Vita Sackville-West dedicated to Woolf her novella *Seducers in Ecuador* (1924), in which the protagonist, Lomax, finds the world radically transformed by the colored spectacles he wears. From the story's beginning, Lomax takes up the tourist's habit of wearing colored glasses. "He already had his blue pair, bought in London; in Cairo he bought an amber pair, and a green, and a black.... [B]ut soon it ceased to be an amusement and became an obsession – a vice"

(Sackville-West 14). The colored glasses change Lomax's view of reality. However, there is a point of convergence between *Seducers in Ecuador* and "Solid Objects" (which does not include blue spectacles) and has to do with where the obsession is located, either in the perception itself as with Lomax, or in the object as with the young man of Woolf's story.

9. While this diary entry for 3 December 1921 does not mention where Woolf had conversed with Russell, she wrote to Vanessa on Nov. 13, "We've been asked to Garsington" (*L2*: 493).

10. See Chapter One on Woolf's association with the journal the *Athenaeum*. "Solid Objects," for instance, was published in the *Athenaeum* in 1920. Judith Killen comments on Woolf's exchanges with Russell ("Virginia Woolf in the Light of Modern Physics" 36–7).

11. Mark Hussey characterized the 1917 Club as a group of "leftist intellectuals, artists and politicians" (*Virginia Woolf A to Z* 191). I am grateful to Judith Killen for pointing out to me the existence of the 1917 Club and Virginia and Leonard's association with it.

12. Woolf spent so much time at the club that she could write to Vanessa at length about scandal among its members (See *L2*: 209–13).

13. The lectures were collected into a volume and published under the same title in 1921.

14. Joanne Wood, "Lighthouse Bodies: The Neutral Monism of Virginia Woolf and Bertrand Russell," *Journal of the History of Ideas* 55.3 (July 1994): 492.

15. In August 1883, the Krakatau volcano, located near the islands of Sumatra and Java, erupted. The blast produced huge tsunamis, the waves of which reached 140 feet above sea level and caused more than 34,000 fatalities.

16. Russell further noted, "I have always ardently desired to find some justification for the emotions inspired by certain things that seemed to stand outside human life and to deserve feelings of awe... the starry heavens... the vastness of the scientific universe..." (*My Philosophical Development* 262).

17. "Lighthouse Bodies: The Neutral Monism of Virginia Woolf and Bertrand Russell," 490.

18. Joanne Wood, "Lighthouse Bodies: The Neutral Monism of Virginia Woolf and Bertrand Russell" 492.

19. Regarding the fallacy of the importance of human knowledge, Russell commented "that the great processes of nebular and stellar evolution proceed according to laws in which mind plays no part" (*My Philosophical Development* 16). Russell's considerations of the problems of mind versus matter span his writing career and of course changed over time. While this text by Russell was not published in Woolf's lifetime, his commentary reflects Woolf's similar sentiments in "The Mark on the Wall."

20. Haldane refers here to a parsec, which is 3.26 light-years.

21. The British and American systems of very large numbers are not equivalent. The British billion traditionally equaled a million million; whereas, in the US a billion equaled a thousand million.

22. Letter to Virginia Woolf, 16 July 1924, *The Letters of Vita Sackville-West to Virginia Woolf* 50.
23. The Alpine Club was founded in 1857 by a group of serious British climbers including upper middle class lawyers, businessmen, dons, and clergymen. Leslie Stephen became a club member in 1858. He was named president in 1865, and edited the *Alpine Journal* from 1868 to 1872 (Noel Annan, *Leslie Stephen: The Godless Victorian* 90).
24. Letter from Vita Sackville-West to Virginia Woolf, 16, July 1924, *The Letters of Vita Sackville-West to Virginia Woolf* 50–1.
25. Letter from Vita Sackville-West to Virginia Woolf, 16, July 1924, *The Letters of Vita Sackville-West to Virginia Woolf* 51.
26. Noel Annan, *Leslie Stephen: The Godless Victorian* 90.
27. The Dolomites are particularly treacherous as most are capped with a loose-grained, crumbling stone debris. Woolf, in fact, was keenly aware of the dangers of climbing in the Alps. She wrote in 1901 to her cousin Margaret Vaughan, who spent her youth in the Swiss Alps (Hussey, *Virginia Woolf: A to Z* 324): "What on earth can you find to do in Switzerland? For goodness sake, don't take to climbing mountains. Every newspaper almost, has a Matterhorn tragedy in it. Are you anywhere near the Matterhorn? I have the vaguest idea of your or any-bodies geography" (*L1*: 43). The much publicized climbing accident involving climbers on Edward Whymper's first ascent of the Matterhorn occurred in 1865, and is discussed in Chapter Two.
28. As an indicator of how ingrained maps are in the popular imagination, as-tronauts and cosmonauts, upon seeing the earth from space, often remarked their own surprise at not seeing visible boundaries demarcating the divisions between nations. Stapledon's novel *Star Maker* was published in 1937, the same year that Woolf was drafting *Three Guineas*. See Chapter Five for a discussion of Woolf's relationship to Stapledon.
29. Sue Roe, *Jacob's Room*, 185, n. 11. Roe makes this point with regard to a scene in Woolf's novel *Jacob's Room* (1922). The character Fanny Elmer, who is in love with Jacob Flanders, walks through London's streets thinking of Jacob (already a casualty of war) as she pauses to look in "the window of Bacon, the mapseller, in the Strand"; she notices a "large yellow globe marked with steamship lines" (*JR* 150).
30. Council on Books in War Time, "A Note on the Maps," *A War Atlas for Americans*. New York, Simon & Schuster, 1944: [i].
31. Council on Books in War Time, "A Note on the Maps," *A War Atlas for Americans*. New York, Simon & Schuster, 1944: [i].
32. Council on Books in War Time, "A Note on the Maps," *A War Atlas for Americans*. New York, Simon & Schuster, 1944: [i].
33. National Geographic Society, *The Round Earth on Flat Paper* by Wellman Chamberlin. The first orthographic maps apparently were designed by the Greek astronomer Hipparchus (c. 190–c. 125 BC) (*The Round Earth on Flat Paper* 55).

34. National Geographic Society, *The Round Earth on Flat Paper* 23. In some cases, the Society simply gave templates of maps to General Staff officers and the Army itself printed them. The Navy, too, used Society maps for navigation, even though the maps were not designed as nautical charts (*The Round Earth* 17).

35. This was the title of a series of lectures on social concerns that Russell drafted in the fall of 1916. The lectures were later published in the US under the title *Political Ideals* (1917).

36. Susan Squier celebrates Haldane's "iconoclastic willingness to embrace different subject positions" (*Babies in Bottles* 250, n. 68).

37. "Virginia Woolf's Poetics of Space: 'The Lady in the Looking Glass: A Reflection.'" *Woolf Studies Annual* 2 (1996): 105.

4 "THE RIDDLE OF THE UNIVERSE" IN *THE WAVES*

An earlier version of this chapter was previously published in *Virginia Woolf and the Arts: Selected Papers of the Sixth Annual Conference on Virginia Woolf*. Ed. Diane F. Gillespie and Leslie Hankins. New York: Pace UP, 1997. 268–76. In this expanded version there have been some revisions to the argument.

1. Jeans used the phrase "space bending back on itself" to describe Einstein's model of a finite and bounded universe in *The Universe Around Us* (69). As noted in Chapter One, Elizabeth Williamson, Smyth's great niece, taught practical classes in astronomy at University College London.

2. Woolf refers to Daniel Defoe's *A Tour thro' the whole Island of Great Britain* (1724–27), in which Defoe provides a literary map of England with in-depth descriptions of London and other major cities, and which includes multiple detailed maps.

3. I am grateful to the Royal Society in London for granting me access to the James Jeans papers archived there, and to Christopher Jeans for allowing me to quote from the papers.

4. In *The Mysterious Universe* Jeans described the earth as "a millionth part of a grain of sand out of all the sea-sand in the world" (4).

5. Virginia Woolf knew Matheson as Vita-Sackville West and Hilda hiked together through the Italian Dolomites in 1929. The BBC Written Archives holds the correspondence between Jeans and Matheson regarding the topics of his talks, as well as Jeans's BBC contractual agreements.

6. Letter to Jeans from C.A. S[iepmann]. The BBC Written Archives Centre, RCont 1 Jeans, 3 Nov. 1930.

7. Letter to Jeans from C.A. S[iepmann]. The BBC Written Archives Centre, RCont 1 Jeans, 2 Dec. 1930.

8. "Virginia Woolf's Photography and the Monk's House Albums," *Virginia Woolf in the Age of Mechanical Reproduction* 232. At least one photo of Siepmann appears in Album 3 (dated 1931) of the Monk's House Albums, along with

photos of Vita Sackville-West and William Plomer (Maggie Humm 233). Bell and McNeillie note that Siepmann stayed with the Woolfs in September 1932 and with them attended a performance of Vita Sackville-West's *The Land* (*D4*: 125).

9. Vita Sackville-West, "Books in General." *The Listener* (19 Nov. 1930): 844.

10. "Books in General." *The Listener* (19 Nov. 1930): 844; Sylva Norman, "The Universe and Its God." *Nation & Athenaeum* (24 Jan. 1931): 546.

11. Hugh Sykes Davies, "The Mysterious Universe." *The Criterion* 10.10 (April 1931): 514.

12. Geoffrey Sainsbury, "Anthropomorphic Universe." *The Adelphi* (January 1931): 339.

13. As noted in Chapter One, Sullivan served the *Athenaeum* as an assistant editor to John Middleton Muray.

14. Roger Fry, "Art and Science." *Athenaeum* 4649 (6 June 1919): 434.

15. Roger Fry, "The Artist's Vision." *Athenaeum* 4654 (11 July 1919): 594 and 595.

16. Roger Fry, "The Artist's Vision." *Athenaeum* 4654 (11 July 1919): 595.

17. J.W.N. Sullivan, "The Scientific Contribution." *Athenaeum* (30 April, 1920): 577.

18. J.W.N. Sullivan, "The Scientific Contribution." *Athenaeum* (30 April, 1920): 577.

19. J.W.N. Sullivan, "The Scientific Contribution." *Athenaeum* (30 April, 1920): 577.

20. Throughout her life, Woolf repeatedly referred to her novels and short fiction as "experiments." Woolf described *The Waves* to Vita Sackville-West as a "complete failure – only a very interesting (to me) experiment" (*L4*: 378).

21. Banfield discusses Fry's admiration for Bertrand Russell's work as well as Fry's interest in "align[ing] art with science" (*The Phantom Table* 250; see also 249–58).

22. Ann Banfield, *The Phantom Table* 249.

23. Quoted in Mark Hussey, *Virginia Woolf: A to Z* 96.

24. Jane Marcus, "Britannia Rules *The Waves*." *Decolonizing Tradition: New Views of Twentieth-Century 'British' Literary Canons* 160.

25. Judith Killen was among the first to point out that references to scientific concepts popularized by Jeans, Eddington, and Einstein permeate *The Waves* ("Virginia Woolf in the Light of Modern Physics." Diss. Louisville: University of Louisville [November 1994]: 93).

26. Judith Killen cites this passage as an example of Woolf's incorporation of Jeans's texts in *The Waves* ("Virginia Woolf in the Light of Modern Physics" 93). For a more complete discussion of passages from *The Waves* that incorporate references to Jeans's work see Chapter Five.

27. Virginia Woolf, *The Waves: The Two Holograph Drafts*. Transcribed and edited by J.W. Graham 363.

28. See Chapter Three for a discussion of Haldane's essay "Possible Worlds."

29. Heidegger, "The Age of the World Picture." *The Question Concerning Technology and Other Essays* 134.

30. Heidegger, "The Age of the World Picture." *The Question Concerning Technology and Other Essays* 128, 134.
31. Heidegger, "The Age of the World Picture." *The Question Concerning Technology and Other Essays* 133–4.
32. Haraway, "Situated Knowledges." *Simians, Cyborgs and Women: The Reinvention of Nature* 196.
33. Virginia Woolf, "The Narrow Bridge of Art." *Granite and Rainbow* 12, 11.
34. Holleyman and Treacher, *Catalogue of Books from the Library of Leonard and Virginia Woolf*. V/s, Section V, 9; Catalogue Index 29.
35. Virginia Woolf, "The Narrow Bridge of Art." *Granite and Rainbow* 18.

5 WOOLF AND STAPLEDON ENVISION NEW WORLDS

1. Quoted in Frank White, *The Overview Effect: Space Exploration and Human Evolution*. 36–7. Russell Schweickart served as Lunar Module pilot for Apollo 9.
2. Quoted in Frank White, *The Overview Effect* 11.
3. Quoted in Frank White, *The Overview Effect* 187. Michael Collins served in July 1966 on the crew of Gemini 10, and in July 1969 as the command module pilot for Apollo 11, the first moon landing mission.
4. The title of Stapledon's novel stems from the final scenes in which the narrator encounters a god-like inventor, the maker of universes.
5. Among the earliest and best photographic images of earth taken from space were those filmed by the US Navy's Viking 11 rocket which carried an aircraft camera to 158 miles in May 1954. Space historian William Burrows describes those images: "Above the horizon, out beyond Earth's marvelously crisp edge, there was the stark blackness of deep space" (*This New Ocean* 135). Images of earth from space had been taken from rockets as early as 1947, but the quality was poor (*This New Ocean* 135). Even the first satellite in space, Sputnik 1 flown in 1957, was capable of only radio transmission.
6. James Pawelczyk, assistant professor of physiology and kinesiology at the Pennsylvania State University. Personal Interview, November 1998. Pawelczyk served in 1998 on the STS-90 Neurolab shuttle mission.
7. Crossley, *Olaf Stapledon* 433, n. 61. See also *D5*: 99 n. 21. Stapledon's letter to Woolf was dated 14 July 1937.
8. R.A. Scott-James, "Virginia Woolf's New Novel." *London Mercury* 35.210 (April 1937): 629–31; Bertrand Russell, "War in the Heavens." *London Mercury* 36.213 (July 1937): 297.
9. In April 1938, as Woolf began "sketching out a new book" which would eventually become *Between the Acts*, she noted her determination that unlike *The Years*, her next book would not "lay down a scheme; call in all the cosmic immensities; & force [her] tired & diffident brain to embrace another whole..." (*D5*: 135).
10. See also Camille Flammarion, *Popular Astronomy: A General Description of the Heavens*. Trans. J. Ellard Gore. New York: D. Appleton and Company, 1931:154.

J. Ellard Gore translated and published Flammarion's *Astronomie Populaire* in Britain in 1894; he later published a second edition in 1907, the year that Sara in Woolf's novel ponders the details of the lunar landscape. The illustrations in Gore's text, however, were not as distinctive as those in the editions published in France. As Leon Stover has demonstrated, H.G. Wells also was inspired by Flammarion's text. In his novel *The First Men in the Moon* (1901) Wells described a frozen lunar surface covered in vegetation. The "cliff-like walls" of enormous craters "showed a disordered escarpment of drab and greyish rock, lined here and there with bands and crevices of snow" (Stover, ed. *The First Men in the Moon* by H.G. Wells 95).

11. Woolf has Kitty read from a 16 April 1880 *Times* [London] news article that reported electric light experiments had been conducted by the British Navy. The *Times* report was taken from an earlier news announcement in the *Gibraltar Chronicle* dated 5 April 1880. The *Times* report read: "On Saturday night at 9:30 o'clock, to the great astonishment of those who were not prepared for it, but who happened to be looking towards the bay, a brilliant light was seen to burst forth suddenly, shooting out a prolonged ray across the water and on to the Rock, which is lighted up in a most vivid manner" ("Electric Light Experiments." *The Times* 16 April 1880: 11).

12. Gardner, Robert, et al., *Conways' All the World's Fighting Ships*. I am grateful to Peter Hingley, historian for the Royal Astronomical Society [London], for his assistance on this point. Additional details from the actual *Times* article Woolf quoted indicate that these naval vessels were investigating the use of an early type of searchlight. The report read: "Owing to the concentration of the light as the instrument necessary to permit of its rays being reflected to a distance, the sphere of its action is unavoidably limited..." ("Electric Light Experiments." *The Times* 16 April 1880: 11). Electric light was still quite new in 1880. The first carbon filament incandescent bulb was exhibited in London in 1879 (*The Timeline Book of Science* 194). As further evidence of the type of light experiments the Royal Navy was conducting at that time, a *Times* article from June 1880 reported the "successful official trial of the electric light was made on board the *Inflexible* at Portsmouth yesterday with the object of ascertaining the amount of horse-power required per light, the cost, efficiency for illuminating, duration of carbons, and other practical questions" ("Naval and Military Intelligence." *The Times* 8 June 1880: 10).

13. Light actually travels at a velocity of 186,282 miles per second, or roughly six trillion miles in one year.

14. C.A. Young's *Elementary Astronomy* (1890) reported on the use of the term "light-year": "It is better, and now usual, to take as the unit of stellar distance the so-called 'light-year'..." (quoted in *The Oxford English Dictionary*, 2nd ed. 1989).

15. "Giant Star Equal to 27,000,000 Suns like Ours." *New York Times* 30 Dec. 1920: 2. Michelson was awarded the Nobel Prize (1907) for Physics, and in 1920 was serving as chair of the Physics Department at the University of Chicago. A research associate at Mount Wilson Observatory,

Michelson became acquainted with some of the leading astronomers in the US and in Britain including Edwin Hubble, George Ellery Hale, James Jeans, Harlow Shapley, and James Ritchey (Livingston, *The Master of Light* 274).

16. Michelson's interferometer produced interference patterns from light waves emitted from two different light sources. The device provided a means of calculating the distance between light sources having very small angular separation. Angular diameter refers to the apparent diameter of a celestial object or how an object appears in a telescope, as opposed to its actual size. As a result of Michelson's work, for the first time, the distance between double stars, or between the limbs of a star, could be determined with relative accuracy. Prior to this, the size and mass of a star could be estimated only by its apparent brightness and by its calculated distance from earth (Arthur Eddington, *Stars and Atoms* 76).

17. "Giant Star Equal to 27,000,000 Suns Like Ours." *New York Times* 30 Dec. 1920: 1.

18. James Kaler claims that Betelgeuse is far larger than Michelson initially thought, and that the red supergiant could overfill the orbit of Jupiter by 30 percent (*Stars* 87). However, Dr. Leo Connolly, an astronomer in the Department of Physics at California State University, San Bernardino, reports that Betelgeuse extends to about 600 solar radii, or to about twice the orbit of Mars, which would be smaller than the orbit of Jupiter.

19. "Measuring the Stars, And Detecting Ether: The Interferometer." *Illustrated London News* 18 April 1925: 677; "Measuring the Stars." *The Times* 12 March 1925: 13. The red giant Mira is not in actuality as large as Betelgeuse. Mira, which varies in size like other red giants, has a diameter of about 200 solar radii and extends to about the size of the orbit of earth around the sun. I am grateful to Dr. Leo Connolly for this information. Larry Webster, chief solar observer at Mount Wilson Observatory, points out that the red giant star Arcturus, which Woolf and Vita Sackville-West often mentioned in their writing, has a radius eighteen times that of our sun; that figure equals roughly eight million miles. By comparison, the radius of Betelgeuse measures over 1,300 times the radius of our sun (James Kaler, *Stars* 87).

20. The Woolfs owned both volumes of poetry by Sackville-West (Elizabeth Steele, *Virginia Woolf's Literary Sources and Allusions* 325).

21. I am very grateful to Stuart Clarke for this information on the early drafts of "The Searchlight." In the published version of the story, the planet Jupiter, the largest planet in our solar system, is mentioned.

22. Eddington, *New Pathways in Science* 29. Gillian Beer noted Eddington's analogy in "'The Least Like to My Own Ideas': Science and Creativity in Woolf's 1930s' Writing," a paper she gave at the 1997 Virginia Woolf conference titled "Virginia Woolf and her Influences." Today, of course, such a model of the atom no longer supports observed phenomena.

23. Judith Killen, "Virginia Woolf in the Light of Modern Physics" 143. Killen also discusses the popular fascination with both atomic physics and cosmology.

24. Judith Killen, "Virginia Woolf in the Light of Modern Physics" 144; *TY* 154.
25. For the sake of clarity, I refer to the *Star Maker* narrator in the singular, but in the novel the narrator's mind melds with other alien intelligences and jointly these intelligences range through the universe observing civilizations in various galaxies.
26. In the late 1920s, when Jeans was first broadcasting for the BBC, he received letters from listeners complaining that they had trouble picking up the broadcasts. These listeners should have been within range of the BBC broadcasts in London, but the broadcast signal apparently was not entirely consistent. See letters to Jeans archived at the BBC Written Archives Centre.
27. In a review of Gilbert Watson's *The Voice of the South* (1905), Woolf noted Watson's comparisons of the wastes of the desert to the vast expanse of the sea. She writes, "All day the little caravan moves on through 'the high sea of the desert'.... By nightfall the green line on the horizon is reached, and they seek shelter in the oasis as in 'an open boat upon the rolling desert sea.' This metaphor of the sea is one that recurs so often that by degrees the two ideas of the desert and the ocean rise and blend spontaneously in the mind" (*E1*: 72–3). In an essay published the same year, "A Walk by Night," Woolf compared the expanses of space to the desolate sea as the "trackless ocean of the night" (*E1*: 81).
28. Stapledon, "Poem 17 from *First Volley, Astronomical*," *An Olaf Stapledon Reader* 306.
29. Stapledon, "Poem 17 from *First Volley, Astronomical*," *An Olaf Stapledon Reader* 306.
30. Stapledon, "Poem 1 from *The Nether Worlds*," *An Olaf Stapledon Reader* 307.
31. Candidus, "The Mystery of Man: From Nothing to Nothing: A Famous Scientist's Dismal Philosophy." *North Mail & Newcastle Chronicle* 7. Dec. 1930. Cited from James Jeans's notebooks of news clippings, which do not contain page numbers.
32. Jessica Burstein, "Waspish Segments: Lewis, Prosthesis, Fascism." *MODERNISM/modernity* 4.2 (1997): 156, 157.
33. Burstein, "Waspish Segments: Lewis, Prosthesis, Fascism." *MODERNISM/modernity* 4.2 (1997): 157. In her essay, Burstein offers a remarkable theory on what she calls "cold modernism" in an explanation of how modernist writers anticipated post-modernist literary strategies.
34. The play also was widely performed throughout Europe and the US (William Harkins, *Karel Čapek* 9).
35. "The Theatre." *London Mercury* 34.202 (August 1936): 347–8.
36. Julian Huxley once noted: "Ants are among the very few organisms other than man which go to war" (*Ants* 85). While there are no earthly varieties of yellow ants, David Pankenier, professor of Chinese at Lehigh University, pointed out at the Inspiration of Astronomical Phenomena Conference II (Malta 1999) that the yellow ants most likely reflect the Čapeks' criticism of western European and American anxieties regarding Asian cultures.
37. Even as I have identified the connections between a fascination in the 1920s with cosmology and insects, so also in the 1990s, with the development of a

new generation of astronomical telescopes like the Hubble Space Telescope, there was an emergence of blockbuster animation movies on insects such as *ANTZ* (1998) and *A Bug's Life* (1998). In fact, the plot of *ANTZ*, with the ant general attempting to position himself as dictator of the colony, reconstructs the major themes of the Čapeks' play. In one poignant scene of *ANTZ*, several insects sit by a fire, gazing up at the stars, and wonder whether other worlds exist beyond their little world. That question is answered when the ant Bala and her worker ant friend, Z, arrive in insectopia, only to nearly meet their end on the bottom of a tennis shoe. It is also interesting to note that in *A Bug's Life*, an entire ant colony is preserved through the technology of the telescope.

38. J.B.S. Haldane, "The Last Judgment," *Possible Worlds and Other Essays* 310.
39. See *The Voyage Out* (1915), *Night and Day* (1919), and *Jacob's Room* (1922), *The Waves* (1932) as well as short fiction selections like "Kew Gardens" (1919) and "The Mark on the Wall" (1917). These represent only a few of the texts that incorporate multiple scenes in which insects, moths, and butterflies are mentioned.
40. Woolf noted in her diary that she was the "lantern bearer" on this occasion (*PA* 144). The event also gets reworked in Chapter Two of *Jacob's Room*.
41. These lines appear in what seems to be the scene that inspired Woolf to remark in her diary: "I don't think I have ever been more excited over a book.... I am doing the scene where Peggy listens to them talking & bursts out. It was this outburst that excited me so" (*D4*: 241).
42. The lines cited translate as: "The mediocrity of the universe shocks and revolts me... the poverty of human beings annihilates me." Interestingly, Lucien Rudaux's *Sur les Autres Mondes* (*On Other Worlds*) (1937), a popular astronomy text, was bound in green leather with a gilt sun and little stars, but this is obviously not the book Peggy reads.
43. I am grateful to Stuart Clarke for information on the publication of the essay.
44. The first biography of Woolf by Aileen Pippett was titled *The Moth and the Star*. Though a perceptive reader of Woolf's work, Pippett does not make the kind of connection between the moth and the star that I am drawing. The title of Pippett's book, she comments in the Preface, resulted from her attempt to "reconstruct this very elusive and complex personality, fragile as a moth and enduring as a star" (*The Moth and the Star* viii).
45. Quoted in Garbedian, "The Star Stuff That is Man." *New York Times Magazine* 11 Aug. 1929: 5:23.
46. I am grateful to my colleague Christina Jarvis for pointing out that it is conjectured that should an extinction level nuclear event occur on earth, only the cockroaches would survive.
47. Holleyman and Treacher, *Catalogue of Books From the Library of Leonard & Virginia Woolf*, V/s, Section V: 9. As early as 1923 in *The ABC of Atoms*, Bertrand Russell had envisioned the military applications of fission: "[A] great deal of work on the structure of the atom was done during the war. It is probable that it will ultimately be used for making more deadly explosives

and projectiles than any yet invented" (5). Russell speculated further that "an enormous amount of energy" must be locked in the nucleus of an atom and would be released if the nucleus could be artificially split (*The ABC of Atoms* 130).

48. This city in northern Spain had been invaded first by rebel Spanish troops, and then attacked by Franco's fascist forces; the women and children of the Basque region were evacuated to London and then placed in safety zones in the British countryside (*D*5: 97, n. 16).

49. In August 1937 shortly after Julian Bell's death, Woolf purchased Jeans's *The Mysterious Universe*, though she had read the book much earlier. This she noted in a diary entry in which she reported having received multiple letters of sympathy regarding Julian, whom, she poignantly commented "stalks beside me, in many different shapes" (*D*5: 107). That same month, the Woolfs obtained a telescope from Elizabeth Williamson, and with the help of Eddy Sackville-West had it set up at Monks House (*D*5: 109).

50. Quoted in Charles Hoffman, "Virginia Woolf's Manuscript Revisions of *The Years*." *PMLA* 84 (Jan. 1969): 80.

51. Elizabeth Steele, *Virginia Woolf's Literary Sources and Allusions* 338.

52. Interestingly, in *Through Space and Time* (1934) Jeans had explained a recent theory that the continents in some past age were nearly all connected and have since drifted apart.

53. This scene becomes conflated with Miss La Trobe's vision for her next play: "It would be midnight; there would be two figures, half concealed by a rock. The curtain would rise. What would the first words be? The words escaped her" (*BTA* 130).

54. Quoted in MacKinnon, Douglas, and Joseph Baldanza. *Footprints: The 12 Men Who Walked on the Moon Reflect on their Flights, Their Lives, and the Future*. 221. Dave Scott, who was commander of Apollo 15, was quoting Norman Cousins in this instance.

55. F.S. Marvin, "The Human Value of the New Astronomy." *Hibbert Journal* 27 (Jan. 1929): 250.

56. F.S. Marvin, "The Human Value of the New Astronomy." *Hibbert Journal* 27 (Jan. 1929): 250.

57. In *Beginning Again*, Leonard noted: "My conclusion was that the first step towards the prevention of war must be the creation of 'an international authority to prevent war' and I examined the minimum requirements for such a league of states if it was to have any chance of success. [Sydney] Webb and I then drew up a formal international treaty for the establishment of such a supernational authority for the prevention of war, based upon my conclusions.... This was the first detailed study of a League of Nations to be published..." (186–7).

58. I am grateful to Peter Schroeder, professor of English at California State University, San Bernardino, for clarifying the Dante lines. Peter kindly pointed out Dante's fascination with linking aspects of astronomy, light, and perspective with religious concepts, and graciously directed me to the closing line of the *Commedia*.

59. Dante, *Dante Alighieri's Divine Comedy: Purgatory.* Trans. Mark Musa, 145, lines 55–7.
60. Dante, *Dante Alighieri's Divine Comedy: Purgatory.* Trans. Mark Musa. 147, lines 73–5.
61. Dante, *The Paradiso of Dante Alighieri*, Trans. Thomas Okey. Canto 33, lines 144–5.
62. Letter to Grace Hubble dated 30 September 1953. See the Edwin Hubble Papers, HUB 676, Box 16.

6 *THREE GUINEAS*: WOOLF'S GLOBAL VISION

1. "Situated Knowledges," *Simians, Cyborgs, and Women: The Reinvention of Nature* 190.
2. "Situated Knowledges" *Simians, Cyborgs, and Women* 190.
3. Emily Dalgarno makes the same argument in the final chapter of *Virginia Woolf and the Visible World* (2001). I wrote this chapter in 1998 and came across Dalgarno's text while doing final proofs for this book project.
4. As David Bradshaw points out, Woolf had multiple connections to the war in Spain. By the mid-1930s, she had become involved with two pacifist organizations, For Intellectual Liberty (FIL), which supported the Republican effort, and the British Section of an organization titled, the International Association of Writers for the Defense of Culture (IAWDC). See Bradshaw, "British Writers and Anti-Fascism in the 1930s, Part I: The Bray and Drone of Tortured Voices," *Woolf Studies Annual* 3 (1997): 3–27.
5. Possibly through her affiliations with pacifist organizations such as For Intellectual Liberty (FIL), Woolf apparently received packets of pictures mailed from the war front (*L6*: 83).
6. "Guernica." *London Mercury* 36.214 (1937): 330–9; italics mine.
7. See, for example, the *Illustrated London News* issues for 18 April 1931: 645; and 5 Nov. 1938: 837.
8. Brothers researched six British papers including four that were pro-Republican (The *Daily Herald*, the *Daily Worker*, *Reynold's News*, and *Picture Post*) and two that were pro-Insurgent or pro-Franco (The *Illustrated London News*, and the *Daily Mail*) (*War and Photography* 4).
9. The *Daily Herald* was a labour-backed daily founded in 1912; its first literary editor was Siegfried Sassoon, the World War I poet whom Woolf knew. E.M. Forster also worked for the paper. Virginia published at least two essays in the paper in the early 1920s (Andrew McNeillie, "Daily Herald," *E3*: 520–1).
10. Jeans's talk was broadcast by the BBC on 24 February 1930.
11. The talks in this series also were later published in a two-volume collection, titled *Points of View* (1930) and *More Points of View* (1930). The Woolfs owned the first volume to this series, edited by G. Lowes Dickinson, whom Leonard met at Cambridge and admired throughout his life. (Holleyman and Treacher, *Catalogue of Books from the Library of Leonard and Virginia Woolf* V/s, V, 22; Catalogue Index 18).

12. Squier offers a fascinating cultural study of the interconnections between emerging visualization and reproductive technologies and literary texts of the modernist period. See *Babies in Bottles: Twentieth-Century Visions of Reproductive Technology* (1994).
13. I am grateful to Susan Squier for pointing out to me Jeans's use of Blake's "Milton," as well as Woolf's use of the same poem in her essay, "Thoughts on Peace in an Air Raid," in which Woolf develops anti-war and anti-eugenics arguments. Perhaps it was in direct opposition to Jeans's talk that Woolf cited Blake in her admonition to fight with the mind instead of with military weapons (CE: 174).
14. Roughly forty letters in response to this single broadcast are archived at The Royal Society in London. I am grateful to The Royal Society for allowing me to research their holdings which includes the largest public collection of Jeans's papers and manuscripts.
15. Letter from E.C. Cull to Jeans, 24 Feb. 1930, Dorking, The James Jeans Papers, The Royal Society, London.
16. Letter from William Brown to Jeans, 25 Feb. 1930, Granville Terrace, The James Jeans Papers, The Royal Society, London.
17. Letter from A.H. Petty to Jeans, 24 Feb. 1930, Inglewood, The James Jeans Papers, The Royal Society, London.
18. Letter from Charles Barton to Jeans, 8 March 1930, Essex, The James Jeans Papers, The Royal Society, London.
19. In 1912, Havelock Ellis published *The Task of Social Hygiene*, in which he argued that birthrates were lowering in the middle and upper classes.
20. The friendship between these families was quite enduring. In 1946, Dr. Stopes was called upon by Jean's second wife, Susi, requesting advice for her older son Michael on how to keep tadpoles alive after they had metamorphosed into frogs: "He doesn't know what to do with them and says they get drowned in the water" (Letter dated 25 July 1946, Stopes Papers, The British Library Manuscripts Collection, Ref Add MSS 58543 ff 47–104).
21. Draft of letter from Marie Stopes to James Jeans, Stopes Papers, The British Library Manuscripts Collection, Ref Add MSS 58543 ff. 36–64v. It is not clear whether the letter was sent. Marie also sent Jeans a draft of a collection of her poems, *Love Songs for Young Lovers*, which Jeans reviewed favorably. Even after Jeans's death, his second wife Susi maintained a long and endeared correspondence with Marie Stopes. Woolf knew Marie Stopes, and as Mark Hussey and others have noted, used Stopes's pseudonym, Mary Carmichael, as one possible name for the narrator of *A Room of One's Own*. In addition, Mary Carmichael is the name of the type of novelist of the future that Woolf praises in Chapter Five of that text.
22. Marie Stopes earned a first class in honors in botany and geology from University College London. She researched fossilized plants to earn a doctorate in paleobotany from the University of Munich.
23. *Marie Stopes and the Sexual Revolution* 134.

24. Christina Hauck, " 'To Escape the Horror of Family Life': Virginia Woolf and the British Birth Control Debate," *New Essays on Virginia Woolf*. 35, n. 28; Rose 134.

25. " 'To Escape the Horror of Family Life': Virginia Woolf and the British Birth Control Debate." *New Essays on Virginia Woolf* 15; see also *D3*: 283–4.

26. Woolf's complex and conflicted position on class and eugenics, Christina Hauck argues, is evidenced in revealing portions of *To The Lighthouse* and *Mrs. Dalloway*. Mr. Ramsay's class position becomes questionable due to his large family (Hauck 16, 26), which is exactly the size of Virginia Stephen's family. Havelock Ellis in 1912 had argued that large families generally were associated with "the pathological and abnormal classes . . . the insane, the feeble-minded, the criminal, the consumptive, the alcoholic, etc." (*The Task of Social Hygiene* 186).

27. Galton was a mountain climbing partner and friend to Leslie Stephen; together they climbed the Col du Geant in Switzerland in the summer of 1857 (Gillian Fenwick, *Leslie Stephen's Life in Letters* 173).

28. The Stephen family appears in a table of families with four or more relations who might be considered prominent literary men, and Leslie Stephen is listed along with his father, uncles and brother in the alphabetical compilation of prominent men of literature (*Hereditary Genius* 163, 180).

29. Suzanne Raitt, *Vita and Virginia: The Work and Friendship of V. Sackville-West and Virginia Woolf* 48.

30. Quoted from a posting by Jill Graham to the Virginia Woolf listserv, VWOOLF@lists.acs.ohio-state.edu, on 4 April 1998.

31. Woolf first met Smyth on 20 Feb 1930. Smyth's talk for the BBC aired on 3 March 1930, and was published back-to-back with the talk given by James Jeans in the volume *More Points of View*.

32. Woolf probably intended to write "sails."

33. In February 1930, Lady Trevelyan offered a BBC talk titled "Towards Utopia: What Women Can Do for Peace." In that talk she puts forward the same arguments that Woolf would develop in *Three Guineas*. She suggested that women should avoid talk "of the villainy of other nations and the need to subjugate them, [and] of the romance and splendour of war"; instead, women should teach children "of the lives of children in other lands" (*Listener* 5, Mar. 1930: 415). Lady Trevelyan's lecture apparently was not part of the BBC Points of View series. Lady Trevelyan may have been wife of Sir Charles Trevelyan, a Labour MP who helped raise funds during the Spanish Civil War for the Basque refugee children (*D5*: 98, 99, n. 20).

34. "Situated Knowledges," *Simians, Cyborgs, and Women* 191.

35. In 1916 Paul von Hindenburg, a very successful German field marshal in World War I, was awarded chief command of the German armies. He was elected as the second president of the German Republic and served from 1925–34. Hindenburg named Adolf Hitler chancellor of Germany in 1933.

36. "OM" stands for Order of Merit, a special honor conferred by a sovereign for distinguished achievement, and FRS stands for Fellow of The Royal Society, the oldest science society in London.

37. David Bradshaw, "British Writers and Anti-Fascism in the 1930s, Part I: The Bray and Drone of Tortured Voices," *Woolf Studies Annual* 3 (1997): 4.

38. David Bradshaw, "British Writers and Anti-Fascism in the 1930s, Part I: The Bray and Drone of Tortured Voices" 7, 23–5. I have offered only a sampling of those involved with these organizations; Bradshaw's detailed lists include many others.

39. Quoted in Bradshaw, "British Writers and Anti-Fascism in the 1930s, Part I: The Bray and Drone of Tortured Voices" 22.

40. Bradshaw, "British Writers and Anti-Fascism in the 1930s, Part I: The Bray and Drone of Tortured Voices" 6.

41. "British Writers and Anti-Fascism in the 1930s, Part I: The Bray and Drone of Tortured Voices" 7.

42. "Science, Art and Society." *London Mercury* 38 (October 1938): 528.

43. Woolf noted in her diary that she had "never forgotten [her] vision of a fin rising on a wide blank sea. No biographer could possibly guess this important fact about my life in the late summer of 1926: yet biographers pretend they know people" (*D3*: 153).

Bibliography

Alexander, Jean. *The Venture of Form in the Novels of Virginia Woolf*. Port Washington: Kennikat, 1974.

Alighieri, Dante. *The Paradiso of Dante Alighieri*. Trans. Thomas Okey. The Temple Classics. 1901. London: J.M. Dent & Sons, 1941.

The Purgatorio of Dante Alighieri. Trans. Thomas Okey. The Temple Classics. 1901. London: J.M. Dent & Sons, 1941.

Dante Alighieri's Divine Comedy: Purgatory. Vol. 3. Verse Translation and Commentary by Mark Musa. Bloomington: Indiana University Press, 2000.

Allen, Carleton K. Letter to Edwin Hubble. 29 Dec. 1936. The Edwin Hubble Papers HUB 102, Box 9. The Huntington Library, San Marino, CA.

Annan, Noel. *Leslie Stephen: The Godless Victorian*. London: Weidenfeld and Nicolson, 1984.

"Asteroid carries collision risk." *The Press-Enterprise* [Riverside, CA] 25 Jul. 2002: A13.

"Asteroid passes in 'close shave.'" *The Press-Enterprise* [Riverside, CA] 21 Jun. 2002: A2.

Back, Anthony. *Constructing Reality: Multiple Perspectives in Ulysses and The Waves*. Stanford Honors Essay in Humanities. No. 24. Stanford: Humanities Honors Program, 1983.

Baldwin, Dean. *Virginia Woolf: A Study of the Short Fiction*. Boston: Twayne, 1989.

Banfield, Ann. *The Phantom Table: Woolf, Fry, Russell and the Epistemology of Modernism*. Cambridge University Press, 2000.

Banks, Joanne Trautmann. "Some New Woolf Letters." *Modern Fiction Studies* 30.2 (Summer 1984): 175–97.

Bartkevicius, Jocelyn. "A Form of One's Own: Virginia Woolf's Art of the Portrait Essay." *Iowa Review* 22.1 (Winter 1992): 123–34.

Barton, Charles. Letter to James Jeans. 8 March 1930. The James Jeans Papers. The Royal Society, London.

Bazin, Nancy Topping and Jane Hamovit Lauter. "Virginia Woolf's Keen Sensitivity to War: Its Roots and Its Impact on Her Novels." *Virginia Woolf and War: Fiction, Reality, and Myth*. Ed. Mark Hussey. Syracuse University Press, 1991: 14–39.

Beer, Gillian. *Arguing with the Past: Essays in Narrative from Woolf to Sidney.* London: Routledge, 1989.

"Eddington and the Idiom of Modernism." *Science, Reason, and Rhetoric.* Eds. Henry Krips, J.E. McGuire, and Trevor Melia. University of Pittsburgh, 1995: 295–315.

Open Fields: Science in Cultural Encounter. Oxford: Clarendon Press, 1996.

Virginia Woolf: The Common Ground. Ann Arbor: University of Michigan Press, 1996.

"'Wireless': Popular Physics, Radio and Modernism." *Cultural Babbage: Technology, Time and Invention.* Eds. Francis Spufford and Jenny Uglow. London: Faber and Faber, 1996: 149–66.

"'The Least Like to My Own Ideas': Science and Creativity in Woolf's 1930's Writing." A paper presented at the Seventh Annual Virginia Woolf Conference titled "Virginia Woolf and Her Influences." Plymouth State College, Plymouth, NY, 1997.

Begley, Sharon. "When Galaxies Collide." *Newsweek* 3 Nov. 1997: 30–7.

Bell, Clive. "Matisse and Picasso." *Athenaeum* 4698 (14 May 1920): 643–4.

Civilisation: An Essay. London: Chatto and Windus, 1932.

Bell, Louis. *The Telescope.* New York: McGraw-Hill, 1922.

Bell, Quentin. *Virginia Woolf: A Biography.* Vol. 1–2. New York: Harcourt Brace, 1972.

Elders and Betters. London: John Murray, 1995.

Berendzen, Richard, Richard Hart, and Daniel Seeley. *Man Discovers the Galaxies.* New York: Science History Publications, 1976.

Bergson, Henri. *Creative Evolution.* Trans. Arthur Mitchell. 1911. New York: Modern Library, 1944.

Matter and Memory. 1912. Trans. Nancy Paul and W. Scott Palmer. London: George Allen, 1962.

Bernal, J.D. *The Social Function of Science.* 1939. Cambridge, MA: MIT Press, 1967.

Bishop, Edward. *A Virginia Woolf Chronology.* London: MacMillan, 1989.

Blake, William. "Milton: A Poem in 2 Books." *The Complete Poetry and Prose of William Blake.* Newly Revised Edition. Ed. David V. Erdman. Berkeley: University of California Press, 1982.

Bowie, Malcolm. *Proust Among the Stars.* New York: Columbia University Press, 1998.

Bradbrook, Bohuslava R. *Karel Čapek: In Pursuit of Truth, Tolerance and Trust.* Brighton: Sussex Academic Press, 1998.

Bradshaw, David. "The Best of Companions: J.W.N. Sullivan, Aldous Huxley, and the New Physics (Part I)." *Review of English Studies* 47 (May 1996): 188–206.

"The Best of Companions: J.W.N. Sullivan, Aldous Huxley, and the New Physics (Concluded)." *Review of English Studies* 47 (August 1996): 352–68.

"British Writers and Anti-Fascism in the 1930s, Part I: The Bray and Drone of Tortured Voices." *Woolf Studies Annual* 3 (1997): 3–27.

"The socio-political vision of the novels." *The Cambridge Companion to Virginia Woolf*. Eds. Sue Roe and Susan Sellers. Cambridge University Press, 2000. 191–208.

Brashear, Ronald and Daniel Lewis. *Star Struck: One Thousand Years of the Art and Science of Astronomy*. San Marino: Huntington Library, Seattle: University of Washington Press, 2001.

Brian, Denis. *Einstein: A Life*. New York: J. Wiley, 1996.

Brothers, Caroline. *War and Photography: A Cultural History*. New York: Routledge, 1997.

Brown, William. Letter to James Jeans. 25 Feb. 1930. The James Jeans Papers. The Royal Society, London.

Burrows, William E. *This New Ocean: The Story of the First Space Age*. New York: The Modern Library, 1999.

Burstein, Jessica. "Waspish Segments: Lewis, Prosthesis, Fascism." *MODERNISM/ modernity* 4.2 (1997): 139–64.

Čapek, The Brothers. *"And so ad infinitum' (The Life of the Insects): An Entomological Review, in Three Acts, a Prologue and an Epilogue*. Trans. Paul Selver. Oxford University Press, 1924.

Cassidy, David. *Einstein and Our World*. Atlantic Highlands: Humanities Press, 1995.

Caughie, Pamela. *Virginia Woolf & Postmodernism: Literature in Quest & Question of Itself*. Urbana: University of Illinois Press, 1991.

Caughie, Pamela L. ed. *Virginia Woolf in the Age of Mechanical Reproduction*. New York: Garland Publishing, 2000.

"Center of the Universe Located by Shapley: It is in the Constellation Sagittarius." *New York Times* 20 Nov. 1928: A1.

Chapman, Clark R. "Statement on the Threat of Impact by Near-Earth Asteroids." http://impact.arc.nasa.gov/congress/1998_may/chapman.html. Accessed on 15 Nov. 2001.

Christianson, Gale E. *Edwin Hubble: Mariner of the Nebulae*. New York: Farrar, Straus & Giroux, 1995.

Clark, Ronald W. *Einstein: The Life and Times*. New York: World, 1971.

Clarke, Stuart N. "A Short Story by Virginia Woolf: 'A Scene From the Past.'" *Virginia Woolf Bulletin* 1 (January 1999): 6–11.

Clerke, Agnes. A *Popular History of Astronomy During the Nineteenth Century*. 2nd ed. Edinburgh: A. & C. Black, 1887.

Problems in Astrophysics. London: Adam and Charles Black, 1903.

"Corrected Path of Eclipse." *The Times* 21 May 1927: 9.

Council on Books in War Time. *A War Atlas for Americans*. New York, Simon & Schuster, 1944.

Crossley, Robert. ed. *Talking Across the World: The Love Letters of Olaf Stapledon and Agnes Miller, 1913–1919*. Hanover and London: University Press of New England, 1987.

Olaf Stapledon: Speaking for the Future. Syracuse University Press, 1994.

An Olaf Stapledon Reader. Syracuse University Press, 1997.

Crowe, Michael. *The Extraterrestrial Life Debate 1750–1900: The Idea of a Plurality of Worlds from Kant to Lowell*. Cambridge University Press, 1986.

Cull, E.C. Letter to James Jeans. 24 Feb. 1930. The James Jeans Papers, The Royal Society, London.

Daugherty, Beth Rigel and Eileen Barrett. *Virginia Woolf: Texts and Contexts*. Selected Papers from the Fifth Annual Conference on Virginia Woolf. New York: Pace University Press, 1996.

Davies, Hugh Sykes. "The Mysterious Universe." *The Criterion* 10.10 (April 1931): 514–16.

Defoe, Daniel. *A Tour thro' the Whole Island of Great Britain*. London: G. Strahan, W. Mears, R. Francklin, S. Chapman, R. Stagg, and J. Graves, 3v., 1724–27.

de Gay, Jane. "An Unfinished Story: The Freshwater Drafts of 'The Searchlight.'" *Virginia Woolf: Turning the Centuries*. Selected Papers from the Ninth Annual Conference on Virginia Woolf. Eds. Ann Ardis and Bonnie Kime Scott. New York: Pace University Press, 2000: 207–15.

Deleuze, Gilles and Felix Guattari. *A Thousand Plateaus: Capitalism and Schizophrenia*. Trans. Brian Massumi. University of Minneapolis Press, 1987.

Dunaway, David King. *Huxley in Hollywood*. New York: Harper, 1989.

"Literary Correspondence: Aldous Huxley and Gerald Heard." *Now More than Ever: Proceedings of the Aldous Huxley Centenary Symposium*. Ed. Bernfried Nugel. Frankfurt am Main: Peter Lang, 1995: 29–42.

"Eclipse Madness." *Nation & Athenaeum* 9 July 1927: 477–8.

Eddington, Arthur S. *Stellar Movements and the Structure of the Universe*. London: Macmillan, 1914.

Stars and Atoms. New Haven: Yale University Press, 1927.

Science and the Unseen World. New York: Macmillan, 1929.

The Nature of the Physical World. New York: Macmillan, 1929.

New Pathways in Science. Cambridge University Press, 1935.

The Expanding Universe. 1933. New York: Macmillan, 1952.

Einstein, Albert. Untitled Essay. *Living Philosophies*. New York: Simon and Schuster, 1931.

"Electric Light Experiments." *The Times* (London) 16 April 1880: 11.

Eliot, T.S. *The Varieties of Metaphysical Poetry: The Clark Lectures and The Turnbull Lectures*. New York: Harcourt Brace, 1993.

"The Burnt Dancer." *Inventions of the March Hare: Poems 1909–1917*. Ed. Christopher Ricks. New York: Harcourt Brace, 1996: 62–3.

Ellis, Havelock. *The Task of Social Hygiene*. Boston: Houghton Mifflin, 1912.

"The End of the World is Still a Long Way Off–But it Will be Very Cold a Million Million Years Hence." *Sunday Worker* [London] 20 Oct. 1929.

Fantoli, Annibale. *Galileo: For Copernicanism and for the Church*. Trans. George V. Coyne. Vatican Observatory Publications, 1994.

Felski, Rita. *The Gender of Modernity*. Cambridge: Harvard University Press, 1995.

Fenwick, Gillian. *Leslie Stephen's Life in Letters: A Bibliographic Study*. Cambridge: Scolar Press, 1993.

Ferris, Timothy. *Coming of Age in The Milky Way*. New York: William Morrow, 1988.

Fiedler, Leslie A. *Olaf Stapledon: A Man Divided*. Oxford University Press, 1983.

Flammarion, N. Camille. *Astronomie Populaire: Description Generale Du Ciel*. Paris: C. Marpon et. E. Flammarion, 1881.

Omega: The Last Days of the World. New York: Cosmopolitan Publishing, 1894. New York: Arno Press, 1975.

Popular Astronomy: A General Description of the Heavens. Trans. J. Ellard Gore. New York: D. Appleton and Company, 1931.

Frayling, Christopher. *Things to Come*. London: British Film Institute, 1995.

Fry, Roger. "Art and Science." *Athenaeum* 4649 (6 June 1919): 434.

"The Artist's Vision." *Athenaeum* 4654 (11 July 1919): 594–5.

Vision and Design. New York: Meridian, 1956.

Letters of Roger Fry. Ed. Denys Sutton. New York: Random, 1972.

Galton, Francis. *Hereditary Genius: An Inquiry into its Laws and Consequences*. New York: Horizon, 1952.

Garbedian, H. Gordon. "Our Universe Bares its Heart: Dr. Harlow Shapley, Who Plumbed Space to Find the Cosmic Centre, Explains the Significance Of This Discovery..." *New York Times Magazine* 24 Feb. 1929, sec. 5: 1, 2, 22.

"The Star Stuff That is Man." *New York Times Magazine* 11 Aug. 1929, sec. 5: 1+.

Gardner, Robert, *et al*. *Conway's All the World's Fighting Ships 1860–1906*. London: Conway Maritime Press, 1979.

Gates, Barbara T. "Retelling the Story of Science." *Victorian Literature and Culture* 21 (1993): 289–306.

Gates, Barbara T. and Ann B. Shteir, eds. *Natural Eloquence: Women Reinscribe Science*. Madison: University of Wisconsin Press, 1997.

Gaye, R.K. Letter to James Jeans. 1 Feb. 1903. The James Jeans Papers, The Royal Society of London.

"Giant Star Equal to 27,000,000 Suns like Ours," *New York Times* 30 Dec. 1920: 2.

Goldman, Jane. *The Feminist Aesthetics of Virginia Woolf*. Cambridge University Press, 1998.

Graham, J.W. "The Drafts of Virginia Woolf's 'The Searchlight.'" *Twentieth Century Literature* 22.4 (December 1976): 379–93.

Graham, Jill. E-mail on Woolf listserv. VWOOLF@lists.acs.ohio-state.edu. Posted 4 April 1998.

Grattan-Guinness, I. "Russell and G.H. Hardy: A Study of Their Relationship." *Russell: A Journal of Bertrand Russell Archives* 2.2 (Winter 1991): 165–79.

"A Great Astronomer Looks at Man a Million Million Years Hence." *Evening News* [Carmelite House] 10, Sept. 1929.

Gropman, Donald, with Kenneth Mirvis. *Comet Fever: A Popular History of Halley's Comet*. New York: Simon and Schuster, 1985.

Haldane, J.B.S. *Possible Worlds and Other Essays*. London: Chatto & Windus, 1928.

The Inequality of Man and Other Essays. London: Chatto & Windus, 1932.

Daedalus, or Science and the Future in Haldane's Daedalus Revisited. Ed. Krishna R. Dronamraju. Oxford University Press, 1995: 23–54.

Hale, George Ellery. Letter to James Jeans. 25 May 1920. George Ellery Hale Papers, Box 23. The Beckman Institute, California Institute of Technology, Pasadena, CA.

Haraway, Donna J. "Situated Knowledges," *Simians, Cyborgs, and Women: The Reinvention of Nature*. New York: Routledge, 1991: 183–201.

Hardy, Thomas. *Two on a Tower*. 1882. London: Macmillan 1964.

Harkins, William. *Karel Čapek*. New York: Columbia University Press, 1962.

Hauck, Christina. "'To Escape the Horror of Family Life': Virginia Woolf and the British Birth Control Debate." *New Essays on Virginia Woolf*. Ed. Helen Wussow. Dallas: Contemporary Research P, 1995: 15–37.

Hebert, Ann Marie. "What Does it Mean? How Do You Explain it All?: Virginia Woolf: A Postmodern Modernist." *Virginia Woolf Miscellanies: Proceedings of the First Annual Conference on Virginia Woolf*. Ed. Mark Hussey and Vara Neverow-Turk. New York: Pace University Press, 1992: 11–19.

Heidegger, Martin. "The Age of the World Picture." *The Question Concerning Technology and Other Essays*. New York: Harper & Row, 1977: 115–54.

Henry, Holly. "Nebulous Networks: Woolf's Rethinking of Jeans's Analogy of the Scientist as Artist." *Virginia Woolf and the Arts: Selected Papers from the Sixth Annual Conference on Virginia Woolf*. Ed. Diane F. Gillespie and Leslie K. Hankins. New York: Pace University Press, 1997: 268–76.

"Eclipse Madness, 1927." *Astronomy & Geophysics: The Journal of the Royal Astronomical Society* 40.4 (August 1999): 17–19.

"From Edwin Hubble's Telescope to Virginia Woolf's 'Searchlight.'" *Virginia Woolf in the Age of Mechanical Reproduction*. Ed. Pamela Caughie. New York: Garland Publishing, 2000: 135–58.

Hentschel, Klaus. *The Einstein Tower: An Intertexture of Dynamic Construction, Relativity Theory, and Astronomy*. Trans. Ann M. Hentschel. Stanford University Press, 1997.

Hintikka, Jaakko. "Virginia Woolf and Our Knowledge of the External World." *The Journal of Aesthetics and Art Criticism* 31.1 (Fall 1979): 5–14.

Hoffman, Charles G. "Virginia Woolf's Manuscript Revisions of *The Years*." *PMLA* 84 (Jan. 1969): 79–89.

Holleyman and Treacher. *Catalogue of Books from the Library of Leonard and Virginia Woolf, taken from Monk's House, Rodmell, Sussex and 24 Victoria Square, London and now in the possession of Washington State University, Pullman, USA*. Brighton: Holleyman & Treacher Ltd., 1975.

Holmes, Arthur. *The Age of the Earth*. 1927. London: Thomas Nelson, 1939.

Holst, Gustav. "Betelgeuse." *Twelve Humbert Wolfe Songs*. Intro. Imogen Holst. Great Yarmouth: Galliard, 1970: 45–8.

Holst, Imogen. *Gustav Holst: A Biography*. 2nd ed. London: Oxford University Press, 1971.

Holtby, Winifred. *Virginia Woolf*. Adelphi: Wishart, 1932.

"Hoover Gets First 12 Books for White House Library." *New York American* 26 April 1930, midnight ed.: 2.

Hubble, Edwin. *The Realm of the Nebulae*. New Haven: Yale University Press, 1936. *The Observational Approach to Cosmology*. Oxford: Clarendon, 1937.

"The Scientist at War." *The Nature of Science and Other Lectures*. San Marino: Huntington Library, 1954: 63–72.

"The War That Must Not Happen." *The Nature of Science and Other Lectures*. San Marino: Huntington Library, 1954: 73–83.

Hubble, Grace. Unpublished Diary titled "Travels 1934." The Edwin Hubble Papers, HUB 74, Box 4. The Huntington Library, San Marino, CA.

Unpublished Diary titled "September 1936 Travel Diary." The Edwin Hubble Papers, HUB 75, Box 5. The Huntington Library, San Marino, CA.

Unpublished Memoirs titled "The Astronomer." The Edwin Hubble Papers, HUB 82 (7), Box 7. The Huntington Library, San Marino, CA.

Unpublished Memoirs titled "Some People." The Edwin Hubble Papers, HUB 82(17), Box 8, The Huntington Library, San Marino, CA.

Humm, Maggie. "Virginia Woolf's Photography and the Monk's House Albums." *Virginia Woolf in the Age of Mechanical Reproduction*. Ed. Pamela Caughie. New York: Garland Publishing, 2000: 219–46.

Hussey, Mark. "*To the Lighthouse* and Physics: The Cosmology of David Bohm and Virginia Woolf." *New Essays on Virginia Woolf*. Ed. Helen Wussow. Dallas: Contemporary Research Press, 1995: 79–97.

Virginia Woolf A to Z: A Comprehensive Reference for Students, Teachers, and Common Readers to her Life, Work, and Critical Reception. Oxford University Press, 1995.

Huxley, Aldous. "To Robert Nichols." 17 Feb. 1930. Letter 303 of *The Letters of Aldous Huxley*. Ed. Grover Smith. New York: Harper, 1969. 330.

Letter to Grace Hubble. 30 Sept. 1953. Edwin Hubble Papers, HUB 676, Box 16. The Huntington Library, San Marino CA.

Huxley, Julian. *Essays in Popular Culture*. London: Chatto and Windus, 1929.

Ants. 1930. London: Chatto and Windus, 1935.

Huxley, Maria. Letter to Grace Hubble. 9 August 1943. The Edwin Hubble Papers, HUB 692, Box 16. The Huntington Library, San Marino, CA.

Letter to Grace Hubble. 9 Jan. 1944. The Edwin Hubble Papers, HUB 1083, Box 16. The Huntington Library, San Marino CA.

"In the Totality Belt." *The Times* 27 June 1927: 14,16.

"Interesting Theories of a Famous Astronomer." *Daily Record & Daily Mail* [London] 10 Sept. 1929: 23.

Jeans, C.M. *"Driftweed" and Later Poems*. Cambridge University Press, 1935.

Jeans, James. *Problems of Cosmogony and Stellar Dynamics*. Cambridge University Press, 1919.

The Universe Around Us. New York: Macmillan, 1929.

Astronomy and Cosmogony. Cambridge University Press, 1929.

Eos, or The Wider Aspects of Cosmogony. New York: E.P. Dutton, 1929.

Untitled Essay. More Points of View: A Second Series of Broadcast Addresses. London: George Allen & Unwin, 1930: 55–71.

The Mysterious Universe. 1930. New Revised ed. New York: Macmillan, 1933.

Letter to Edwin Hubble. 22 Feb. 1938. The Edwin Hubble Papers, HUB 718, Box 16, The Huntington Library, San Marino, CA.

Through Space and Time. 1934. New York: Macmillan, 1947.

The Stars in Their Courses. 1931. Cambridge University Press, 1954.

The Universe Around Us. 1944. 4th ed. Cambridge University Press, 1960.

Jeans, Susi. Letter to Marie Stopes. 25 July 1945. Stopes Papers. The British Library Manuscripts Collection, London (Ref Add MSS 58543 ff 47–104).

Kaler, James B. *Stars*. New York: Scientific American Library, 1992.

Kern, Stephen. *The Culture of Time and Space 1880–1918*. Cambridge: Harvard University Press, 1983.

Killen, Judith. "Virginia Woolf in the Light of Modern Physics." Dissertation. University of Louisville, November 1984.

King, Henry. *The History of the Telescope*. New York: Dover, 1955.

Kronk, Gary. "Comet Hysteria: Comet Hale-Bopp, the California Ritual Suicide, and Comet Hysteria through the Centuries." <http://www.maa.mhn.de/Comet/Hale-Bopp/hbhysteria.html>. Accessed on 12 Dec. 2001.

Latour, Bruno. *Science in Action: How to follow scientists and engineers through society*. Cambridge: Harvard University Press, 1987.

We Have Never Been Modern. Trans. Catherine Porter. Cambridge: Harvard University Press, 1993.

Laurence, Patricia. "The Facts and Fugue of War: From *Three Guineas to Between the Acts*. *Virginia Woolf and War: Fiction, Reality, and Myth*. Ed. Mark Hussey. 1991: 225–46.

Leaska, Mitchell. *The Novels of Virginia Woolf: From Beginning to End*. New York: John Jay Press, 1977.

Lee, Hermione. *Virginia Woolf*. London: Chatto & Windus, 1996.

LeMahieu, D.L. *A Culture for Democracy: Mass Communication and the Cultivated Mind in Britain Between the Wars*. Oxford: Clarendon Press, 1998.

Levenback, Karen. *Virginia Woolf and the Great War*. Syracuse University Press, 1999.

Lightman, Bernard. "Constructing Victorian Heavens: Agnes Clerke and the 'New Astronomy.' " *Natural Eloquence: Women Reinscribe Science*. Eds. Barbara T. Gates and Ann B. Shteir. Madison: University of Wisconsin Press, 1997: 61–75.

"Light-year." *The Oxford English Dictionary*. 2nd ed. 1989.

Livingston, Dorothy Michelson. *The Master of Light: A Biography of Albert A. Michelson*. New York: Scribner's, 1973.

MacKinnon, Douglas and Joseph Baldanza. *Footprints: The 12 Men Who Walked on the Moon Reflect on their Flights, Their Lives, and the Future*. Washington, DC: Acropolis Books, 1989.

"Mankind Just An Accident: Ice Age of Universal Death Must End the World." *Daily Herald* [London] 5 Nov. 1930: 1.

Marcus, Jane. "Britannia Rules *The Waves*." *Decolonizing Tradition: New Views of Twentieth-Century 'British' Literary Canons*. Ed. Karen R. Lawrence. Urbana: University of Illinois Press, 1992: 136–62.

Marvin, F.S. "The Human Value of the New Astronomy." *Hibbert Journal* 27 (Jan. 1929): 244–53.

"A Mathematical Universe." *Hibbert Journal* 29 (1930): 401–10.

McCrea, William H. "Jeans Centenary Talk." *The Quarterly Journal of the RAS* 19.2 (June 1978): 160–6.

McNeillie, Andrew. "Daily Herald." *The Essays of Virginia Woolf.* Vol. III. London: Hogarth, 1986: 520–1.

McRae, Murdo William, ed. *The Literature of Science: Perspectives on Popular Scientific Writing.* Athens: University of Georgia Press, 1993.

"Measuring the Stars." *The Times* [London] 12 March 1925: 13.

"Measuring the Stars, and Detecting Ether: The Interferometer." *Illustrated London News* 18 April 1925: 677.

Meyer, Gerald Dennis. *The Scientific Lady in England, 1650–1760: An Account of Her Rise, with Emphasis on the Major Roles of the Telescope and Microscope.* Berkeley: University of California Press, 1955.

Meyerowitz, Selma. *Leonard Woolf.* Boston: Twayne, 1982.

Millhauser, Milton. "In the Air." *Darwin.* A Norton Critical Edition. Ed. Philip Appleman. 2nd ed. New York: W.W. Norton, 1979: 27–31.

Miller, Ron. "The Astronomical Visions of Lucien Rudaux." *Sky & Telescope* (Oct. 1984): 293–5.

Milne, E.A. *Sir James Jeans: A Biography with a Memoir by S.C. Roberts.* Cambridge University Press, 1952.

Milner, C. Douglas. *The Dolomites.* London: Robert Hale, 1951.

Mitchell, S.A. "The Return of Halley's Comet" *American Review of Reviews* 41.4 (April 1910): 443–4.

Morrell, Ottoline. *Memoirs of Lady Ottoline Morrell: A Study in Friendship, 1873–1915.* New York: Alfred A. Knopf, 1964.

Moszkowski, Alexander. *Einstein the Searcher: His Work Explained from Dialogues with Einstein.* Trans. Henry L. Brose. New York: E.P. Dutton, 1921.

Myers, Greg. "Science for Women and Children: The Dialogue of Popular Science in the Nineteenth Century." *Nature Transfigured: Literature and Science, 1700–1900.* Ed. Sally Shuttleworth and J.R.R. Christie. Manchester University Press, 1989.

"Mystical Mathematics of the City of Heaven," *Illustrated London News* 22 Nov. 1930: 922–3.

"NASA's Current Efforts/Future Plans: NEO's" <http://impact.arc.nasa.gov/may/>. Accessed on 12 Dec. 2001.

"The Nation and Athenaeum." *British Literary Magazines: The Modern Age, 1914–1984.* Ed. Alvin Sullivan. Vol. 4. New York: Greenwood Press, 1986: 269–72.

National Geographic Society. *The Round Earth on Flat Paper: Map Projections Used by Cartographers.* By Wellman Chamberlin. Drawings by Charles E. Riddiford. Washington, DC: National Geographic, 1950.

"Naval and Military Intelligence." *The Times* [London] 8 June 1880: 10.

Nicholson, Nigel. Letter to the author. 1 March 1998.

Norman, Sylvia. "Eclipse Madness." *Nation & Athenaeum* 41.14 (9 July 1927): 477–8.

"The Universe and Its God." *Nation & Athenaeum* (24 Jan. 1931): 546, 548.

Ochoa, George and Melinda Corey. *The Timeline Book of Science*. New York: Ballantine, 1995.

"On the North-East Coast." *The Times* 30 June 1927: 18.

The Oxford English Dictionary. 2nd ed. Vol. VIII, 1989: 928.

Pais, Abraham. *Einstein Lived Here*. Oxford University Press, 1994.

Petty, A.H. Letter to James Jeans. 24 Feb. 1930. The James Jeans Papers. The Royal Society, London.

Phillips, Patricia. *The Scientific Lady: A Social History of Women's Scientific Interests 1520–1918*. New York: St. Martin's Press, 1990.

"Photography Records a Stellar Explosion." *Illustrated London News* 18 June 1938: 1097.

Pippett, Aileen. *The Moth and the Star: A Biography of Virginia Woolf*. Boston: Little, Brown & Co., 1955.

"Plans of London Public." *The Times* 29 June 1927: 16.

"The Progress of Science. New Views on the Universe." *The Times* [London] 5 Jan. 1925: 18.

Radin, Grace. *Virginia Woolf's The Years: The Evolution of a Novel*. Knoxville: University of Tennessee Press, 1981.

Raitt, Suzanne. *Vita and Virginia: The Work and Friendship of V. Sackville-West and Virginia Woolf*. Oxford: Clarendon Press, 1993.

Reston, James, Jr. *Galileo: A Life*. New York: HarperCollins, 1994.

Roberts, S.C. "A Memoir" In *Sir James Jeans: A Biography*. By E.A. Milne. Cambridge University Press, 1952: ix–xvi.

  The Evolution of Cambridge Publishing: The Sandars Lectures 1954. Cambridge University Press, 1956.

Roe, Sue. ed. *Jacob's Room*. By Virginia Woolf. London: Penguin Books, 1992.

Rose, June. *Marie Stopes and the Sexual Revolution*. London: Faber and Faber, 1992.

Rouse, Joseph. "What are the Cultural Studies of Scientific Literature?" *Configurations* 1.1 (Winter 1993): 57–94.

Rudaux, M. Lucien. *Sur les Autres Mondes*. Paris: Librarie Larousse, 1937.

Rusk, Rogers. *Atoms, Men and Stars*. 1937. Freeport: Books for Libraries Press, 1971.

Russell, Bertrand. *Our Knowledge of the External World as a Field for Scientific Method in Philosophy*. London: Open Court Publishing, 1914.

  "Dreams and Facts." *The Athenaeum* 4643 (25 April 1919): 232–3.

  The ABC of Atoms. New York: E.P. Dutton, 1923.

  Icarus, or the Future of Science. New York: E.P. Dutton, 1924.

  The Analysis of Matter. New York: Harcourt, 1927.

  "A Free Man's Worship." *Mysticism and Logic*. New York: W.W. Norton, 1929: 46–57.

  Mysticism and Logic. New York: W.W. Norton, 1929.

  "War in the Heavens." *London Mercury* 36.213 (July 1937): 297–8.

  The Analysis of Mind. 1921. London: George Allen & Unwin, 1951.

  An Outline of Philosophy. London: George Allen & Unwin, 1956.

  My Philosophical Development. New York: Simon and Schuster, 1959.

  The Autobiography of Bertrand Russell. Vols. 1–2 Boston: Little, Brown and Company, 1967, 1968.

Russell, Doug. "Popularization and the Challenge to Science-Centrism in the 1930s." *The Literature of Science: Perspectives on Popular Scientific Writing*. Ed. Murdo William McRae. Athens: The University of Georgia Press, 1993: 37–53.

Sackville-West, Vita. "Full Moon." *Orchard and Vineyard*. London: J. Lane, 1921: 56.

Seducers in Ecuador. London: The Hogarth Press, 1924.

"Spring." *The Land*. London: William Heinemann, 1930.

"Books in General." *The Listener* 19 Nov. 1930: 844.

Solitude: A Poem. London: The Hogarth Press, 1938.

The Letters of Vita Sackville-West to Virginia Woolf. Ed. Louise DeSalvo and Mitchell A. Leaska. New York: William Morrow, 1985.

Sainsbury, Geoffrey. "Anthropomorphic Universe." *The Adelphi* (January 1931): 338–41.

Savory, Jerold. "Punch." *British Literary Magazines: The Victorian and Edwardian Age, 1837–1913*. Vol. 3. Ed. Alvin Sullivan. New York: Greenwood Press, 1983: 325–9.

"Science and Sentiment Are Best Sellers!" *Sunday Express* [London] 29 March 1931: 8.

Science in War. New York: Penguin, 1940.

Scott-James, R.A. "Virginia Woolf's New Novel." *London Mercury* 35. 210 (Apr. 1937): 629–31.

Seeley, Tracy. "Virginia Woolf's Poetics of Space: 'The Lady in the Looking-Glass: A Reflection.'" *Woolf Studies Annual* 2 (1996): 89–116.

Seymour, Miranda. *Ottoline Morrell: Life on the Grand Scale*. New York: Farrar, Straus & Giroux, 1992.

Shanks, Edward. "Do We Matter?" *Evening Standard* [London] 5 Nov. 1930: 7.

Shapley, Harlow. "What Are the Stars?" *The Universe of Stars*. Based on Radio Talks from the Harvard Observatory. Rev. ed. Ed. Harlow Shapley and Celia Payne. Cambridge: Harvard Observatory, 1929: 3–9.

Sharov, Alexander, and Igor Novikov. *Edwin Hubble: The Discoverer of the Big Bang Universe*. Cambridge University Press, 1993.

Smith, Adrian. *The New Statesman: Portrait of a Political Weekly, 1913–1931*. London: Frank Cass, 1996.

Smith, Beverly E. "New Statesman and Society." *Consumer Magazines of the British Isles*. Ed. Sam G. Riley. Westport: Greenwood Press, 1993: 134–8.

Smith, Geraint. "We're all doomed (or at least we might be) as giant asteroid heads for Earth." *Evening Standard* (London) 12 March, 1998: 1.

Smith, Robert. W. *The Expanding Universe: Astronomy's "Great Debate," 1900–1931*. Cambridge University Press, 1982.

Smyth, Ethel. Untitled Essay. *More Points of View: A Second Series of Broadcast Addresses*. London: George Allen & Unwin, 1930: 75–92.

Smythe, Francis Sydney. *Edward Whymper*. London: Hodder and Stoughton, 1940.

Spender, Stephen. *World Within World*. New York: Harcourt, 1951.

The Struggle of the Modern. Berkeley: University of California Press, 1963.

Untitled Essay. *Recollections of Virginia Woolf by her Contemporaries*. Ed. Joan Russell Noble. London: Cardinal, 1989: 219–25.

Spurgeon, Dickie. "The Athenaeum." *British Literary Magazines: The Romantic Age, 1789–1836*. Ed. Alvin Sullivan. New York: Greenwood Press, 1983: 21–4.

Squier, Susan. "The Modern City and the Construction of Female Desire: Wells's *In the Days of the Comet* and Robins's *The Convert*." *Tulsa Studies in Women's Literature* 8.1 (Spring 1989): 63–75.

Babies in Bottles: Twentieth-Century Visions of Reproductive Technology. New Brunswick: Rutgers University Press, 1994.

Stapledon, Olaf. "Science, Art and Society." *London Mercury* 38 (October 1938): 521–8.

Star Maker. 1937. To The End of Time: The Best of Olaf Stapledon. Ed. Basil Davenport. New York: Funk & Wagnalls, 1953: 221–412.

The Legacy of Olaf Stapledon: Critical Essays and an Unpublished Manuscript. Ed. McCarthy, Patrick, Charles Elkins and Martin Harry Greenburg. New York: Greenwood, 1989.

"*Interplanetary Man?*" in *An Olaf Stapledon Reader*. Ed. Robert Crossley. Syracuse University Press, 1997: 218–41.

"*Poem 1 from The Nether Worlds*," in *An Olaf Stapledon Reader*. Ed. Robert Crossley. Syracuse University Press, 1997: 307.

"*Poem 17 from First Volley, Astronomical*" in *An Olaf Stapledon Reader*. Ed. Robert Crossley. Syracuse University Press, 1997: 306.

"Stars Seen Now as They Were 'Inconceivable Ages Before Man.'" *Illustrated London News* 15 Nov. 1930: 873.

Stebbing, L. Susan. *Philosophy and the Physicists*. London: Methuen, 1937.

Steele, Elizabeth. *Virginia Woolf's Literary Sources and Allusions: A Guide to the Essays*. New York: Garland, 1983.

Virginia Woolf's Rediscovered Essays, Sources and Allusions. New York: Garland, 1987.

Steer, George. "Guernica." *London Mercury* 36.214 (1937): 330–9.

Stephen, Leslie. *The Playground of Europe*. 1871. New York, Longmans, 1910.

An Agnostic's Apology, and Other Essays. London: Watts, 1937.

Stokley, James. *Stars and Telescopes*. New York: Harper, 1936.

Stopes, Marie. Draft Letter to James Jeans. Stopes Papers. The British Library Manuscripts Collection, London (Ref Add MSS 58543 ff. 36–64v).

Stover, Leon. *The Prophetic Soul: A Reading of H.G. Wells's Things to Come. Together with His Film Treatment Whither Mankind? and the Post Production Script*. McFarland & Company, 1987.

The First Men in the Moon: A Critical Text of the 1901 London First Edition, with an Introduction and Appendices. By H.G. Wells. Jefferson: McFarland & Company, 1998.

Sullivan, J.W.N. "Science and Literature." *Athenaeum* 4650 (13 June 1919): 464.

"Stellar Universes." *Athenaeum* 4671 (7 Nov. 1919): 1155–6.

"An Abstruse Theory," *Athenaeum* 4723 (5 Nov. 1920): 621.

"Einstein's Problem." *Athenaeum* 4698 (14 May 1920): 641–2.

"The Relativity Discussion at The Royal Society." *Athenaeum* 4685 (13 Feb. 1920): 213–4.

"The Scientific Contribution." *Athenaeum* 4696 (30 April 1920): 577–8.

Taylor, Henry. *Autobiography of Sir Henry Taylor 1800–1844*. Vol. 1 London: Longmans, 1885.

Tennyson, Alfred. "The Dawn." *The Poems of Tennyson in Three Volumes*. Ed. Christopher Ricks, 2nd ed., Vol. III: 247–8.

"The Biological Telescope." *New Statesman and Nation* 2.24 (8 Aug. 1931): 171–2.

"The Progress of Science. New Views on the Universe." *The Times* [London] 5 Jan. 1925: 18.

Thomson, G.P. *The Atom*. 1930. London: Oxford University Press, 1962.

Thomson. J.J. *Recollections and Reflections*. New York: Macmillan, 1937.

Trevelyan, Lady. "Towards Utopia: What Women Can Do For Peace." *Listener* 5 March 1930: 415.

"The Universe. Sir James Jeans on Astronomy." *The Times* 13 Sept. 1929.

Walpole, Hugh. Letter to Edwin Hubble. 11 Sept., 1934. The Edwin Hubble Papers, HUB 987, Box 20. The Edwin Hubble Papers, The Huntington Library, San Marino, CA.

Wells, H.G. *In the Days of the Comet*. London: Macmillan, 1906.

The Outline of History: Being a Plain History of Life and Mankind. Rev. Ed. London and New York: Cassell, 1920.

"The Star." *Twenty-Eight Science Fiction Stories of H.G. Wells*. 1932. New York: Dover Publications, 1952: 680–91.

The First Men in the Moon: A Critical Text of the 1901 London First Edition, with an Introduction and Appendices. Ed. Leon Stover. Jefferson: McFarland & Company, 1998.

"We're all doomed (or at least we might be) as giant asteroid heads for Earth." *Evening Standard* [London] 12 March, 1998: 1.

Wersky, Gary. *The Visible College: The Collective Biography of British Scientific Socialists of the 1930s*. New York: Holt, Rinehart & Winston, 1979.

White, Frank. *The Overview Effect: Space Exploration and Human Evolution*. 2nd ed. Reston: American Institute of Aeronautics and Astronautics, 1998.

Whitehead, Alfred North. *The Concept of Nature*. Tarner Lectures Delivered in Trinity College November 1919. Cambridge University Press, 1920.

Whitehead, Alfred. *Science and the Modern World*. Lowell Lectures, 1925. New York: Macmillan, 1967.

Science and Philosophy. New York: Philosophical Library, 1948.

Whittier-Ferguson, John. *Framing Pieces: Designs of the Gloss in Joyce, Woolf, and Pound*. Oxford University Press, 1996.

Whitworth, Michael. "The Clothbound Universe: Popular Physics Books, 1919–39." *Publishing History* 40 (1996): 53–82.

"Virginia Woolf and Modernism." *The Cambridge Companion to Virginia Woolf*. Cambridge University Press, 2000: 146–63.

Whymper, Edward. "The Fatal Accident on the Matterhorn." *Peaks, Passes and Glaciers: Selections from the Alpine Journal.* Ed. Walt Unsworth. Seattle: The Mountaineers, 1981: 46–52.

Wilford, John Nobel. "Fireworks in Deep Space as Two Galaxies Collide." *New York Times* 22 Oct. 1997: A24.

Wood, Joanne A. "Lighthouse Bodies: The Neutral Monism of Virginia Woolf and Bertrand Russell." *Journal of the History of Ideas* 55.3 (July 1994): 483–502.

Woolf, Leonard. "Daedalus and Icarus." *Nation & Athenaeum* 34:25 (22, March 1924): 890.

"Ad Astra?" *Nation & Athenaeum* 45.26 (28 Sept. 1929): 829.

Beginning Again: An Autobiography of the Years 1911 to 1918. New York: Harcourt, 1964.

Downhill All the Way: An Autobiography of the Years 1919–1939. London: The Hogarth Press, 1967.

Woolf, Virginia. *Between the Acts.* The Definitive Collected Edition of The Novels of Virginia Woolf. London: The Hogarth Press, 1990.

The Captain's Death Bed and Other Essays. New York: Harcourt, 1950.

The Common Reader. New York: Harcourt, 1925.

The Complete Shorter Fiction of Virginia Woolf. 2nd ed. Ed. Susan Dick. San Diego: Harcourt Brace Jovanovich, 1989.

"The Death of the Moth." *The Death of the Moth and Other Essays.* New York: Harcourt, 1942: 3–6.

The Diary of Virginia Woolf. Vol. I–V Ed. Anne Olivier Bell and Andrew McNeillie. New York: Harcourt, 1980–4.

The Essays of Virginia Woolf. Vol. I–IV. Ed. Andrew McNeillie. London: The Hogarth Press, 1986.

"Flying Over London." *Collected Essays Vol. IV.* New York: Harcourt, 1967: 167–72.

Freshwater: A Comedy. Ed. Lucio P. Ruotolo. New York: Harcourt, 1976.

Granite and Rainbow. Ed. Leonard Woolf. New York: Harcourt, 1958.

"Half of Thomas Hardy." *Nation & Athenaeum* 44 (24 Nov. 1928): 289–91.

A Haunted House and Other Short Stories. New York: Harcourt, 1949.

"Incongruous Memories" in Jocelyn Bartkevicius, "A Form of One's Own: Virginia Woolf's Art of the Portrait Essay." *Iowa Review* 22.1 (Winter 1992): 126–9.

Jacob's Room. Ed. Sue Roe. London: Penguin, 1992.

"The Journal of Mistress Joan Martyn." *The Complete Shorter Fiction of Virginia Woolf.* Ed. Susan Dick. New York: Harcourt Brace Jovanovich, 1985: 33–62.

"Leslie Stephen." *The Captain's Death Bed and Other Essays.* New York: Harcourt, 1950: 69–75.

The Letters of Virginia Woolf. Vols. I–VI Ed. Nigel Nicolson and Joanne Trautmann. New York and London: Harcourt, 1978–80.

The Moment and Other Essays. New York: Harcourt, 1948.

"The Moment: Summer's Night." *Collected Essays Vol. II* New York: Harcourt Brace, 1967. 293–7.

Mrs Dalloway. 1925. New York: Harcourt, 1981.

Night and Day. London: The Hogarth Press, 1971.

Orlando: A Biography. London: The Hogarth Press, 1990.

A Passionate Apprentice: The Early Journals 1879–1909. Ed. Mitchell Leaska. San Diego: Harcourt Brace Jovanovich, 1990.

"Robinson Crusoe." *Nation & Athenaeum* (6 Feb. 1926): 642–3.

Roger Fry: A Biography. New York: Harcourt, 1940.

A Room of One's Own. New York: Harcourt, 1957.

"The Searchlight." *A Haunted House and Other Stories*. New York: Harcourt, 1944: 120–5.

"The Sun and the Fish." *Collected Essays IV*. New York: Harcourt, Brace & World, 1967: 178–83.

"The Symbol." *The Complete Shorter Fiction of Virginia Woolf*. Ed. Susan Dick. New York: Harcourt Brace Jovanovich, 1985: 282–4.

"Thoughts on Peace in an Air Raid," *Collected Essays IV*. New York: Harcourt Brace, 1967: 173–7.

Three Guineas. New York: Harcourt, 1966.

To the Lighthouse. New York: Harcourt, 1981.

"To Vita Sackville-West." 3 Dec. 1939. *The Letters of Vita Sackville-West to Virginia Woolf*. Eds. Louise De Salvo and Mitchell A. Leaska. New York: William Morrow, 1985.

Virginia Woolf's Reading Notebooks. Ed. Brenda Silver. Princeton University Press, 1983.

The Voyage Out. Ed. Lorna Sage. Oxford University Press, 1992.

The Waves. New York: Harcourt, 1978.

The Waves: The Two Holograph Drafts. Transcribed and Ed. J.W. Graham. University of Toronto Press, 1976.

The Years. The Definitive Collected Edition of The Novels of Virginia Woolf. London: Hogarth, 1990.

Index